Inside
New England

Jud in his Museum

Inside
New England

Judson D. Hale

BAUHAN PUBLISHING
PETERBOROUGH, NEW HAMPSHIRE
2010

Library of Congress Cataloging-in-Publiscation data:

Hale, Judson D.
Inside New England / Judson D. Hale.
p. cm.
Originally published: New York : Harper & Row, c1982.
With new introd.
Includes bibliographical references.
ISBN 978-0-87233-140-2 (pbk. : alk. paper)
1. New England—Social life and customs—Anecdotes. 2. New England—Social life and customs—Humor. 3. New England—History—Anecdotes. 4. New England—History—Humor. I. Title.
F4.6.H34 2010
974—dc22

2010028583

Wood engravings by Randy Miller
www.randymiller.com

Photographs of Jud by Ian Aldrich
www.ianaldrich.com

Cover design by Henry James

Typeset by Sarah Bauhan
in Adobe Jenson Pro

Also by Judson D. Hale:

The Education of a Yankee: An American Memoir
Discovering Our Faraway Brother

BAUHAN PUBLISHING LLC

7 MAIN STREET PETERBOROUGH NEW HAMPSHIRE 03458

603-567-4430

WWW.BAUHANPUBLISHING.COM

Printed in Canada

To my uncle,

ROBB SAGENDORPH (1900-1970)

Founder of **Yankee Publishing Incorporated**

*"Yankee magazine is the expression and perhaps indirectly the
preservation of that great culture in which every Yank was born
and by which every real Yank must live."*

—R.S., September, 1935

CONTENTS

ACKNOWLEDGMENTS

Thanks and thanks and ever thanks ... to those who helped me with the original edition and have encouraged me to have another up-to-date go at it. They include Susan Peery, Clarissa Sititch, Karen Albrecht, Marie Waltz, Bill Austin, Tim Clark, Deborah Navas, Mel Allen, Carole Allen, Dick Heckman, Sandy Taylor, Paul Fraser, Joan and Bob Hayes, Ernestine Blodgett, Gedy and Charles Moody.

... to those who helped with the original edition who have since passed away. They include: Rob Trowbridge, Larry Willard, Vrest Orton, John Pierce, Ed Brummer, Bill Conklin, George Kendall, Jim Meath, Esther Fitts, Martha Jennison, Lorna Trowbridge, and Austin Stevens.

... to Jamie Trowbridge who, as CEO of Yankee Publishing Inc., graciously accepted from me the copyright of this book, which I had recently obtained from Harper & Row (now Harper Collins). It was my gift of gratitude to the family enterprise that I feel so fortunate to have been a part of since 1958. Also to Sarah Bauhan and Gordon Peery for helping make possible this new, revised edition.

... to my past and present-day editors, Larry Ashmead, now retired from Harper & Row, who came up with the idea of my writing this book in the first place; and Ian Aldrich, my editor for this revised edition, who diligently, skillfully, yet gently, examined every sentence, at times suggesting appropriate changes, which in every case I gracefully accepted.

... to Sally, mother of our three sons, mother-in-law of their wives and grandmother of our eight grandchildren, whose encouragement, advice, and unfailing support were invaluable in the creation of both the past and current editions of this book.

And finally, to those who lived in Vanceboro, Maine, during the 1930s and 1940s as well as those living in Dublin, New Hampshire, from 1958 to the present day. Throw in a little of Boston, where I was born, and I visualize a sort of window into the New England I've celebrated and loved all my life.

—J.D.H.

INTRODUCTION

Since writing this book, there have been so many ice-outs on my beloved Lake Winnipesaukee, so many spring launchings of the swan boats in Boston's Public Garden Lagoon, and the three maples outside my bedroom windows here in Dublin, New Hampshire, have changed to orange oh so many times. And, yes, over those years my once-blond hair has turned to white. Any yet, despite people raving about all the changes that have been occurring throughout our six states, I'm reminded every day that the essence of New England has remained a constant. As David Shribman recently wrote in the *Boston Globe*, "It's the mental landscape of the place [New England] and the intellectual architecture of its people that makes it forever identifiable, forever evocative, forever distinct." David Watters, editor of the *Encyclopedia of New England*, agrees. "We've found that New England," he wrote, "is a remarkably persistent notion."

My own experiences seem to always support that "notion." For instance, not long ago my wife, Sally, and I were driving up to Bartlett, New Hampshire, on a *Yankee* magazine "House for Sale" assignment. Somewhere a bit south of Conway, Sally said her stomach was a little upset and maybe at the next convenience store we passed, we could stop and buy some TUMS. We found one in Tamworth. As I entered the store, I walked by an old fellow sitting quietly in a rocking chair next to the door. At the counter, I asked the proprietor for some cherry-flavored TUMS.

"We have TUMS," the man replied," but not the cherry flavored."

"Well, do you have the orange flavored?" I asked. He said he didn't.

"Lemon?" No.

"Well then," I said, a little exasperated, "I guess I'll just take the plain TUMS."

As I was walking out the door after paying, the old fellow in the rocking chair looked up at me and said, "Looks like you're gonna have to rough it."

That's a little anecdote I'd surely like to have included in this book but, of course, I couldn't. It occurred recently. It's today's story in today's New England. Sometimes I tell it as part of one of the speeches I still occasionally give and, particularly if it's a New England audience, they absolutely roar with laughter. It's a hilarious little tidbit, true, but I don't think it's all *that* funny. So why do they react so enthusiastically? I think it's because it somehow touches a chord in all our hearts. It's true, current, and yet sort of an old-fashioned New England story that supports the notion that our so-called "image" not only endures to this day but might also be *real*. Furthermore, it's possibly an indication that it's always been real, always been an integral part of our American culture and, as such, worth nurturing, protecting, and, for sure, celebrating, often with humor, at every opportunity. Harvard professor and noted author the late Van Wyck Brooks wrote, "Generally speaking, Americans have a stake in New England. They're deeply implicated in it as the seat of their deepest, their stoutest, their greatest tradition. Their blood is mixed perhaps with other strains and perhaps they have long lived in other regions but New England is the ark of the covenant still. How fares this ark? Into what hands has it fallen? For it meant much to Americans that this old region should fare well as their palladium of truth, justice, freedom and learning."

I would say to Professor Van Wyck Brooks, don't worry. New England is still New England—perhaps now more than ever. To anyone who disagrees, maintaining that the New England we love is weakening or even disappearing, I point to places like Lowell, Newburyport, Providence, Concord, Boston, and hundreds of other communities throughout our six states, big and small, who have, in just the thirty years since I wrote this book, undertaken through historic preservation societies, land trusts, planning boards, and all sorts of other citizen efforts to live up to the faith that we will, indeed, preserve and safeguard our New England culture—image and all. (For one thing, it's essential for our tourist industry.)

But is it all too large a task? Too unrealistic in this fast-changing world? Well, if you feel that way, let me suggest you contemplate what Shakespeare's Hamlet told his mother. It's a quote that pretty much solves every conceivable problem. "Assume a virtue if you have it not," said Hamlet, "for use almost can change the stamp of nature."

So maybe one can say this book endeavors to assume New England's charming, inspiring, humorous, sometimes puzzling idiosyncrasies, customs, beliefs and behaviors that rather mysteriously comprise our treasured image. Or, in simpler terms and more clearly reflecting my own view, it reveals the real New England—then, now and always.

"Can you tell me how to get to Penacook?" a man, with his wife and two children in a New York-licensed car stopped to ask me recently as I was taking my daily three-mile walk. At that particular moment, it so happens I was deep in thought, planning what I might say in this introduction. So, without forethought, my response to his question reflected what was on my mind.

"Well," I replied slowly, "if I was to go to Penacook," and here I paused for several seconds, "I don't believe I'd start from here." I even pronounced it "staht" and used two syllables in "he-ah."

The man froze for a few seconds, staring at me, before bursting out laughing. Then, alas, I absolutely spoiled it all by telling him to go north on Rt. 202 out of Peterborough and eventually exit off I-93. He'd have told the story for years if only I'd just left it be. It might have even eventually found its way into a future book about New England. Darn.

Judson D. Hale
September 2010

1

SMALL-TOWN LIVING

We're Not Quaint and There's Plenty to Do All Winter

Regular natives and wealthy natives ঽ◈ tourists, summer people, year-round summer people, the socially elite, working professionals, and the dirt poor ঽ◈ "The Club" and why wealthy people own country equipment ঽ◈ "them" and "us" ঽ◈ fifteen specific differences between summer people and townspeople ঽ◈ the code of the deer hunter ঽ◈ small-town characters— The Historian, The Doer, The Eccentric, The Good Cook, The Mystery Man, That Woman, The Celebrity, The Voice, The Do-Gooder, The Force, and The Gossip ঽ◈ how to avoid driving the town fire truck ঽ◈ ministers I've known and a secret romance in the community church ঽ◈ raising money selling hearing-aid batteries ঽ◈ how not to run for town office ঽ◈ conducting an effective conversation ঽ◈ why one doesn't ask the yacht club commodore if he wants to sell his boat ঽ◈ outsiders' five "country dream" occupations ঽ◈ should a real natural-born sonofabitch be "true to himself"?

THE ORIGINAL SMALL-TOWN MOLD was cast in New England. "Oh, what a nice little village," a traveler in Ohio or Indiana or Illinois or Wisconsin might say. "It seems almost like New England." Not that it necessarily looks like New England—rather, it *seems* like New England. Attempts to articulate that common feeling and its appeal, or lack thereof, result in differing evaluations and emphases:

"It's not a faceless society—that's the great attraction," *Yankee* magazine's late publisher Rob Trowbridge liked to say.

"Freedom is what the new Yankees are seeking in New England towns," the author Chard Powers Smith once wrote. "Freedom to think their own thoughts and lead their own lives."

"New England small towns can be narrow, gossipy, cruel, and cliquish—and there's no tolerance at all," wrote an editor friend of mine after returning to his own city of Baltimore, Maryland, after an unhappy year in Dublin, New Hampshire.

"There's nothing to do around here. Small towns are dullsville. All of New England is dullsville." That from a nineteen-year-old Dublin, New Hampshire, native.

To be sure, there are as many opinions and descriptions of small-town living in New England as there are points of view. By "points of view," I mean that a country person in the plumbing business is not apt to enjoy relating humorous stories about the difficulties of convincing a country plumber to come to one's home to fix the leaky faucet. A wealthy summer person is full of such stories.

So before I blatantly describe in this first chapter the uniquely New England small-town cast of characters, their opinions, and how they function, I must, in the interest of perspective, "place" myself.

I was born in Boston of well-to-do, socially prominent Bostonians, raised on a dairy farm in Vanceboro (population 150), Maine, and educated at private schools around New England, including Choate and Dartmouth; I spent three years in the U.S. Army as an enlisted man, and have been a working (for *Yankee* magazine and *The Old Farmers Almanac*), taxpaying member of the Dublin (population 1,600), New Hampshire, community since 1958. So while I am a native New Englander, I am native to neither Vanceboro nor Dublin. And never will be. I know my "place" and, to the end of this book, I write from it . . .

The social structure of every New England town can be basically divided into two categories, the "haves," known as summer people, and the "have-nots," known as townspeople. Simple as that. But since the entire world can be divided in the same way (excluding the terms "summer people" and "townspeople"), I'll refine summer people to include, in order of respect, tourists, regular summer people, year-round summer people, and the very wealthy, socially elite. Townspeople can be broken up into the working professionals who are longtime residents but originally from outside, and the natives. Natives can be divided into very wealthy natives and regular natives, but it would appear the term "native" doesn't apply to a native if said native is *very* wealthy.

Not included in the social structure are the dirt poor. They live in shacks or roofed-over cellars at the end of town roads, have car bodies strewn about their yards, and are ignored by everybody. As I discovered several years ago when we published an investigative article entitled "The End-of-the-Road People," even mentioning this group of New Englanders makes everybody angry—including the proud end-of-the-roaders themselves! Although they are there, they're somehow off the chart.

Therefore, the lowest rung on the social ladder is the "tourist."

The late Walter Muir Whitehill, head of the Boston Athenaeum for so many years, used to quote the prophet Jeremiah in discussing tourists. "When ye entered, ye defiled my land, and made mine heritage an abomination." If reminded that a number of tourists are wonderfully fine people, he would say he was not referring to *all* tourists, just those "tripping gawkers . . . who rush through the state dressed as if for the beach, scattering beer cans behind them."

"What do you people do after the summer tourists all go home?" I once overheard a tourist ask the weary proprietor of the Dublin General Store.

"Oh, just fumigate," he replied. "Fumigate and keep on living."

When, with the passing of many years, a year-round summer person has worn out several sets of snow tires and long underwear, paid property taxes many times, toughed out a few winters without either Florida or Arizona, raised a succession of vegetable gardens, and become a legal resident, "you qualify for the highest attainable accolade," wrote Jim Brunelle in his book *Over to Home and From Away.* "You are now 'from away'? Strive for nothing beyond this. You've had it."

The working professional people don't necessarily work in town. Many commute as much as an hour. They fix up old colonial homes, assume effective roles in town government and town organizations, and because they make more money than the natives but much less than most of the socially elite, they are often a communications link between the two groups.

The socially elite have their own club, known among themselves as "The Club," which includes a few of the professionals, but not too many, and no natives. A distinguishing characteristic of the year-round members of the socially elite is their love of country equipment. All own four-wheel-drive vehicles and many, when they are not "South," plow their own driveways, much to the private disgust of the natives, who feel they don't do it correctly.

One doctor friend of mine carried this country-equipment inclination to the point of obsession. He bought a six-ton bulldozer. I happened to be present the first morning he tried it out. It had been delivered on a flatbed trailer the day before and during the previous evening he had read the literature, started the engine, worked the huge blade, and turned in place. Now he was ready to really use it. He decided his first job was to scrape the corn stubble off the top of his garden. The engine roared and the huge thing lumbered slowly into his garden as he lowered the blade. From my vantage point at the doorway of his garden house, I immediately detected a new, more labored sound to the engine, and the amount of smoke being emitted from here and there was alarming. But he kept going. When I saw the mountain of earth slowly rising in front of him, I realized what was happening. His blade was set too low. I ran down to the garden, shouting at him to stop, but he couldn't see through all the smoke, and couldn't hear me over the strained pounding of the engine. He didn't stop until his entire garden was transported some thirty or forty feet to an area on the north end of his property formerly devoted to a raspberry patch. His subsequent efforts to make things right resulted in about an acre of his land looking like, as he himself was to remark later in the day, "a training ground for giant woodchucks."

Nonetheless, I must say that bulldozer of his was one beautiful -looking machine.

On many town issues, particularly those involving "growth," politics can make for strange bed-fellows, aligning the politically conservative socially elite with the town's liberal leaning residents. For instance, just such an alliance, favoring protecting the town from change, defeated a couple of proposed shopping centers in Lenox, Massachusetts, back in the early 1970s and muddied the usually predictable social waters in that town to the point where, as writer Jeff Wheelwright later described in *Yankee*, the policeman on the corner had hair down to his shoulders and "the bearded, longhaired owner of the new art gallery talked about forming a people's polo team."

Certainly there are exceptions, surprising alliances on occasion, and innumerable crossovers among the social groups I've mentioned. A working professional in one town can be a tourist in another. A summer person can, technically speaking, be a native. And then there are those individuals whom no one can figure out. But the basic social current runs consistently.

"It's us against them!" I remember a Dublin resident, one of the fairly new working professionals in town, saying dramatically at town meeting as he was speaking out against a state-proposed bypass road of the village area.

"The funny thing about that," I heard the woman behind me, a native, whisper to her husband, "is that it's the 'them' that's been here longer than the 'us.' "

"Us and them," "rich and poor," "haves and have-nots," "summer people and townspeople"—that division, by whatever words, is everywhere, although the uniquely New England *regional mix* of manifestations pertaining to each side can be easily recognized in terms of behavior modes and small-town attitudes.

For instance . . .

Summer people favor maintaining their town roads as narrow, dirt roads. Townspeople would like to widen and hard-top them for ease in plowing.

Summer people favor cross-country skiing. Townspeople favor snowmobiling.

Summer people keep horses. Townspeople do not—unless for harness racing.

Townspeople are suspicious that zoning laws will hurt their ability to make a living as well as their right "to do with my own property as I damn well please." Summer people favor strict zoning in order to protect the quiet, noncommercial atmosphere of an area. Overall, townspeople favor individual rights. (Particularly when the individual is them.) Summer people favor group rights. (Particularly *their* group.)

Summer people sail, play tennis and golf, wear sneakers, and drink martinis. Townspeople have outboard motorboats, play no outdoor games at all, wear visor caps, and drink beer and "sippin' whiskey." (Also, during the winter, summer people's coats extend down below the knees. Townspeople's coats are three-quarter length at most.)

Summer people are against growth. Townspeople are in favor of growth. Both are against "progress."

As former *Vermont Life* editor Brian Vachon once pointed out to me, summer people cut their kids' hair at home. Townspeople's kids go to a barber.

Summer people label themselves with car bumper stickers ("Split Wood Not Atoms"). Townspeople do not.

Townspeople utilize snowshoes as a means of getting around the woods when the snow is deep. Summer people consider snowshoeing a sport.

Summer people value the scenic views from their homes. I marveled at mine of Mount Monadnock to the man, a native, who was building my house in 1959. "Well, after you've lived here for a while," he said, "you'll get so the view won't bother you no more."

Summer people are Episcopalian. Townspeople are not.

Townspeople meet for coffee in the morning at certain places— the diner, the general store if it serves coffee, which it often does, and so on. Summer people meet later in the day at "The Club." For tennis, not coffee. (Working professionals meet at Rotary and other formal or informal gatherings that involve meals.)

Summer people enjoy having long driveways. Townspeople prefer homes close to the road.

Summer people feel that they do not understand townspeople. However, they make sincere efforts to do so. Townspeople feel they *do* understand summer people. And they are aware of the efforts summer people make to conform to acceptable "native" behavior.

Townspeople hunt deer (and raccoons). Summer people hunt birds. (Lots of crossovers here—except that summer people do not hunt raccoons, and although *some* summer people travel to faraway northern places to hunt deer, they do not poach deer.)

There are innumerable exceptions, of course.

Of all the attitudes and behavior modes I have attributed to the two groups, it may be that the last mentioned, deer hunting, is the most divisive. Deer hunting in northern New England towns is a veritable way of life, as foreign to the average summer person as the world of horse shows and fox hunting on horseback is to the average New England native.

In the town in which I was raised, Vanceboro, Maine, and in most northern towns today, deer hunting was and is a way of life year-round. Not just during the season. Oh, sure, there are game wardens and they'll throw the book at any outsider caught poaching (hunting out of season) or jacking (hunting at night with a light). They'll prosecute natives for illegal hunting activities, if they have to. The subtle and important point here is that they will often find ways to not *have* to.

I was aware of all these deer-hunting subtleties at an early age. In fact, the first bona fide illegal deer I *remember* seeing was on a June afternoon in the early 1940s when I was eight or nine years old. A number of my father's old farmhands (the young ones were off in the war) and others were gathered at the Vanceboro store after the day's work. I was there too—hanging around as usual for a free candy bar or tidbit one or another of the men usually enjoyed giving "Roger Hale's young fella"—when I heard one of them say to our farm foreman, Russell Nichols, "Got any deer lately, Russ?" Immediately there was an embarrassed and uneasy silence, with the most embarrassed being the questioner. Not because it was not deer season (which, of course, it wasn't) but because he'd forgotten for a second that the game warden was a member of the gathering that afternoon.

"Why, sure I have!" Russell boomed after a split-second hesitation. "Biggest ol' buck in the State-o-Maine. Got 'm with one shot right between the eyes. He's out there waitin' for me in the truck right now if you wanna go see 'm." Everyone laughed uproariously, including the game warden. What a good joke!

Of course, I left the group, the men still laughing and back-slapping, and meandered right out to Russell's truck parked in back of the store. There, under a large canvas or burlap covering, was one of the largest buck deer I was ever to lay eyes on. A little warm, too.

I still think that if Russell had denied the deer, looked uneasy, and generally acted in a guilty manner, the game warden would have had to look in the truck on his way out and, of course, would then have had to fine him. Such was the code. And I have reason to believe it's no different today.

By noting some of the different attitudes within the small New England town social structure, I don't mean to imply that there is no common ground. There is. We all share a pride in the town, a concern for the individual members of the community who may be in trouble, a love of everyone's children, rich or poor, and a hope that they don't all leave after high school or college graduation. (Many do—but come back eventually. At least enough do to keep the population about steady.) We mourn each other at funerals, celebrate our births and weddings together, cluck together at scandals, struggle against the elements together, and march together to the cemetery each Memorial Day. Also, we continually support each other, day in and day out, year in and year out, with car honks, waves, good mornings, short weather analyses, and all such other small but unifying support features inherent in the life of a small town.

Everyone is aware, too, of certain residents who unknowingly represent characters who inevitably exist in every community. Every single one.

For instance, there is:

The Historian—usually an elderly man (or a long-winded one, depending on your point of view) and almost always a native. He will tell you, often without even being asked, exactly where the old hotel once stood, the names of all the people who stayed there each summer, and what the weather was like the day before, the day, and the day after it burned to the ground.

The Doer—usually a male member of the working professionals. He is chairman of the church executive committee, serves as town selectman, raises money for the area hospital, convinces "The Club" to allow townspeople to play their golf course during the spring and fall, and his wife is the president of the Women's Club.

The Eccentric—who exists from town to town in many forms, man or woman, native or summer person, but whose actions are ever so slightly strange. One of my favorites in this category was a man living in Peterborough, New Hampshire (a few miles from Dublin), who had an inordinate love of beavers. His property bordered a large beaver pond. Each morning for a number of years the man stood at the edge of the pond calling to the beavers. "Here, beaver, beaver, beaver! Here, beaver!" is what he yelled repeatedly, with evidently no reaction whatsoever from the beavers. I'm told that after some three years of this on a daily basis, one morning a single beaver finally emerged from the water near the shore in front of him, waddled up to our Eccentric, and, rumor has it, bit him quite severely on the hand.

The Good Cook—always a native and usually a woman. At church suppers, pieces of her lemon meringue pies are taken from the serving tables (by those oblivious of proper conduct) *before* the main-course dishes, just to be sure. She can cook and manage a baked-bean-roast-beef-and-hot-fresh-rolls supper for three hundred people—served exactly at the announced time, every dish piping hot, and with bottomless cups of incredibly good coffee. In marked contrast to The Good Cook, The Good Cook's husband is quite skinny.

The Mystery Man—one of the very few people in town whose ancestry and place of birth cannot be determined. Also, no one is quite sure what he does for a living or if he ever had a wife and family. Or why he leaves town for ten days every three months except during odd-numbered years. The Mystery Man causes extensive frustration.

That Woman—she may not be pretty in the classic sense, but there's something vaguely exotic—and cheap—about her appearance. She wears her hair long, uses elaborate facial makeup, and she elicits from each and every other woman in town, whether she's a summer person or a townsperson, an instant and irrevocable hate. On sight.

The Celebrity—who either commanded the Second Army in Europe during World War II, wrote a screenplay early in the career of a major Hollywood star, or whose father briefly served as an ambassador to a small country whose name nobody in town can pronounce. The Celebrity, more often than not, wears an ascot.

The Voice—man or woman, townsperson or summer person, The Voice sings at every town occasion in which solo singing is called for. During group singing of hymns in church, The Voice sings louder than is called for. And holds his or her notes a split second longer than anyone else does. The Voice is a soprano or a tenor, depending on sex, and is quick to lead sing-alongs, beginning with "Moonlight Bay," at parties. The Voice once choked during a church Christmas solo, and no one present has ever mentioned the incident from that day to this.

The **Do-Gooder**—a wealthy elderly woman who, in a pinch, could qualify for the role of The Eccentric. She has waged a lifelong crusade against cruelty to animals, once suggested that an African-American be invited to speak on integration as part of the Thursday afternoon summer lecture series at "The Club," and occasionally holds a seminar at her mansion for the purpose of "breaking down the silly barriers between summer people and townspeople." The seminar, incidentally, results in a most stimulating and lively discourse among the summer people present. There are, of course, no townspeople there.

The **Force**—always a woman and always a native. Her blessing is absolutely crucial to the success of most any church, school, or town organization project. She never speaks out at meetings, and in private, speaks out only to her most intimate friends. Since the opinions she expresses, even privately, are always in the negative, any project about which she has failed to utter a single word is considered to have her heartfelt support. How her considerable power is derived has always been a mystery to me.

Finally, there's **The Gossip**—usually a native and always, due probably to stereotyped attitudes, a woman. Of course, every man and woman in all social levels is a gossip. As Thornton Wilder once said, "In our town we like to know the facts about everybody." But The Gossip, either the general-store owner's wife, the postmaster, the librarian, or at least someone with ready access to people on a day-to-day basis, is *counted* upon by everyone in town to either confirm or deny the latest rumors. She always confirms them. And adds to them. Also, she is an unwitting tool for a few wily residents who use her to spread *their* version of certain common information.

In the days of party telephone lines, The Gossip obtained a great deal of her information from that particular source. My mother, being a professional singer, was often away from our farm in Vanceboro, and the nightly telephone calls to her were important to my father. However, during most conversations, the line would noticeably weaken when a certain Mrs. Armstrong (not her real name), The Gossip in Vanceboro in those days, picked up her receiver to silently listen in. On one particular night, my father lost his patience when the line suddenly weakened to the point where he could barely hear my mother's voice.

"Mrs. Armstrong," he shouted, "will you please get the hell off the line!"

A voice immediately came in from somewhere, and we have always assumed it was that of Mrs. Armstrong.

"Oh, Roger Hale," it said, "you never say anything interesting anyway!" And slam went a receiver.

There are also, of course, The Idiot, The Lover (male or female), The Drunk, and a few others, but I'm in enough trouble with this chapter already.

There is a "coming together" evident in a small town after the summer is over. Social divisions become noticeably fuzzier. Town organizations spring back to life with renewed vigor and almost all are socially integrated to some extent. An exception is the volunteer fire company. It's all townspeople. And unlike some other town organizations, it is active all summer too.

Although, as I've stated, I am not a native of my town, and although I belong to "The Club," I proved to be an exception to the unwritten and unspoken "townspeople only" social rule and was a member of Dublin's Volunteer Fire Company for more than fifteen years. I was and still am inordinately afraid of fires and I have no aptitude in mechanical matters. However, upon arriving in town in 1958, I felt it was my duty to join the company simply because the fire station was located only a hundred yards from my office. When the siren sounded, I was one of those readily available. The first man to reach the firehouse after the alarm began to wail always jumped into the ten-wheel, multi-ton fire truck, started it up, and commenced to move out in the direction indicated by the truck radio. Late-arriving firemen would hop aboard as the truck moved or would bring the second or third fire truck. Others would follow in their own vehicles.

I was very often that first man to arrive at the station, which constituted a problem. To put it simply, I could never remember how to start or how to shift the many gears in that big truck—or, for that matter, how to tune in the radio.

The solution to my problem presented itself in about 1965. It was around that time that the company purchased waterproof fire coats and helmets for us volunteers to use during a fire. They were hung on the rear of the truck. The first time the alarm sounded after purchase of this equipment, I was once again the first arrival at the station. Instead of jumping in the cab and struggling with the gears, I ran to the rear of the truck to fetch my new coat and helmet. Running back forward, I noted to my immense relief that someone else was already in the driver's seat starting the engine. So at every subsequent fire, I made certain I took a long enough period of time fetching a coat and helmet to avoid the driver's job. Often this required initially running around and around the truck a number of times until someone else finally arrived, but no one ever caught me on that particular ruse. During a fire alarm, the main thing is to *run*. It really doesn't matter to anyone where you're going or why.

After serving some fifteen years of what I considered to be my stint, I submitted my letter of resignation. I was becoming more rather than less apprehensive about fires, due in no small part to the increasingly sophisticated equipment available to us. Also, I was growing a bit weary of replacing sportsjackets, oxford shirts, ties, and expensive slacks, which, even with the new fire coats, I inevitably ruined.

In spite of my fears and all the rest, I miss the fire company. I particularly miss those times after the fire was out, when a can of beer or a little whiskey was passed around while we were still hosing down. The tension and wild intensity of the preceding hours lifted and groups of men gathered near those on the hoses to jaw and laugh and summarize what had happened to each of them. There was a euphoric feeling of having worked, endured under trying circumstances, and succeeded together. ("We've never lost a cellar hole," we always said.)

I have never, before or since, felt more a part of what I might call the central spiritual core of the town than I always did during those special times after fighting a fire with the men of the Dublin Fire Company.

The church is another organization close to the heart of a small New England town. But while the volunteer fire company is the enduring bastion of townspeople or natives, the church involves all social levels, particularly during the fall, winter, and spring. In the summer, many towns like Dublin, New Hampshire, open an Episcopal chapel for the summer people. But while larger towns naturally have several churches of various denominations open year round, innumerable small communities all across New England have, over the past fifty years or so, reduced down to one church, usually known as the community church. It's nondenominational in spirit—i.e., open to all—but its background and traditional support is often Congregational or Unitarian.

A small-town community church has a difficult time encompassing its members' various religious backgrounds, and its popularity among the various social groups swings from high to low to in between. Sometimes Episcopalians will have a dominating influence. During that time, more year-round summer people than usual will attend and possibly even Communion will be offered, to the distress of several townspeople. Then perhaps some ex-hippies will gain the upper hand. There will be an awkward few minutes in each service where everyone holds hands. Quite a bit of guitar playing too. When this sort of deviation subsides, and subside it always does, the natives and working professionals assume command once again and run the organization in the straightforward, no-frills, comparatively unemotional, traditional manner in which it's been run for centuries.

The ebbs and flows of community church life are dictated to a large degree by the sort of minister in residence. Ministers come and go with a fair amount of regularity, and it is during those periods *between* ministers that the church experiences its ultimate harmony. A search committee, including all town social factions, is formed and it regularly meets with the congregation as a whole to report on progress as well as to invite discussion and expression of views on what the church "needs." On these occasions, person after person rises to explain what the church means to him or her and what marvelous attributes ought to be part of the new minister's character.

"He or, as the case may be, she [both will be expressed, but "he" is meant] should be understanding but firm; have great faith in God but not jam that faith down our throats."

"He must love little children and be able to be someone you can go to when you're in trouble."

"He must be able to give a good sermon and be very involved in the community."

"He must have a love for people all over the world and inspire others to love likewise."

Everyone agrees with what everyone says. The church is never happier. And often the search process can last over a year, with guest ministers from surrounding towns filling in on Sundays.

The man or woman eventually hired, of course, is simply the nicest person available at the moment the church feels it really is time to choose somebody.

Unfortunately for small-town ministers, they are expected to be approximate replicas of Jesus Christ. No human frailties allowed. Over the years, I have known and liked many town ministers and most have had more apparent human frailties than many people I've enjoyed less. The first minister I ever knew—in Vanceboro—

suffered from a severe stutter, particularly with the word "Christ." It's unfortunate he wasn't a Unitarian, because the entire service would come to a halt over and over while he would silently struggle with that particular all-important name until it would finally burst forth in a minor explosion.

Alcohol was the problem of another minister I knew well. Probably precipitated by self-doubt. "Do you think being a minister in this town or anywhere makes any sense, Jud?" he would ask me as we sipped a cocktail on my screened-in porch from time to time. During sermons, he often forgot where he was going. His point would remain dangling in the air somewhere for his flock to guess at. "And as John once said in those never-to-be-forgotten words . . . those never-to-be-forgotten words . . . those . . ." I would hurt for him.

Ministers' wives are carefully observed too, and one, particularly vivid in my own memory, happened to be observed far more carefully than most. She was a handsome woman and very concerned about health, eating the correct foods, exercising, and so forth. She also felt that the sun's rays are important to the well-being of one's body. So during the summer, she would sunbathe in a well-hidden area behind the church parsonage, often without a stitch of clothing on. About a quarter of a mile up the hill from the parsonage was the only garage and gas station, which, in those days, served as a meeting place for male townspeople after four o'clock. A few beers were consumed and the day was reviewed.

I would happen over there on occasion and was, therefore, a witness to a harmless little ritual that started quite by accident one summer afternoon and was then deliberately continued off and on for two subsequent summers. It began when someone in the group used the wall telephone in the garage to call the minister on some matter then being discussed. The minister was not there. The phone was allowed to ring a number of times in case he was outside. He wasn't. But his wife was. And suddenly someone in the group caught a fleeting, distant glimpse of her running for the parsonage back door—stark naked!

Well, several days later at the garage gathering, it was a consensus (it being a bright, sunny afternoon) that the minister ought to be telephoned. If he was there, he would be asked whether or not a church supper was being planned for that month, or some such, and if he was not there . . . well, let it ring for a while, because he might be outside. This time *everyone* caught a fleeting, distant glimpse of a stark-naked lady racing for the parsonage back door. When she answered the phone, an unimportant message was given for her husband.

I believe it was several weeks before someone brought a pair of binoculars to the garage gathering. That someone, as I recall, was none other than one of the church deacons, and it was that very same church deacon who, after the minister and his wife were divorced several years later, eventually became her second husband.

Too bad that church histories and church annual reports seldom, if ever, include the *romantic* stories of small-town church life.

Besides the many organizations connected with town government, such as the Zoning Committee, the School Committee, the Budget Committee, the Recreation Committee, and others, to which one must be elected, larger New England towns have countless organizations one can simply join. There are the Masons, the Rotarians, the Chamber of Commerce, the Lions, the DAR (if you qualify—see Chapter 6), various art, music, and literature groups, and so forth. Residents of small towns, particularly the working professionals, go outside their own communities to join such organizations in nearby larger towns.

Besides the town government, the church, "The Club," and the volunteer fire company, very small towns usually have the Women's Club, the Historical Society, and possibly the Grange, although the Grange is fading in New England.

Attendance at the meetings of these small-town organizations is often meager. When I was the civil defense director of Dublin during the early 1960s, I was called upon to address the Dublin Women's Club on the procedures to be taken in the event of a nuclear war. Seven people were present. Two left the meeting halfway through my talk and went into the kitchen to start the coffee to be served afterward. So four ladies (one lady was very obviously asleep) listened blandly as I told them that we would soon all very possibly be blown to smithereens. I received a round of pleasant applause, and then we all waded into the coffee, cookies, and cakes.

Some years later, I was asked to speak to that same group about *Yankee* magazine. I don't recall the number in attendance, but I do remember the introduction.

"It is indeed a pleasure to introduce and welcome Judson Hale," the elderly lady who was program chair said, in a frail and wavering voice, "who will tell us all about the *Yankee* magazine. After his talk, we will adjourn for refreshments and begin to enjoy ourselves."

To function well in a small New England town requires patience, humility, common sense, compassion, and a strong natural instinct for the sensitivities of others. Of these, patience may be the most difficult for an outsider to learn or accept.

A member of the Grange in Brattleboro, Vermont, once told me proudly that from the program of recycling hearing-aid batteries, the Grangers had raised about seventy dollars for their scholarship program.

"You mean you personally raised seventy dollars for the Brattleboro Grange by recycling hearing-aid batteries?" I asked.

"Heavens, no," he replied. "I mean all the Grange organizations throughout the state of Vermont have raised that amount recycling hearing-aid batteries." Their efforts continued at that pace for some time—but eventually enough was collected to send a blind student to college.

In the same way, ladies of the church will knit socks, mittens, and hats, or sew aprons, doilies, and potholders, for months prior to the church fair. Several days before the fair, they'll cook countless pies, cakes, bread, and cookies, and then they'll spend eight or ten hours setting up the fair, managing the tables throughout the day, and cleaning up afterward.

"Well, how did it go?" I usually ask my wife as she returns home, exhausted, in the evening of a church-fair day.

"Really well," she might say. "I think when all our expenses are accounted for we may net almost $125!"

For some people not accustomed to New England small-town ways, it might appear more logical to save literally hundreds of woman-hours by simply convincing one generous person to take a half minute and write out a $125 check to the church. But of course, that would be missing most, if not all, of the point.

"Go slowly," advised the late Vrest Orton, owner of the Vermont Country Store in Weston, when asked if he might have any advice for newcomers to a small New England town. "I wish that some of the newcomers from metropolitan centers who just *love* our rural ways," said Vrest, warming to this subject, "would, if they arrive on Monday, wait until at least Friday before they start running for office and telling us, at town meetings, why we are wrong and how to run the town."

It is impossible to explain this adequately to a newcomer if said newcomer does not have the natural instinct to feel it.

"But I'm only running for the Board of Selectmen because I want to show the townspeople that this town *means* something to me, that I *care* about it, that I'm willing to *work* for it. I know I can *improve* things for *everyone*. What does it matter how long I've been here?"

Those are almost the exact words of a capable, hard-working friend of mine who had just moved to Dublin from a city in New York State. And in spite of my urgent appeals to him that he be patient and wait a few years before running for the town's top job, he continued his campaign, sending out letters to every resident in which he explained his opinions and made suggestions for town improvements, printing and handing out bumper stickers, buying space in the local paper, and calling upon each and every voter in town. He received a friendly reception wherever he went, and the night before the election, he told me he was confident he was going to win.

"I've been through every name on the checklist," he said, "and my 'definite yeses' alone will put me over the top—even without some of the 'maybes.' "

On election day, I believe, he received three votes. Even I didn't vote for him. His opponent, not incidentally, had done absolutely nothing during the campaign except to sign his name, verifying he would serve if elected.

Vrest also advised new town or state officeholders to "keep your mouth shut, and listen to those who have had experience. Until you know what is going on, vote no."

Patience is an asset in simple day-to-day functioning too. Here's a typical conversation that may illustrate the point:

"Morning, Bill—looks like it'll turn out to be a pretty nice day after all."

"It will, Jud, if it don't rain."

More weather talk, possibly involving an anecdote or two related to previous days in which the weather had been similar to that of the day of the conversation, then:

"Too bad about the young Arnold girl."

"Well, these young people—they just won't learn these days. They've got no sense. "

Further discussion about the Arnold girl, young people, and possibly the Arnold girl's father and uncle, "who weren't much good either."

"Well, Bill, we've all got our problems, right?"

"If we didn't, Jud, why, we just wouldn't be happy!"

Laughter. And a good summarizing laugh is the signal that the real purpose of the conversation can now begin.

"Say, Bill, I was wondering whether you might know of somebody who could come up to my place sometime and take a look at that chimney of mine. The fireplace still smokes something awful. I know how busy you are, but . . ."

"How high does that chimney of yours extend up over the

roofline, Jud?"

Long back-and-forth discussion about the chimney, the damper, the fireplace, and the man who built it.

"I knew it wasn't exactly right when you first had it put in, but I didn't want to say anything at the time."

"Well, I sure know it now, Bill. You were right. Do you think there's any possible way it can be fixed?"

"Oh, sure. It can be fixed, all right. Cost you a little money. But oh, sure, it can be fixed."

Long pause. Long, *long* pause. It is at this specific critical juncture that you win or you lose.

"Well, I've got to go up by your way tomorrow afternoon, and I'll stop by and take a look. . . ."

"Thanks, Bill. I'd appreciate it." I win. Bill might not stop by my house the next afternoon—in fact, he probably won't. But he is now committed. My fireplace problem will be fixed. Eventually.

In contrast to patience, the other good attributes for functioning effectively in small towns—common sense, humility, compassion, and a good instinct for the sensitivities of others—are certainly obvious to everyone. I mean, one would assume most wealthy summer people would know that the habit of not paying bills to local businesses for months and months is particularly rankling to townspeople.

It would seem obvious, too, that if one wished to get along well and happily in a small New England town, one would not hire work from outside; in a letter to a local newspaper advocating that newer people be taxed more, one would not refer to one's own property as "my ancestral lands"; one would think twice before giving one's worn-out clothing to a family one considers poor; one would not ask the commodore of the local yacht club how much money he'd be willing to take for his boat; one would be very careful about decorating one's garden for the annual garden club tour by hanging one's underwear on various casually displayed clotheslines to simulate the gay informality of an Italian garden; during a burial service at the cemetery, one would not refer to the bereaved wife of the recently deceased resident as "the widder of the corpse"; one would not put one's opinion at a church meeting into the form of a motion when it is obvious there are several people present who still do not agree; one would not show up at the Memorial Day parade in a costume; one would resist the temptation to take, as seconds, the last piece of The Good Cook's lemon meringue pie at a church supper; and finally, one would not call the town moderator a liar during town meeting.

I have been witness to each and every case of misjudgment listed above. No doubt I've committed similar ones. Everyone has. Actually, I guess the moderator, then my uncle, the late Robb Sagendorph, *Yankee's* founder, was not exactly called a liar. Rather, he responded to some criticism from the floor by saying angrily, "Ben, do you mean to call me a liar?" The retort was, "No, Robb, I don't. But ain't you?"

To function at all, it is necessary to be able to make a living. A variety of steady work isn't always available in small towns, so commuting becomes for many country New Englanders as much a part of their daily routine as it is for urbanites living near cities all across America. It seems to me, however, that the work most outsiders dream about when they contemplate "throwing in the towel and moving to a small New England town where I can lead the good life" is one of the following: owning and running a country inn or a country store, being the editor or publisher of a country newspaper, fishing for lobsters, or becoming the proverbial jack-of-all-trades.

I am quick to advise anyone to just as well forget the lobster fishing. To be sure, one legally needs only to possess a proper lobster-fishing license, but in reality, the requirements are more complicated. First of all, your father must have been a lobsterman. Maybe even your grandfather. Interlopers are not regarded with kindness. After placing out in the ocean a number of your brand-new "poverty boxes," as lobstermen call their traps (no lobsterman ever admits to doing well in the business—although *many*, in fact, do), in an area not your own (and there's nothing written down or even stated verbally to stipulate who "owns" what area), you might find two half hitches around your buoy spindles the next time you go out to check them. That's the first warning. The second could be damaged traps. If you still haven't caught on, don't be overly surprised if your boat springs a leak and sinks to the bottom.

I discourage the jack-of-all-trades idea too, unless one possesses an exceptional skill or talent in a craft or service. Service includes the professions—and many communities are in need of professionals willing to endure, or wanting to enjoy, small-town life. Up in northern Vermont, New Hampshire, and Maine, for instance, school boards have advertised for teachers in *Field and Stream*. Plowing driveways, sugaring in the spring, cutting firewood, doing some painting, some carpentry and plumbing, some fishing and clamming, driving a truck—all these together, and more, constitute the "getting by" profession that is really townspeople's territory. Newcomers can break in, but only marginally. Few can ever really learn to juggle their time and customers around as effectively as the native who has done it all his life.

Author Jim Brunelle writes about one of the most successful jack-of-all-traders in his town, one Jonas Hall, who said a man was better off eight months behind in his work than merely four months behind. "Jonas argued that once a man got eight months behind, he could pretend he was four months ahead. He'd lose a year that way but he would gain peace of mind and probably what he was going to do in the year he'd lost wouldn't amount to anything anyway."

Owning or working for a small-town newspaper entails, like every sort of country work, comparatively low financial reward, long hours, and, most important, an entirely different perspective on what exactly is *important*. As *Vineyard Gazette*'s former editor and owner Henry Beetle Hough once said, "The President of the United States would probably not get his name in our paper. Except in election returns. Or unless he came to Martha's Vineyard."

Frederick J. Harrigan, a longtime editor and publisher in Colebrook, New Hampshire, disclosed that when he sold out any edition of his *News and Sentinel* and got back on press to print more copies, it was because that edition had more than the usual complement of weddings and/or obituaries of people with lots of relatives. "It tends to keep your ego in place," Harrigan said.

Owning a historic old inn with a good restaurant and lounge is perhaps the ultimate dream. As Norman Simpson, author of *Country Inns and Back Roads*, wrote, it's a realistic dream for those who possess such qualities as "showmanship, a good head for business, and an attitude toward people that is service-oriented." He has words of warning too. "If your marriage is shaky, forget it. . . . And if you have an alcohol problem, the problem will increase." Also, new inn owners must get past "the dangerous year." That, according to Simpson, is the third year, when new owners think they've made it, expand quickly, "and then go down the tube."

A former flight attendant I talked with, who with her husband bought the Barrows House in Dorset, Vermont, in 1972, confessed that in reality "running an inn is like being on an airplane that never lands."

Yet the appeal remains. Most old New England inns have long histories, traditions, warmth, and gentility, and they manifest the spirit of the communities they serve. As Henry David Thoreau once said, "The gods who are most interested in the human race preside over the tavern. . . . The tavern compares favorably with the church. The church is the place where prayers and sermons are delivered, but the tavern is where they are to take effect. And if the former are good, the latter cannot be bad."

For reasons I cannot fathom, most new owners of New England inns come from New Jersey. Some make the grade. The majority, unfortunately, do not—but then ever more New Jersey-ites are dreaming in the wings.

Owning and operating the general store in a New England town is equally attractive to daydreamers. And attractive to some realists too, who go ahead and buy a store, work seventy or more hours a week, build up a good inventory, and then sell. If they have done it all right, in the right town, at the right time, they can make a killing. I know about one Maine store that realized a net profit after taxes in 1977 of $17,000 and paid each of its three owners—two brothers and the wife of one—a weekly $150 wage. That isn't much until you consider that the store also provided their food and upstairs living quarters. Finally—and this is where the real money is—they sold the store four years later for three times the amount they paid for it—not counting inflation. Some other stores around New England are, of course, only barely getting by. Still, country stores don't seem to change ownership as rapidly as do country inns. And country stores are more often bought by townspeople or natives than are country inns.

I knew a native country-store owner in northern Maine who also owned stores in two nearby towns. The rumor was that he would charge the town residents in each of his three stores more than he would charge the out-of-towners. This would cause many residents to go to one of his stores in a neighboring town, where, to justify the trip, they would tend to buy many more things than they would ordinarily have bought.

Certainly a pitfall in storekeeping today is extending credit. Most don't. A hunting friend of my father's who had been raised in Lewiston would recall how "Big Jim," a Lewiston general-store owner, wouldn't get much business when people had cash in their pockets. During those prosperous times, they would buy at the chain supermarkets, where the prices were lower. But when crops failed or times were generally hard, Big Jim's store was always crowded with people buying on credit.

"One year," my father's friend enjoyed recalling, "Big Jim had so darn much business he almost went bankrupt."

Today, as anyone who has traveled backcountry New England will confirm, there are still plenty of old-fashioned general stores. In fact, there's one for every small community. "But do you know of any that are for sale?" visiting out-of-staters will often ask me.

My uncle Robb Sagendorph probably had the best answer for that question. He'd simply reply, "I don't know of any that aren't."

I actually don't feel comfortable giving advice to the many outsiders who come to our *Yankee* office inquiring about moving to Dublin or another small New England town. We're never bored or lonesome. Some people would be. There are some unique standards of right and wrong in a New England community, but many people are unable to recognize them. If your car is stuck in the snow, probably the first town resident who happens by will pull you out, no matter how precious his time. But there are those who will never understand why he won't accept any money. When someone says to me earnestly, as did a woman from Philadelphia recently, that she wants "to sit by the fireplace and knit mittens with the country people and become their friend," I know there isn't the remotest chance she ever will. Nor will she ever know why.

Perhaps the safest and best advice one can give to inquirers is, as so many philosophers have said in so many ways, "be true to thyself." If you're not a native, don't ever give a thought to trying to become one. If you're a scholarly person, don't change your manner of speaking among a group of townspeople who may not have received as much education. They may, in fact, be smarter. If your inclination is to wear a coat and tie, wear your coat and tie. No matter what you wear, you won't pass for a native the second you open your mouth. If you like people, you will be liked in a New England town. If you don't, you won't.

Which brings me to the question of whether or not a real, natural-born sonofabitch ought also to be "true to himself." Although I haven't as yet been presented with the opportunity (to my knowledge), I've often contemplated how I would advise such a person. And I'm inclined to believe that the rule should hold true. Maybe, after living in town for three or four weeks, a newcomer like that would run for some town office like tax collector. He'd probably win, too.

2

THE FOOD

Making a Decent Clam Chowder and Other Culinary Observations

The much-maligned New England boiled dinner ❧ duff and other indigestibles ❧ Lizzie Borden ❧ breakfast ❧ red flannel hash ❧ clam chowder and why New Yorkers put inner tubes in theirs ❧ baked beans and codfish balls on Sunday morning ❧ why nobody fishes for scrod ❧ how to tell haddock from cod ❧ the "codfish aristocracy" ❧ hulled corn or samp or hominy ❧ the only legal Rhode Island jonnycake ❧ the man responsible for "pie timber" and apple pie order ❧ our favorite food—with green stuff and a long googy thing in it ❧ the correct way to cook a lobster ❧ how not to make strawberry shortcake ❧ clambake and tea party etiquette ❧ the first maple syrup gatherer ❧ the first hamburger ❧ the first grinder ❧ the first to fry a clam ❧ how the doughnut hole really came to be—and other theories ❧ why New England sailors never drank water ❧ the drink used for blasting stumps ❧ a decent cup of tea ❧ why I was thrown off the Yankee recipe-testing committee, and the worst chicken Eve ever eaten ❧ and the best New England biscuit

BACK IN THE YEAR 1677, Massachusetts sent King Charles II of England a handsome gift. It consisted of ten barrels of cranberries, two barrels of samp (actually dried cracked corn), and about three thousand codfish, salted and dried and looking for all the world like a shipload of roofing shingles. The colonists were hoping this gesture might soften the king into relaxing the crippling restrictions of the Acts of Trade and Navigation. The king received the package—and the Trade Acts remained unaltered.

Maybe they should have included maple syrup in the package. The colonists had learned to make it by then from the Native Americans, who, as historian Marc Lescarbot wrote in 1609, "get juice from the trees and from it distill a sweet and agreeable liquid." But Charles probably would not have been impressed with maple syrup either. Too strange and assertive a taste. Even today, maple syrup is virtually unknown in Europe. (To be sure, sugar-maple trees are not native there.)

New England cooking and New England food have never impressed non-New England gourmets in other regions of the world. Ask for their impressions of it and they'll immediately describe "the New England boiled dinner," which, in a less rarefied form, is simply corned beef and cabbage. I enjoy a boiled dinner, but those preparing it today are fortunately a bit more cognizant of good taste and health than during the time when New England's food reputation was being established. A Rhode Island traveler in 1704, as recorded in Richard Hooker's *Food and Drink in America*, described one cook's corned beef as having evidently been "boil'd in her dye kettle." He went on to say, "I, being hungry, gott a little down; but my stomach was soon cloy'd and what cabbage I swallowed serv'd me for a Cudd the whole day after."

Possibly New England whalers should take some of the blame. The fact that they abided each day for months on end the meals served aboard their ships can be interpreted to mean they knew no better, either at sea or at home. One of the everyday foods enjoyed on whaling ships was something called "duff." It consisted of a quantity of flour, moistened with equal parts of salt and fresh water, and stirred together with a lot of "slush," or lard, as well as yeast. The whole doughy mixture was then boiled in a bag until, as one whaleman's journal records, "it can be dropped from the topgallant crosstress upon the deck without breaking." Another reference to duff describes it as "not only indigestible, but difficult to masticate and more fit to be used as shot for storming ports and towns than to be eaten."

Furthermore, if mental associations have something to do with taste—and I would be of the opinion that they do—then New England's choice of names for some of its dishes have been, let's say, unfortunate. Leaf through some of the old-time New England recipe books, as *Yankee* writer Annie Proulx once did, and you'll find the likes of Mud Pie, Burnt Leather Cake, Bumpy Stew, Nameless, and Lazy White Pickles. The last, Annie says, conjures up "visions of faded, large cucumbers lounging indolently on an antebellum veranda." One notices innumerable mistakes in these old recipe books too. Typical is a recipe in a nineteenth-century Vermont cookbook for making a lemon-cheese sandwich that neglected to include the cheese. Thus the reader was left with two damp, sour pieces of bread. Does nothing much to enhance New England's culinary reputation.

I am, however, sympathetic to mistakes, and while *Yankee* magazine has, I would hope, done much over the years to portray New England food in a more favorable and delicious light, we've inadvertently gone the other way too. Years ago we always simply took the word of an author that a particular submitted recipe had been carefully tested. The *last* time we were so trusting was when we printed a recipe for refrigerator bran muffins that the author assured us she'd made many times. Turns out there was a little problem. She listed, by mistake I would assume, baking powder rather than baking soda. Judging from the hundreds of understandably irate letters we subsequently received from our subscribers, this little one-word boo-boo turned refrigerator bran muffins into compact little cakes of cement. Since that unhappy occasion, we've tested all *Yankee* recipes ourselves.

Testing, I might add, doesn't automatically eliminate typographical errors. For instance, many years ago one of our typesetters inadvertently left out a most important word in a rhubarb jam recipe—"sugar." So instead of creating jam, our readers found themselves with a sort of astringent rhubarb soup, which prompted one disgruntled New Hampshire lady to add a postscript to her letter pointing out the omission.

"All your recipes," she said, "give me gas."

I wrote her back, saying, "I'm so sorry." (What else could I say?)

Lizzie Borden further smirched the reputation of New England food. That wretched breakfast the Borden family ate on the fateful morning of August 4, 1892, in Fall River, Massachusetts, has been described in almost every account of the Borden murder case, including those in countless books, poems, movies, television shows, and plays. Before Lizzie gave her mother "forty whacks" with an ax later that morning, the family dined, as you are no doubt aware, on cold mutton, bananas, and black coffee. If only it had been baked beans, codfish balls, and cider . . .

So what is New England cooking really like? Or better still, what is New England food? Well, as we'll all have to admit, it does include the New England boiled dinner. After all, if you're going to have to keep a fire going all day for a good part of the year, as we do here in this region, you might as well be cooking something at the same time. It can be stretched to accommodate hard times too. Throw just about anything into the boiling pot and it won't much hurt—or help. But the standard combination is meat (most often corned beef), cabbage, turnips, parsnips (sometimes), carrots, and potatoes. With today's plastic cooking bags, you can heat up a nice batch of Indian pudding for dessert, right in there with everything else. All in all, very uninteresting, but certainly nourishing, easy, economical, fairly tasty—and wonder of wonders, noncontroversial. Well, there is a *mild* controversy over whether or not to add beets, but most New Englanders see no harm in it. Or at least they'll readily add beets to the entire ground-up boiled-dinner mixture several days later—and fry up "red flannel hash" in a skillet.

The vast majority of other bona fide New England dishes do indeed involve raging controversies that have, in most cases, lasted for centuries. Probably because most every good cook has his or her secret variations. Clam chowder, baked beans, codfish, lobsters, maple syrup, jonnycake, hulled corn, apple pie—New Englanders are always arguing with each other and with outsiders as to the proper ingredients and/or correct preparation procedures.

Like most New Englanders, I believe strongly that there are correct ingredients and cooking procedures. It's not a matter of taste. But by the word "correct" I really mean "traditional"— the recipes and procedures used first and longest by native New Englanders over many, many years. The incorrect recipe for jonnycake, for instance, could very well result in something that to a number of people would taste better than jonnycakes made from the correct recipe. Or perhaps someone would prefer to go the non–New England route and put heavy cream in her fish chowder. Fine. But then it simply isn't representative of the traditional food of this particular six-state region. Continuity and consistency in many, many things, including food, are in large measure responsible for the development of a true "region," whether that region be New England, Appalachia, or Texas.

Of all New England dishes, clam chowder probably evokes the strongest feelings. In 1939, for instance, a bill was introduced into the state legislature in Maine suggesting that to make a clam chowder with tomatoes be deemed illegal. Almost passed too.

To some, the vehement objection of New Englanders to the presence of a tomato in their clam chowder might appear odd. After all, it was a Newport, Rhode Islander, Michaele Felice Corne, who, probably around 1835, was the first to dine on tomatoes. (Thomas Jefferson, in 1781, was the first in this country to grow them.) Before this, most people in England believed the "tomata," as it was usually spelled, or "love apple," caused all sorts of diseases, including cancer. In fact, it is suspected in some quarters that Michaele Felice Corne inaugurated the clam chowder controversy by dunking his tomatoes in his chowder. The Corne family today, as I understand it, adamantly asserts this "vicious rumor" to be untrue.

Nonetheless, of all today's native New Englanders, only Rhode

Islanders will put at the end of their clam chowder recipes, "if desired, add a can of tomato soup." A lifelong friend of mine from Barrington, Rhode Island, who is otherwise an excellent cook, actually does add tomato soup to his chowder. He once told me about a visit to California, during which he entered a restaurant just north of San Francisco that proclaimed on a sign in the window: "Real Rhode Island Clam Chowder."

"Where are you from?" the waiter asked as the order was given.

"Rhode Island," my friend replied.

"You don't want any," answered the waiter.

But Manhattan or New York clam chowder is not just New England clam chowder with tomatoes. The entire base is different. Traditionally, it is a spicy vegetable soup to which someone one day decided to add some clams.

And therein is one of the main reasons the presence of tomatoes in clam chowder so upsets most of us—it reminds us of how stubborn and ridiculous New Yorkers are to persist in calling their vegetable *soup* a clam *chowder*. (Every New Englander knows that a chowder is always based on milk. A stew, on the other hand, while somewhat similar to a chowder, doesn't have potatoes and contains more solids than liquids.)

Perhaps the controversy goes further. "Any fool knows that Manhattan clam chowder is far superior to New England clam chowder," once wrote a New York columnist. "It is superior because it comes from Manhattan. The other comes from New England."

Now, that's really getting down to the nub of it! Both sides feel superior—but I trust that no New Englander would feel the need to say so. I personally prefer the lighter, more subtle chowder darts anyway, such as: "The best thing to use in Manhattan clam chowder is pieces of old automobile inner tubes. They wear well and do not interfere with the tomatoes." That quote is from a July 1958 edition of the *New York Herald Tribune*. Probably the writer was a Maine summer person.

I must allow that the New Yorkers scored a devastating victory over New England in that same year of 1958 when it was discovered

that "Manhattan clam chowder" was being served at the American
Pavilion at the World's Fair in Brussels. What was even more appalling
was the rumor I heard at the time to the effect that the chefs in the
American Pavilion kitchen couldn't understand what all the fuss was
about. They really thought they were serving clam chowder!

There is one thing about which New Yorkers and New
Englanders could agree, however. As Harold Shook, proprietor of
a little lunch counter that once sat next to our *Yankee* office said to
me years ago in reference to his ninety-year-old father, "Chowder
is a godsend to him since his teeth left."

It has been said that there is no official recipe for Boston baked
beans. One cook will say that molasses must be the sweetening
ingredient. Others, particularly Vermonters (naturally), declare
maple syrup to be the best. Some people like them cooked with
tomato ketchup for a spicy taste or include onions and mustard.
Salt pork suits most, but bacon is delicious to others, and I guess
there are beans made with no pork at all. Native Americans pit-
cooked their beans in maple sugar and included a nice big lump of
bear fat. As we all know, church groups and fire companies around
New England are still putting on "bean-hole suppers" as money
raisers, though I don't know of anyone who buries his beans in a
deep, hot (from coals) hole in the ground for twenty-four hours
simply for family use. Everyone does agree that beans should be
cooked slowly, and when starting with dry beans, you soak them
overnight. However, there's plenty of disagreement about the
beans themselves. Cooks in central Maine swear by Jacob's cattle
beans; Vermonters prefer yellow-eyes; and Bostonians wouldn't
have anything but pea beans.

My grandparents and their ancestors, on both sides, were
Boston (and Newburyport, Massachusetts) natives; they felt that
the real Boston baked beans were navy (pea) beans artfully cooked
with pork and molasses. My father's mother would occasionally
bury an onion in the bubbling beans, but never tomatoes. Never.

Her brown bread, a must companion to baked beans, as everyone knows, was made with various flours but always included corn-meal and was always steamed. And I recall she cut it with a string rather than a knife.

She also emphasized the importance of the bean pot. (In fact, if my recollection is correct, she so appreciated the wonderful bean pot she used all her life that she mentioned it in her will.) Above all, the bean pot must be big enough to serve everyone at the table on Saturday night and with enough left over to warm up in a frying pan for Sunday morning breakfast.

Eating baked beans and codfish balls (call them cakes, if you must) on Sunday morning is as "Boston," says Evan Jones in his book *American Food*, "as reading *The Transcript* and taking visitors to see the glass flowers at the Peabody Museum."

Of course, as far as Maine is concerned, the word "Boston" needn't be included in the same breath as traditional New England baked beans. According to a Lewiston, Maine, newspaper, every bean in a real Maine bean pot "should be treated like a voter in an election. You must understand each bean to bake a collection of them." Down Easters maintain that the Boston variety of baked beans tends to become a sort of brown paste that ought better to be called "bean butter." Well, Maine and Massachusetts are always sniping at each other.

Sadly, baked beans don't seem to be included as much on New England restaurant menus today. The same can't be said for "scrod." And yet, as any marine biologist will tell you, nobody ever went fishing for scrod and there's no fish in the ocean off New England or anywhere else by that name. Here, briefly, as researched by Robert X. Perry for *Yankee* in 1974, is how "scrod" came to be:

Years ago, a fishing schooner would work the Grand Banks for ten days or so. The first day's catch would be gutted and iced down in the bottom of the hold and each following day's catch would be added until the vessel was full. Then, under full sail, she'd speed to the Boston fish pier, where the catch would be auctioned off. Now, Boston's famous Parker House (now known as the Omni Parker House and still featuring those "Parker House rolls") did not want to serve fish that came out of the bottom of any ship's hold. It would be old, flabby, and maybe soft from the weight of each succeeding day's catch on top of it. The Parker House wanted only the small, choice, firm fresh fish from the top layer.

Of course, the Parker House maître d' couldn't predict what sort of fish would be on the top layer. If he printed the menu featuring haddock and the top layer turned out to be pollack—well, he might get away with it in Kansas City, but not in Boston. So what to do? The answer was simple. He coined a name for a new seafood. He called it "scrod." (Maybe he was making a contraction of "sacred cod"?)

He could serve scrod every day of the week and his customers would know that they were getting the very best from the latest arrivals at the fish piers. Haddock, cod, pollack, and hake are all related and all caught off the New England coast. In fact, if both haddock and cod are fresh, properly prepared, and cooked without skin, I really can't tell the difference. And I'm told by chefs today that most scrod is either young cod or haddock. In Newfoundland, the word refers only to a "young cod"—in the pound and pound-and-a-half range. And in the New England fishing trade generally, you'll hear "scrod" used today as a size designation, such as scrod haddock, scrod cod, or scrod pollack. But it seems clear that the Parker House chef, whoever he was back then, gets credit for originating the term.

Incidentally, it's easy to tell cod from haddock if their skins are on. It is part of the cod's New England mystique, you see, that it became the "sacred cod" because it was the fish Christ used when he fed the multitudes, and even today the marks of his thumbs and forefingers are plainly visible on the codfish. As to the haddock, well, the devil thought *he* could multiply fish and feed the multitudes too. So he grabbed a cod, but it wriggled and slid through his red-hot fingers, burning two black stripes down its sides. And so it became a haddock! Fisherman still use these markings to differentiate between the cod and the haddock.

Whether or not you enjoy eating scrod or maybe Cape Cod turkey (boiled salt codfish mixed with potatoes—and sometimes pickled beets) or those wonderful codfish balls I so well remember having on Sunday mornings, and other recipes involving salted cod (which you can still buy in New England—though most of it is caught and salted in Nova Scotia), the codfish is certainly one of the main characters in the story of New England food—and for that matter, in New England history.

"The codfish was to us," said Samuel Adams, "what wool was to England or tobacco to Virginia, the great staple which became the basis of power and wealth."

Power and wealth in terms of our codfish dates back to what was once labeled the "codfish aristocracy," a contemptuous term used for those who shipped codfish to the Caribbean (and elsewhere) to feed the plantation slaves. Returning, ships would bring back molasses for the New England rum distilleries. At one time, some 1,200 fishing vessels and 10,000 New England fishermen were netting cod in the North Atlantic to satisfy the world's appetite for the "beef of the sea." From that so-called codfish aristocracy emerged one of New England's most prestigious, influential, and justly admired families—the Cabots.

Today, a large codfish (or is it a haddock?), carved from a single block of white pine, hangs between two central columns in the Massachusetts House of Representatives—a symbol of all the codfish has meant to New England. It faces north when the Democrats hold the majority, and south when the Republicans do. The symbolism of that escapes me.

Some of our traditional New England food has not caught the fancy of the country as a whole, as have lobsters, clam chowder, Boston baked beans, scrod, Indian pudding, cranberries, and apple pie. (Yes, we claim apple pie too!) I mean, there aren't many who have much craving for white field corn, with hulls removed, that's been boiled in water for many hours with just a little salt until it's become a sort of mush. And yet the dish, once a hearty staple on New England tables, hasn't disappeared. You can still buy it in a few places, dried or cooked in a can. It's known as hulled corn. Or samp. Or hominy.

My late friend Vrest Orton of the Vermont Country Store in Weston maintained that samp is actually kernels of corn ground coarse for breakfast cereal, hulled corn is roughly as described above (no hulls), and hominy is another name for cornmeal cooked in water. I've heard others say that samp and hulled corn are the same except that samp was used only for yellow corn and hulled corn used only for white corn. And I've heard it vice versa. But I'll go along with Vrest, because they actually made all this stuff at his store, using the old-fashioned methods, including grinding corn into cornmeal on a stone mill.

All these corn terms—samp, hulled corn, cornmeal mush, hominy, regular cornmeal—are familiar to most of us New Englanders, though that doesn't mean we are always able to explain the subtle differences on command. (Just an hour or so ago, for instance, I was totally confused on the issue.) We all know that hominy grits are now purely Southern, although they were invented by Northerners—the Algonquin Indians.

Purely "Rhode Island" is jonnycake, made with stone-ground cornmeal, salt, butter, and *milk*—or stone-ground cornmeal, salt, butter, and *water*—shaped into patties, and fried. The controversies surrounding this old-time favorite are just about hopeless to resolve. Not only have Rhode Islanders been fighting among themselves for years over whether to use milk (the Newport County jonnycakes) or water (the "South County jonnycakes"), but New Englanders cannot agree on how to spell the word (Johnnycake, journey cake, jonnycake), whether Native Americans or the settlers originated them, how to grind the corn, how to cook them, their size, or exactly what type of corn to use.

Traditionalists maintain that the only real jonnycakes are

those made with whitecap flint corn, a corn that can be difficult to find. But demand for it and "real" jonnycakes seems to be on the upswing. In recent years a few devoted Rhode Island farmers have started growing the stuff while the University of Rhode Island's cooperative extension service, as it has for years, maintains a seed supply and furnishes limited amounts to such growers as Old Sturbridge Village, Mystic Seaport, and Prescott Farm in Middletown, Rhode Island, all of which must use fields carefully located about a quarter of a mile distant from any other cornfields. This isolation is necessary to prevent cross-pollination of the right stuff with the wrong stuff!

"We are purists," a Jamestown, Rhode Island, past president of the four-hundred-member society once recalled, "and any purist will tell you that the flavor and texture of a jonnycake made with flint corn is entirely different from that made with white dent corn or any other commercially grown corn."

The Rhode Island Legislature firmly agrees with the society's stand on this matter. About sixty years ago, it passed a law making it illegal to call jonnycakes made with anything other than flint corn a "Rhode Island" jonnycake. To be absolutely truthful, I cannot tell the difference, but then Rhode Island is the one and only New England state in which I have not lived. While growing up in Maine, my own childish idea of jonnycake was a short of shortcake covered with sliced cooked apples and cream. We called it "Apple Jonathan" and it was absolutely delicious.

Apples are, of course, one of New England's greatest contributions to American food, with American apple pie rating right there with Mom and our flag. As we all know from our grade school history books, apples were spread across this country by a Leominster, Massachusetts, man by the name of John Chapman, otherwise known as Johnny Appleseed. Actually, Johnny never went beyond the Mississippi, but when he died in 1845 (his tombstone in Fort Wayne, Indiana, reads "He Lived for Others"), one of his orchards in Indiana contained over fifteen thousand seedlings and there were hundreds of others spread out over thousands of square miles from the banks of the Monongahela through Ohio and out across Indiana. Settlers carried his seeds for "pie timber," as it was called, farther west on the Oregon Trail until, thanks to our own dear Johnny, practically the entire nation became apple country.

"A glorious unity," said Henry Ward Beecher of apple pie, "in which sugar gives up its nature as sugar and butter ceases to be butter and each flavorsome spice gladly vanishes from its full nature that all of them by common death may rise into the new life of the pie."

"Good apple pie is rarer than Democrats in Vermont," said New England writer Edward Elwell Whiting, but of course that was some time ago.

Henry Ward Beecher had stern thoughts on ingredients too. "Nothing," he wrote, "is so fatal to the rare and higher graces of apple pie as inconsiderate and vulgar spicing."

My family always felt one should go easy on the spices in apple pie during the fall and early winter. They saved them to accentuate the fading flavor of the apples in the later months, and at that time cinnamon was favored over the usual nutmeg. As to consistency, "Never so thick as to feel that we are biting into a feather bed, nor so thin that our teeth click."

It was also very important to arrange the apple slices in "apple pie order," meaning in regular circles on the pie plate (already covered with the dough of the lower crust), each slice overlapping another. There were two concentric circles, one around the outer rim and one inside the first, each uniform in character. On this base were laid other slices, perhaps less precisely, particularly toward the central part of the circle. Makes my cheeks ache just to think about it!

Apples somehow have a way of affecting our hearts too. Whenever we've published something in *Yankee* magazine mentioning some of the old-time apple varieties—the Yellow Newtown, the Northern Spy, the Greening, the Roxbury, Pumpkin Sweets, the Jonathan, the Snow, the Delicious—it's as if we've honored people's long-gone beloved relatives. Letters pour in from elderly New Englanders living around the country, who give their opinions of each variety along with apple anecdotes and favorite apple recipes. Invariably, many ask if any of these old apple varieties are still grown somewhere. They are, but most not in commercial quantities. In North Grafton, Massachusetts, for instance, an orchard "museum" (Creepy Hill Orchard) was established and then, in 1975, moved to Sturbridge Village, where many old-time apple varieties are grown today.

I also well remember the clove apple on my grandmother's parlor "whatnot" years ago. I guess today it's known as a "pomander." But it remains, a small apple solidly embedded with cloves and guaranteed to last for half a century. Probably a little longer.

Back in Pilgrim days, when a storm hit Plymouth, Massachusetts, lobsters tossed ashore piled up in windrows some two feet high along the beaches. Lobsters were so plentiful and so easily gathered that they were considered food for only the very poor. In their book *Eating in America*, Waverly Root and Richard de Rochemont report that in 1622, when a group of new colonists arrived in Plymouth, Governor William Bradford was deeply humiliated because his colony was so short of food that the only "dish they could present their friends was a lobster."

Today, Maine lobsters (along with lobsters caught off every other New England state with a coastline) are probably regarded by Americans as the most special of all New England foods. Certainly the restaurant prices for them are special. Lobster is often the one item on the menu for which no price is given. In those cases, it's best just to order your Maine lobster and fume over the price afterward, since one should be able to enjoy lobster without mental encumbrances.

Lobster is one of the few New England foods over which very little controversy boils (or broils). Some novices feel one shouldn't eat the "green stuff," otherwise known as tomalley or the liver, or the long, googy string running the lobster's length (the alimentary canal or, ugh, lower intestine), but that's merely ignorance. You can, and as far as the "green stuff" is concerned, you should. Many New Englanders, even, are of the opinion that the meat in very small lobsters is more tender than in large ones. I used to think so too, until someone presented me meat from a twenty-pounder and it was as tender as can be. (I still like the small ones best, though.) The real test would be to take a bite from the likes of the six-foot lobsters which the early Dutch settlers of New Amsterdam recorded in their journals. I find that size hard to believe, but every two or three years a man-size lobster is caught off New England and photographed for a local newspaper.

Cooking the lobster isn't all that controversial either. It's just that most people don't do it correctly. They waterlog them. Don't know how many restaurant lobsters I've had where the water simply pours out of the claws when you break them. That means they were precooked and then reheated. Still good, of course. But there are better ways to prepare them.

For my authority on that, I'll use the late Bertha Nunan of Cape Porpoise, Maine, whose family has been in the lobster business for three generations and is still operates Nunan's Lobster Hut, a little restaurant between Route 9 and the salt marsh in Cape Porpoise.

"I put in two inches of water, whether I'm cooking two lobsters or fourteen lobsters," Mrs. Nunan explained to anyone who wanted to know her secret. "I take a salt container and with the spout open I pour it three times around the pot, then *plop* at the end (about three teaspoons). When the water is boiling, I put in the lobsters, put the lid on, and steam them for twenty minutes. Not a minute less or a minute more. That's how Grandfather, Captain George Nunan, showed me and I've done it his way ever since. When the twenty minutes is up, I draw up my butter and serve the lobster with a dish of vinegar as well."

Bertha had one more piece of advice. Lobsters, she pointed out, are scavengers and can get pretty greasy from the bait, so she always washed out the pot with salt water and put fresh salted water in for each batch of lobsters.

That's it. Simple, but there's definitely no better way to cook lobsters.

A few additional, opinionated, particularly New England culinary dos, don'ts, and observations:

❖ Strawberry shortcake must be made with biscuits. Never cake. And the strawberries should be sliced. Never mashed.

❖ Refrain from including raisins in real New England brown bread. Incidentally, plum pudding, plum duff, plum porridge, and plum cake are all made with raisins. No plums.

❖ Use maple syrup rather than sugar on your morning grapefruit. Use it on ham and in your iced tea too. I even like it on prunes if I'm feeling a bit that way. But use the "fancy" or "grade A" maple syrup, not the cane sugar or brown-sugar blend.

❖ Pancake batter should be quite thin, with less baking powder than is used for those excessively large and puffy (but good) New York "griddle cakes." Real New England pancakes, thin and fairly small, are served at Boston's Omni Parker House and other knowledgeable places.

❖ There are too many complicated procedures for putting on a proper New England clambake to list them here. But if you're *attending* a clambake, here's how you proceed, as described to me years ago by the late Joseph C. Allen, then eighty-two years old, of Vineyard Haven, Massachusetts:

"Take off your coat and fold it up and lay it on the grass some distance off. A pretty fair distance so nobody can heave their shells into it. Take your knife, fork, and spoon and lay them on top of the coat to keep them clean. Roll up your shirtsleeves high, and slew your necktie around aft so it hangs down your back, then haul up close and turn to! When you have tucked away all you can, hunt up your knife, fork, and spoon and use them to scrape off your pants and shirt-front. Your coat and tie will be clean."

❖ At a proper New England tea party, the tea must be served in a pot of china or pottery, never a metal pot (unless, of course, the metal is silver). Also, the tea must always be poured by a woman. And the *same* woman until the party is over. Finally, never ask for some "more" tea. Sounds greedy. Even with your second or third cup, simply ask for "some tea."

❖ With sweet potatoes, do not combine either pineapples or melted marshmallows. (A New England home economist quoted in the Boston Globe years ago said she would just as soon serve ice cream topped with sauerkraut or brook trout smothered in chocolate sauce.)

❖ Julia Child emphasized French cooking, but her advice was often as practical and sensible as was her mother, who hailed from western Massachusetts. On bread-making, for instance, she said: "Some people go on and on about how necessary it is to knead bread by hand, to get the feel of it through their fingers, up through their arms and down their spines—as if their soul was more important than their taste. I use every mechanical aid possible to make cooking easy."

Sound advice. Sometimes, of course, today's cooking implements can be too complicated or ambitious. And so could the old gadgets used by New England cooks years ago. In a November 1969 issue of *Gourmet*, several of these contrivances are described, including a combination cookie cutter/pie crimper/spice grinder/grater/apple quarterer/cherry pitter, all in one masterpiece. *Gourmet* commented on it aptly: "Just holding it posed a distinct problem of having the hand cut, crimped, ground, grated, quartered and pitted simultaneously."

❖ Roast chicken should invariably be accompanied by squash, mashed potatoes, peas, and creamed onions. Spinach and sweet potatoes go with ham and if you're serving pot roast you *must* have mashed potatoes, carrots, and green beans cooked with a little salt pork.

❖ Finally, if a New Englander, or anyone else for that matter, first tells you that she or he has cooked a special dish all herself or himself and then earnestly asks you to taste it and give your "honest opinion" of it—well, do please remember that *anything* but an honest opinion is called for.

New Englanders love to be first. So does everyone. But because the country more or less began in New England (yes, I know— in Virginia too), New Englanders can claim a tremendous number of "firsts." Including certain people who first ate or first cooked certain foods. And yet New Englanders themselves don't always agree as to which New Englander was the first to eat or cook that certain food.

We all go along with the fact that one Samuel Cunnabell of Bernardston, Massachusetts, was the first white man to "gather sap in a basket and boil it in a tub." There's not much disagreement, either, on the fact that the hamburger was invented at Louis' Lunch in the year 1900 in New Haven, Connecticut.

"Hey, Louis," a customer said to Louis Lassen, Sr., one day as he was preparing a hamburger plate, "put that hamburger on two pieces of toast and let me get out of here." The rest, of course, is history. At this writing, Louis' Lunch, now operated by fourth-generation owner Jeff Lassen, is still going strong, though it's moved from its original location on George Street to a spot on Crown Street.

And everybody knows that the "grinder" was first made in New London, Connecticut. "Grinders" went on to become "poor boys" in Sacramento, California, "garibaldis" in Madison, Wisconsin, "zeppelins" in Morristown, Pennsylvania, "musalattas" in New Orleans, "torpedoes" in Gary, Indiana, "rockets" in Cheyenne, Wyoming, "Italian sandwiches" in Allentown, Pennsylvania, "bombers" in Buffalo, New York, "submarines" in Jacksonville, Florida, and "hoagies" in Newark, New Jersey, but a grinder is a grinder by whatever name. Its originator was Benedetto (Benny) Capalbo, born in Salerno, Italy, who immigrated to New England in 1913 and for years operated a neighborhood grocery store in the heart of New London's Italian section. He made grinders for family and friends for a long time before selling his first grinder in 1926.

I'm not aware of any claims as to who first swallowed an oyster. William Makepeace Thackeray, while on a lecture tour of America in 1855, said that after swallowing his first oyster he felt "as if he had swallowed a baby." Whoever actually *did* do it first was very brave or, possibly, demented.

We do know, however, who first began eating clams. It was probably some prehistoric Native American. But New England claims one Ruth Alden Bass, a Duxbury, Massachusetts, housewife who noticed one day that pigs in the community were busy along the seashore routing up clams and eating them. She noticed the clams didn't harm the pigs and actually seemed to make them happy. So she tried a few, liked them, and then she was happy! So began clams on the half shell, clam fritters, clam omelets, clam pie, clam chowder, littleneck clams—well, the list could continue for pages. Ruth Alden Bass had taken one giant gulp for humankind.

But while Ruth Alden Bass may or may not have been the first to *eat* a clam, who was the first to *fry* a clam? That question inevitably stirs up one of the many smoldering "first food" controversies that continue unabated and unresolved here in New England.

Most people credit Lawrence H. Woodman, who operated a small concession stand on Main Street in Essex, Massachusetts, with being the first to serve fried clams. The year was 1916. As reported by Frederick John in the June 1979 *Yankee*, on the reverse side of Lawrence and Bessie Woodman's wedding certificate were recorded their most important family events. The first two lines give the birth dates of their two oldest sons, Wilbur and Henry. The third notation reads: "We fried the first fried clam—in the town of Essex, July 3, 1916."

"There's no doubt my father invented fried clams," says Mrs. Nancy Story of Essex, as quoted by Frederick John, "and if somebody else did it, I'm certain that person, or those close to him, would have come forward by now."

Following publication of that article, people came forward. We received tons of mail! And while none doubted that the Woodmans fried some clams on July 3, 1916, and believed themselves to be the first to do so, all claimed earlier fryings.

"My uncle Hosea B. Quint, who had a fish market near the corner of Boston and Myrtle streets in West Lynn, fried clams every Friday in his shop as early as 1910."

"When she was a young woman, my now eighty-seven-year-old mother worked as a waitress in 1912 at the Chase House, Salem Willows, Massachusetts. She tells me that the 'shore dinner' she served consisted of fish or clam chowder, fried lobster, *fried clams*, fried perch, and french-fried potatoes. Price: 75 cents. She states that the same menu was served at this popular summer restaurant years before she started working there."

"I have personally eaten and seen clams prepared and fried by both my grandmother and my father, prior to 1913." (This from Bath, Pennsylvania!)

"Abe Noyes of Lynn, Massachusetts, ran a fried-clam stand in Nahant for several years prior to 1916."

I note that Richard J. Hooker in his book *Food and Drink in America* makes mention of a Dr. Alexander Hamilton, a Maryland physician, eating "his first fried clams," with rye bread and butter, at the Narrows Ferry on Staten Island in 1744. Let's just hope the New Yorkers don't get wind of this.

Perhaps we can all agree on a certain scientific law that seems to hold true in all cases. To wit: "The flavor of fried clams is in inverse proportion to the square of the distance from the ocean to the place where they are fried."

How did the doughnut develop a hole? Not a pressing question in today's troubled times. Probably not a pressing question at any time. But I can't resist bringing it up here because I really do think, after a great deal of research, I have finally come up with the true answer that can settle the question for future generations (and *their* "troubled times").

There are, of course, countless theories—maybe even some I haven't heard. And I remember a Vermont gentleman telling me, with a twinkle in his eye, how, during the Second World War, German U-boat crews were fed holeless doughnuts and how they landed a group of saboteurs whose mission it was to capture the original doughnut hole recipe, which they believed to be in the Rockport, Maine, area, but which had been stolen by a Vermonter from Dorset and buried "for the duration" on Bromley Mountain, and how the Army to this day still classifies the whole episode as "top secret." Tales of this sort abound.

Mark Whalen, once reputed to be Vermont's only Democratic RFD postman, claimed a Vermont ancestor of his invented the doughnut hole. He wrote my uncle Robb Sagendorph about it in a letter that I still have. "Due to my folks' voracious nature and inherent desire to get something for nothing," he said at one point, "they have took to eating the hole in the doughnut and this practice is giving them wind on the stomach. Sittin' by the fireplace all day toasting their shins, eating doughnuts, holes and all, and washing them down with hard cider, is giving their faces a strained colicky look, and we're getting to be known as the 'yellow-bellied, blue-shinboned Yankees.'"

The most serious and widely believed theory of the doughnut hole's origin is the one declared the winner, over many other theories submitted, at the Great Doughnut Debate held at New York City's World's Fair in 1939 and judged by a number of well-known people, including Elsa Maxwell. A similar debate, with the same winner resulting, occurred around the same time at Maine's Hotel Association annual convention, which a number of New England's top governmental officials, including Governor Barrows of Maine, attended. Both groups, after examining affidavits, letters, and other documents, declared that Captain Hanson Crockett Gregory of Rockport, Maine, invented the doughnut hole.

"Young Hanson Gregory," the New York group wrote, "was in

the kitchen of his home watching his mother make fried cakes. He asked her why the centers were so soggy. She said that for some reason they never got cooked. Then the boy decided to poke out the center of some uncooked cakes with a fork. His mother cooked them. They were the first (ring) doughnuts."

In 1947, just a century after this incident supposedly occurred, a bronze tablet was placed on the old Gregory home. It reads: "In commemoration. This is the birthplace of Captain Hanson Gregory who first invented the hole in the doughnut in 1847. Erected by his friends, November 2, 1947."

Another popular version also recognized Captain Gregory but claims that the hole was born around 1870, aboard Gregory's ship at sea. The good captain, as the story goes, was at the wheel of his ship during a storm one night, and knowing his fondness for cake, the ship's cook brought him one. Just as he was about to bite into it, however, the ship was struck by a mountainous wave that forced the captain to grasp the wheel with both hands. Not wishing to lose the cake—naturally—he jammed it down over a spoke on the wheel and proceeded to bring his ship back on course.

When the wheel returned to its original position, the captain saw his cake on the spoke, safe and ready to eat. But now, voila, it was of course a doughnut. So he ordered his cook to make holes in all future "cakes" that were to be served to the ship's helmsmen.

Joe Allen, in one of his columns in the *Vineyard Gazette*, cruelly crushed this pleasant little seafaring tale by pointing out that Gregory's ship (and I refuse to believe that, as some assert, it was named the *Donati*) was in all probability steered by means of a tiller.

Now, for the true and final answer to the whole question, I suggest we examine closely the word "doughnut." In the early days it was not spelled that way, but rather "dough-knot." Isn't the key right there in that simple little fact? It was called a "dough-knot" because early cooks in New England and elsewhere rolled the dough into a sort of slender rope and twisted the ends together to form a ring.

That's the theory I subscribe to. Definitely. Or do you suppose it is indeed possible that it all began when a Native American in Plymouth, Massachusetts, in 1623 shot an arrow clean through a muffin, which in turn gave several Pilgrims standing nearby a pretty good idea?

New Englanders are no more fond of drinking hard liquor than inhabitants of any other section of the country. But as with so many other things, we've been at it longer! William Weeden in his *History of New England* estimates that 1.14 barrels of cider per capita were drunk in Massachusetts in the year 1767. I assume that most of that, if not all, was hard cider.

Horace Greeley wrote about his father's boast that he had never lived a day through thirty annual summer hayings without liquor, but that curiously enough, there was a certain Irishman who mowed and pitched one entire haying drinking only buttermilk. The man attracted considerable curiosity and attention because he accomplished more with much less fatigue than his associates. Greeley observes that the report about the Irishman was received with as much incredulity as if it had been certified that he lived wholly on air.

Harold Fisher Wilson, who made a sociological study of northern New England in the 1930s, mentions a letter from a man who, having grown up in New Hampshire, describes how from his father's barn he could "see seventeen farms that had been drunk up by their occupants."

Of course, in the United States as a whole in the nineteenth century, drinking hard liquor was common. The Yankee was a hard and steady drinker. It's been said that "the very culture of the wilderness was alcohol," and I would say that today, to an unfortunate extent, the culture of the north country is still alcohol. We all know it and none of us much likes anyone to talk about it. It just doesn't sound right to say that hard and steady drinking plays a part in our New England heritage.

But it does.

Drinking was a big part of military life in the old days too. It remains that way, but now we rightly call it a "problem," while years ago it was simply policy. And at least in the navy, that policy was *rum*.

Recently, in an old newsletter put out by Ocean Science and Engineering, Rockville, Maryland, I noted a fascinating item describing a voyage of the U.S.S. Constitution, or "Old Ironsides." Here's some of it:

> On the 23rd of August, 1813, the U.S.S. Constitution carrying its regular cargo set sail from Boston with 475 officers and men, 48,600 gallons of fresh water, 7,400 cannon shot, 11,600 pounds of black powder and 79,000 gallons of rum. Her mission was to destroy and harass English shipping.
>
> Making Jamaica on the 6th of October, she took on 826 pounds of flour and 68,300 gallons of rum. Then she headed for the Azores. Arriving there on the 12th of November, she provisioned with 550 pounds of beef, and 64,300 gallons of Portuguese wine.
>
> On the 18th of November, she set sail for England. In the ensuing days, she defeated 5 British men of war, captured and scuttled 12 English merchantmen, salvaging only the rum.
>
> On the 27th of January, her powder and shot were exhausted. Unarmed she made a night raid up the Firth of Tay. Her landing party captured a whiskey distillery and transferred 40,000 gallons aboard. Then she headed home.
>
> The U.S.S. Constitution arrived at Boston on the 20th of February, 1814, with no cannons, no shot, no food, no powder, no rum, no whiskey, and 48,600 gallons of stagnant water.

That may not be an accurate account. They must have used a little water (rum and water?). Then again, maybe not.

While rum and other spirits are popular and widely consumed in New England today, the traditional New England drink is, of course, cider. Preferably hard cider. Sure, there's always been plenty of sweet cider handy for when the minister calls, but there are also favorite cider recipes, such as "Hard Cider Eggnog," "Old Hard," and "Whitcomb's Dynamite Special." The latter, in an old nineteenth-century recipe book, is described with the following postscript:

"Don't ever venture to drink it. It's great for blasting rocks or blowing out stumps. If you owe somebody a grudge, a slug of 'Whitcomb's Dynamite Special' will square accounts permanently."

An old New England custom, not necessary since the invention of freezers, was to take barrels of cider and bury them in the ground in the fall. In the spring, the barrels were dug up and the contents put through some sort of filter, after which the cider would be "clear as wine, with a kick that would put a mule to shame." The holes were called cider holes and the result was generally known as applejack, which has "a muzzle velocity," a New Hampshire neighbor of mine once told me, "like a six-inch howitzer cannon!"

Tea, more popular in New England than in any other part of the country, is written and talked about in the same exaggerated manner as is hard cider. We seem to need to boast about how strong our drinks are.

"Laboratory tests have proved that tea prepared in the Maine fashion is far more corrosive than nitric acid and only misses being the universal solvent by an eyelash," wrote one Down East newspaper columnist some years ago. And he was only half joking!

"To be at its best, Maine tea should be prepared out of doors," he went on to say. "In a pot made of double-thick armor plate. A pound of tea in a tablespoon of water is the ration generally observed in mixing the ingredients. This mixture is boiled for two days or until the foliage within a radius of three miles has been withered by the strong fumes it gives off."

Roger Finn reports the time when the Finn School had its beginnings, in Concord, Massachusetts. One day a Miss Hay was reading a story to grade 1 and came upon the word "straight." She paused for a minute to establish the meaning of it. Some told her that the edge of the table was straight. Others chose a ruler. There seemed to be complete understanding by all until, inevitably,

Sammy, age six, said, "No, that's not what it means. In my house it means 'without ginger ale.'

Spoken like a true New Englander!

In any case, along with most other New Englanders, wherever in the world we may live, I prefer traditional New England food above any other (including slumps, grunts, Bettys, buckles, and pandowdies—all good New England desserts). But I'm no gourmet. In fact, I was thrown off the *Yankee* magazine recipe-testing committee, on which I served for several years, when it dawned on a number of the committee members that I had never been critical of a single recipe.

"Mmm, this is really good," was my typical reaction. It never varied. I loved everything. That attribute, they decided, is useless on a recipe-testing committee.

The only universal food—as opposed to the traditional baked beans, Indian puddings, lobsters, and so forth—that I can rank right up there with New England cuisine is chicken. In all forms. Cooked any old way. As a matter of fact, I can honestly say I've never had a chicken I didn't enjoy. The proof of this came forth conclusively the night I bought a small container of chicken from a coin-operated dispenser at our printer's, then outside Hartford, Connecticut, while I oversaw *Yankee's* manufacture by the third shift. I didn't happen to notice the directions on the wrapper, which directed the purchaser to place the chicken in a nearby microwave oven for cooking. I ate the chicken without taking that rather important, if time-consuming, additional step in its preparation. It was the worst chicken I have ever eaten. But it was pretty good.

Although I may be a throwback to those old-time New England whalers who abided "duff" and the like without complaint, most New Englanders, unlike me, are discerning. And like me, they value our regional food traditions as well as individual foods. Sometimes tradition and age may gain the upper hand.

For instance, I received a letter in 1976 from a New Englander living in Aiken, South Carolina, on the subject of New England biscuits.

"If age denotes quality," she wrote me, "then I have 'the best New England biscuit.' It was recently found in an old trunk that's been in my family for years—carefully wrapped in a piece of muslin with a now-faded and wrinkled note which reads: 'Mrs. Phoebe Dorne Patton died on the 20th of April, 1828, and she baked this biscuit on the day of her death.' I don't know much about Phoebe Dorne Patton but she must have cooked very good biscuits—since only one was left."

3

THE HUMOR

Is This the Road to Freeport?

The lost tourist and those devastating one-liners ❧ anatomy of a Down East joke ❧ why Mass-achusetts and New Hampshire humor books don't sell ❧ some Boston stories ❧ humor that isn't supposed to be funny ❧ the difference between folk art and a goat-milking stand ❧ how to put down (1) outsiders, (2) the federal government, (3) wealthy people, (4) Democrats, (5) Texans, and (6) ourselves ❧ Sherman Adams remembers ❧ little morals masquerading behind the laughter ❧ understated versus overstated ❧ side-bill gougers, lying, and down gullible trail ❧ the recipe for field mouse pie ❧ jokes that are too hot to handle ❧ why the motion passed to breed Ruthie Pratt one more time ❧ dialect and the census-taker story ❧ the test of drunkenness ❧ and a joke that isn't funny at all

MOTORIST: "IS THIS THE ROAD TO FREEPORT?"
DOWN EASTER: "What part of Freeport do you want to go to?"
    MOTORIST: "Well, I don't know—just Freeport."
    DOWN EASTER: "Want to see someone?"

MOTORIST (*annoyed but still patient*): "I was looking for a Mr. Anderson who runs a restaurant."

Down Easter: "Mr. Anderson don't run the restaurant. He sold it to a man named Hawks."

MOTORIST: "Well, then where is the garage?"

DOWN EASTER: "It ain't where the restaurant was. It's moved."

MOTORIST (*purple in the wattles*): "And where has the garage moved to?"

DOWN EASTER: "I thought you wanted to see Mr. Anderson." And so forth.

New England humor more or less starts, at least in the minds of most Americans, with the lost tourist or city person asking directions of some grizzled old Maine or Vermont country native and receiving in return a devastating one-liner.

Such as:

"I'd like to get to Orange."

"Don't know a thing to hinder."

Or:

"Does it matter which road I take to Portland?"

"Not to me it don't."

Or (and *everyone* in America knows this one):

"Can you tell me how to get to Wheelock?"

"Well, now, if I were going to Wheelock, I don't think I'd start from here."

There are those scholars, many of whom take humor far too seriously, who feel that wry, understated New England humor is kept alive by magazines like *Yankee*, newspaper columnists, and "humorists" on the lecture circuit, such as the late Marshall Dodge (killed by a hit-and-run driver in Hawaii in January of 1982) of "Bert and I" fame. New York advertising agencies attempt to pick up on the theme by, say, depicting a Maine fisherman, complete with the heavily accented delivery of the inevitable droll one-liners. Most New Englanders, I think, have learned over the years not to allow those god-awful commercialized attempts at "Yankee humor" to bother them. I achieved an inner peace in this regard by realizing that my turning stomach was a reaction to the advertisement and that *any* reaction was probably the basic goal of the advertiser.

In all fairness I should add that the character with the Yankee twang who used to do the old Pepperidge Farm commercials always rang more true to me. Recently I found out why. He was one Parker Fennelly, who spent the first twenty years of his life on Mount Desert Island, Maine.

The real surprise to visitors, however, is that there is a true brand of New England humor. The accent exists! The droll but wise one-liners? Yes. Strike up a conversation with the bona fide New England native (born here—parents too), and the perceptive listener will hear them. Humor in every individual region of the United States consists of all the common attributes of humor in general—plus a small, subtle dose of its very own brand of humor. New England is no exception.

Several winters ago, I was in Port Clyde, a beautiful Maine fishing village, doing a story for *Yankee*, and I had the following conversation between myself and a lobsterman on tape. Here it is, word for word:

"Is that a lobster trap you're building?"

"Yep." (I remember realizing then, by the expression on his face, what a damn fool question I'd asked.)

"Is that how you keep busy in winter months?"

"Yep." (Ditto to the fool question.)

"How many do you build in a year?"

"Maybe fifty. Maybe one-fifty." (Now I was getting somewhere.)

"Is that lobster trap your own design?"

"Nope."

"Do you own your own boat?"

"Yep."

"How big is she?"

"Forty-five-footer."

"Where is she now?"

"On the bottom. Winter storm."

"Do you intend to sail her again?"

"Not where she is."

"Do you plan to raise her?"

"Yep, probably."

The only change one would have to make in the above would be to omit the last two lines, ending with "Not where she is."

Then presto, a real Down East story that can be related back home with much enjoyment and praise for those "grand characters who are up there"—of course, it should be *down* there—"on the coast of Maine." There is no question that New England humor is perpetuated by the snob appeal inherent in the telling and appreciating of the stories nationwide. But there are some grand characters living down along the coast of Maine! And in Vermont too.

The late writer Bill Conklin used to tell a true "asking directions" story that occurred several years ago when he was moving from "away" to the town of Walpole, New Hampshire. He'd somehow wound up across the Connecticut River from Wapole, in the town of Westminster, Vermont, and although he could plainly see the church spires of Walpole, he couldn't find the road to the bridge that would get him there. Finally, he stopped to ask directions. The classic setup.

"Can you tell me how to get across to Walpole?" he asked an elderly gentleman walking along beside the road.

"Well, turn right a few hundred yards down this road, cross the bridge, and you'll be there," the man said in what appeared to be a very un-Vermontlike response to a tourist asking directions.

But then, after a short pause, he added, "I wouldn't go there, though."

"Why shouldn't I?" Bill asked, at once apprehensive.

"Didn't say *you* shouldn't," he replied. "Said *I* wouldn't."

Vermont and Maine are the only two New England states associated with New England humor, perhaps a bit unfairly. Cape Cod creeps in on occasion, but one seldom, if ever, hears a "New Hampshire story" or a "Connecticut joke." For that matter, no one has ever heard of South Dakota humor or Michigan humor. They are not regions.

Vermont is a region. Maine is a region. Cape Cod is a region. Massachusetts is not a region, nor is Rhode Island or Connecticut. New Hampshire isn't, either. New England, as a whole, *is* a region. Texas is a region and so is the South. A "region," I submit, is an area with which its residents associate themselves with far more than ordinary pride. Thus I've found that at regional publishers' meetings I've attended around the United States, a New Hampshire person will say he or she is "from New England." A Vermont resident will say "from Vermont."

Incidentally, there *is* a New England Society in St. Louis (as well as other New England societies around the country), but I've never run across a St. Louis Society here in New England.

Keith Jennison of Castleton, Vermont, author of a few books on New England humor, explained once, "While my books on Maine and Vermont were selling well, I did one on New Hampshire. The book didn't sell copy one. I also did a book that had pure Massachusetts—Boston—humor in it. That didn't sell at all. I guess Maine and Vermont are magic words."

Well . . . Maine and Vermont are regions. Regional pride and regional humor go hand in hand. It may be, too, that the non-regional humor on television and radio has supplanted to some extent the country regional humor in the more urban areas of New England.

I'd make an exception with Boston, however. As Keith Jennison says, Boston humor may not sell—but I submit it is there. It's based on snobbism, certainly a common denominator to much humor all over the world.

For instance . . .

It seems a Boston man had lost his wife. As soon as telephone communication was established between the "Hub of the Universe," as Bostonians refer to it, and heaven, he put in a call to her.

"Hello!" he shouted. The connection wasn't all that good.

"Hello!" she shouted back from the other end.

"Is that you, Artemesia?"

"Yes, dear. It is."

"Well, my love, how do you like it up there?"

"Well, it's very nice," she replied, "but of course, it isn't Boston."

Boston's stories about Philadelphia have been for ages a part of the city's humor too. Today's sports rivalries between the two cities is in no way a recent phenomenon. The feud between Boston and Philadelphia goes back to the days of Benjamin Franklin, whom Philadelphia claims but who everyone knows was born in Boston.

Years ago I heard the story of the Bostonian proudly showing his native city to a friend from Philadelphia. Having taken his guest to all the historic points of interest, he asked him if he didn't think Boston a wonderful city.

"Yes, it's very nice," said the Philadelphian. "But I don't think it is so well laid out as Philadelphia."

"No," replied the Bostonian, "but it will be when it's as dead as Philadelphia."

Pretty harsh. But of course, true. In terms of balance, however, it could be mentioned here that Mark Twain, a Western writer often associated with the understated New England type of humor, once explained that Boston is known as the "Hub of the Universe" because the hub is the slowest part of the wheel.

E. B. White once wrote that "humor can be dissected as a frog can, but the thing dies in the process and the innards are discouraging to any but the pure scientific minds." The humor that occurs unconsciously may well be the very best indication of the nature of a region's humor. If a person isn't intending to be funny, then there are no preconceived notions influencing that person's ability to be funny. Like all spoken humor, unconscious humor requires the participation of at least two people—one to be funny; the other to think it's funny.

An undertaker friend of my sister's told her of the time he was summoned by a farmer living up in the hills of Albany, Vermont, a long way from town. He told the undertaker to please come and pick up the body of his wife. When the undertaker arrived at the farm after a rough drive up a winding dirt road, he was met by the farmer outside the front door of the house. "She ain't dead yet," he said, "but you can come in and wait."

The farmer was simply being practical, so practical as to be funny to at least the undertaker and my sister. And me.

As another example of raw, pure New England humor, consider this story that Bill Conklin swore occurred precisely as follows. And, surprise, it occurred in neither Vermont nor Maine!

"At an old barn on a back road in New Hampshire, my wife and I came upon an Antiques & Collectibles sign that led us into the barn and the presence of one of those Yankee proprietors right out of 'Bert and I.'

"I at once spotted a curious contraption, a rectangular pine platform mounted on four short legs. One end of it held a wooden upright with a hole cut out of the middle, exactly resembling a miniature stock for punishing, say, a midget of old New England days.

"On inquiring about its purpose, and waiting a long minute while the proprietor decided if he was going to tell me or not, there finally came a muttered 'That's a goat-milking stand.'

"To me, newly transplanted from the flatlands, it seemed a marvelous piece of pure folk art.

" 'Look at that,' I exclaimed to my wife. 'You could use it for a planter, or a coffee table, or to display *objets*.'

"The silence was palpable. Then the flat, nasal, disgusted voice came from behind us, where the proprietor stood.

" 'You could use it,' he said, 'to milk a goat.'

Professor Edward Ives of the University of Maine, who studied New England humor for many years, said it is very difficult to define New England humor as something that is found only in New England. "Nine times out of ten," he said, "you can find the same story somewhere else."

Well, you might *find* the goat-milking-stand story somewhere else someday, but it couldn't have *happened* anywhere but here in New England.

Driving through Burlington, Vermont, one night, I spotted a twenty-four-hour diner, went in, and allowed a grizzly old counterman to wipe my elbow with a damp cloth while I studied the menu.

"I'll have apple pie à la mode."

"Want ice cream on it?"

"I *said* à la mode."

"Well, *that's* with ice cream."

I wonder who was laughing at whom?

One attribute of the bona fide New England punch line is that there isn't a single word that can be appropriately said afterward. When you've been Down Easted or Vermonted, that's that. The next spoken words must begin conversation on an entirely new subject. I recall the time an unconscious blast of New England humor rendered me speechless for the remainder of the time I was with the person I had dropped in on—and to this day I cannot conjure up a suitable retort.

It was during the years I was editing *Yankee's* monthly column "Small Business and Crafts" and a woman in Stoddard, New Hampshire, wrote me about her button collection, which I decided to go over to see and photograph. She took me into her living room and invited me to examine the contents of a very large button basket. Seated in the room was an elderly gentleman who uttered not a word. When the woman briefly introduced us (it was her father), he simply nodded. While the button collector and I discussed various unusual button specimens in the basket, the silent spectator slowly rocked and unashamedly stared at the sight of a grown man who would waste his time talking to a woman about buttons. After a rather long period of time, his curiosity finally overcame his Yankee reticence. He looked me straight in the eye, and completely without facial expression, said:

"Ain't you got no folks?"

Then there is the *conscious* type of New England humor,

which most often involves a gentle or devastating put-down. Done deliberately. Maybe even with malice! Those people we New Englanders enjoy putting down with humor are: (1) tourists; (2) wealthy people (even wealthy New England natives—there are plenty of them, you know, even though they are never, ever labeled as such); (3) outsiders or "outlanders" and city people; (4) the federal government; (5) Democrats; and 6) ourselves.

I've already discussed tourist put-down humor. It's mainly the "asking directions" line of stories. Others involve old chestnuts, such as the tourist asking the local storekeeper if she has lived in the area all her life and the storekeeper replying, "Not yet."

Wealthy people are the butt of put-down humor all over the world. That's simply one of the prices a wealthy person must pay for being wealthy. New England humor is no exception. Perhaps that's one of the reasons (for others, see Chapter 6) many old-time New England natives of wealth wear clothes until they become threadbare, drive ordinary (but quality) cars, and have an ingrained tendency toward stinginess in everyday matters. There is a horror at being "fancy." But of course, all that accomplishes very little. As far as New England humor is concerned, the rich are fancy. Period.

Here's a typical example, extracted from the detached pages of an old nineteenth-century book I've had in my files for years. You'll note that not only is the punch line a put-down of rich, fancy people, but the entire tone of the telling is pretty darn belligerent as well. It's a little dated but the sentiments are still around. . . .

> Men may be important on Wall Street and their very presence may cause city men to tremble. But those big fellows are just human beings to the average New England countryman. A pompous, chesty, egotistical city man only makes a fool of himself when he tries to show off. One such man, who thought of himself as a big shot, had to leave his summer home in the mountains in a hurry and telegraphed to the president of the railroad asking to have the 10:24 southbound stop at a certain nearby rural station. Upon reaching the station that night, he asked the station agent if he had received orders to flag down the 10:24. "No, I hain't." "Well, aren't you going to flag that train?" "No, I hain't." The big shot was all of a dither, for he heard the train approaching in the

distance. As the train hove into sight far down the track, he grabbed a lantern the agent had left sitting on the platform and swung it violently up and down in his best imitation of a railroader. The 10:24 came to a stop. "You'll hear about this," said the big shot to the agent.

"Teehee," snickered the agent. "If you hadn't been so high and mighty, I might have told you the 10:24 always stops here."

Outsiders overlap the wealthy to a certain extent—probably because if someone can either move to the country or travel, he must have money. So an outsider is most often a summer person.

"Nice little town, so old and quaint. But I suppose you have a lot of oddballs too."

"Oh, yes, quite a few. You see 'em around. But they're mostly gone after Labor Day."

The federal government is the butt of New England put-down stories because the federal government often offends the old-time New Englander's attitude of frugality. In fact, of the thousands of Calvin Coolidge jokes, ninety percent involve his legendary frugal attitude toward money or the simple frugality of his words. And the juxtaposition of this supposedly stingy, dry Vermonter heading up the big-spending federal government, so often snarled in the wordiness of red tape, easily created a humor situation over and above the good sense of humor manifested by Cal himself.

"Let's walk and save a nickel," said a friend to then ex-President Coolidge, as they were leaving their New York hotel for Grand Central Station.

Replied Cal, in reference to the higher cost of a Fifth Avenue bus ride back then, "Let's walk down Fifth Avenue and save a dime."

But the typical federal-government put-down could be exemplified by the story of the man whom a policeman in a New England town observed throwing ten-dollar bills out the window of his car. Stopping the driver, the policeman said he intended to arrest him.

"On what grounds?" the man asked.

"Insanity is the charge, mister."

"Insanity, nothing," came the angry retort. "I'm just as sane as you are. I guess I have the right to throw my money from my car if I please."

"Well, then you must be drunk. Nobody sober goes down my street throwing money away like that."

"I beg your pardon," the man replied, "but it so happens I haven't had a drink in five years. Any of my friends will tell you that."

The exasperated policeman paused, but suddenly came up with the solution to his problem.

"OK, no more of your back talk now. You're under arrest for impersonating a federal officer."

Since the days of Roosevelt and even beyond, the Democratic party has been associated with the antithesis of New England thrift, and so, like the federal government, which the Democrats have been in charge of off and on, the Democrats are a favorite subject of New England humor. I should quickly add that Democratic jokes cannot be turned around to become Republican jokes. Democratic jokes are not like worldwide ethnic jokes, in which, often, most any ethnic minority can be substituted for another ethnic minority.

For instance, if "Republican" were substituted for "Democratic" in the following story told by former New Hampshire Governor Sherman Adams, it would not be funny.

The Governor's story concerns a boy in a Vermont village near his home town (Adams was raised in Vermont) who decided to go to college. His parents were willing to help him but were unsure about some of the ideas he might pick up.

"Sure enough," said Governor Adams, as recorded on tape for a *Yankee* article by writer Richard Meryman, "the boy came back from college a Democrat. The family was very upset about that and considered he had been under the auspices of evil. To make matters worse, the boy founded the local Democratic movement and on the Fourth of July organized a parade. His father pulled down all the shades in the house and wouldn't let anybody look out to see what was going on. But then he got curious and picked up just the corner of the shade and took a peek. In horror, he turned to his wife and said, 'My God, Samantha, they've stolen our flag!'"

Here's one more, as told by the late Professor Allen Foley of Dartmouth College and involving a Texas Democrat and a Vermont Republican. It takes place in Texas, and has a double whammy because New Englanders enjoy putting down Texans (and I'm sure the reverse is true—Texas is a bona fide region after all) just about as much as they enjoy putting down Democrats.

"How come you are a Republican?" the Texas Democrat asks the visiting Vermont native (there's no such thing as a native Vermont tourist).

"I come from Vermont and my father was a Republican," replies the Vermonter.

"Oh, I see," says the Texas Democrat. "So I suppose if your father had been a horse thief, you would have been a horse thief too."

"No," says the Vermonter. "In that case I would have been a Democrat."

There are, of course, countless Democrats in New England.

So how do New England Democrats counter all these old-time New England "Democrat stories"? Well, one of their most effective means is to utilize the "wealthy, fancy people stories" and substitute "Republican." Maybe that's not always fair, but fairness and accuracy have nothing whatsoever to do with New England or any other kind of humor.

It might well be that all these put-down stories would constitute a sort of mean streak in New England humor if it were not for the fact that the group of people we enjoy putting down most of all is ourselves. Every so-called New England trait—such as frugality, independence, laconism, shrewdness, elderliness, reluctance to be beholden to anybody—is turned around and used in the punch lines of New England jokes.

"Good morning, Mr. Spence, and how are you this lovely morning?"

"'Tain't none of your business and I wouldn't tell you that much if you wasn't my neighbor."

Movie producer Frank Pierson, in another Dick Meryman interview for *Yankee*, said that New England jokes are told with little morals "masquerading behind the laughter." He tells about two Maine fishermen who lose contact with their mother ship and drift for days and weeks in their dory. For food, they grab sea birds that land on their heads, and drink the blood. Finally, far off on the horizon, they see the smoke from a passing steamship. One of the fishermen tears off his shirt and is waving it in the air and screaming and crying. The other one says:

"Jed, don't do nothing to make you beholden to them."

And writer Edwin Valentine Mitchell, in his book *It's an Old State of Maine Custom*, recalls the story of the stranger being shown around town who remarked to his guide how extraordinarily old the townspeople seemed to be.

"Seems as if everybody we meet is old," says the stranger.

"Yes," the guide admits, "the town does have a lot of old folks."

"I see you have a beautiful cemetery over there," remarks the stranger.

"Yup," is the laconic answer. "We had to kill a man to start it."

The late Marshall Dodge was raised in New York City and was a product of Saint Paul's School and Yale. However, he is very definitely—and I think appropriately—associated with New England humor. The "Bert and I" records that he made with fellow Yale man Robert Bryan have sold nationwide, and Dodge lived in Maine as more or less a professional New England humorist. Dodge contrasted humor in New England with humor in the western area of the United States on the basis of the characteristics of the land itself. He felt that the geographical tightness of New England, increased by the tightness of its resources, leads to understated humor.

"The easterner withdraws into himself," he said, "as much out of a desire for freedom as in deference to his neighbors."

The openness of the West, on the other hand, enhanced by the greater richness of soil and mineral resources, leads to expansive or exaggerated humor. Davy Crockett bragged he was half horse, half alligator, and a touch of earthquake; he could outrun, out-jump, throw down, drag out, and whip any man in all Kentucky. In contrast, when a Maine man hears a good joke, he sometimes finds it is all he can do to keep from smiling.

Charles Pratt agrees with Dodge. In his book *The Island*, he notes that the tendency of New England people to avoid hyperbole is stronger among coastal people than among those people who live inland, and even stronger on the offshore islands. Pratt suggests that the sea makes people feel small and powerless, whereas the land, with the woods and the hills, gives them comfort and strength. According to this theory, we should find that the humor of the Maine woods is overstated and that Maine coastal humor is understated.

And that, it would seem, is precisely what we do find.

Of course, this geographical theory might run into trouble in a consideration of Vermont's essentially understated humor. But Dodge would have answered that the sea is not the only confining geographical element. The Vermont hills can be as confining as the shores of an island and the rocky Vermont fields as unyielding as those in Maine. Maybe.

For over thirty years, Joseph Allen, a lifelong resident of Martha's Vineyard island, answered letters from readers of *Yankee* in a column we called "Sayings of the Oracle." Here's a sample letter to Joe, written by a man from Lincoln, Maine (near Bangor), demonstrating the typically exaggerated "inland humor" that so often begins in a mildly outrageous fashion, grows more preposterous, and ends in a crescendo of whoppers.

> Dear Oracle: I noted you mentioned in your column a while back the side-hill gougers. We have 'em up here in Lincoln too—only we call 'em lumcumsouse. They have two long right legs and two short left legs and the left-handed lumcumsouse have legs vice versa. The only way you can shoot 'em is to put your gun in the fork of a tree and bend it into a curve. Then when you fire you have to be careful or if you should miss

the bullet will go round the hill and get you in the back. Sometimes if you shoot too high it will get 'em the second time around, as gravity pulls the bullet down. Shot one one day. It was above me a ways. It started to slide down the hill and as it went by, I jumped on board. By the time it reached the bottom of the hill, friction had generated so much heat it was well cooked and ready to eat. Delicious.

Joe's laconic though sympathetic reply was typically understated. "Thanks for the dope," he wrote. "We never knew before that they were good eating."

E. B. White was of the opinion that "tall stories can be unspeakably boring." In fact, he went on to write, "It is possible to be quite tall without being a bit funny." Of course, E. B. White lived on the coast of Maine and, following the Marshall Dodge geographical theory of humor, could be expected to feel that way.

But there are tall stories and tall stories. Even though I was raised in Vanceboro, Maine, and that's "inland," I tend to agree with White insofar as those tall stories that give themselves up totally to outrageousness.

"His pigs were so lean it took two of them to make a shadow." Or: "His pigs were so lean they could crawl out through the cracks in their pen and he finally stopped that by tying knots in their tails."

"When the bear charged me, I stood my ground, put my hand right into his mouth down his throat through his intestines and out the other side. Then I grabbed his tail and gave it a yank and pulled that bear inside out. The bear kept running, but it was in the other direction."

Then there is that exaggerated humor which gently tests the gullibility of the listener. It wavers over and under that subtle line of believability, at least in the beginning of the stories, thereby representing, perhaps, a combination of the inland and coastal brands of New England humor. Here's an example from the "Vermont diary" of Mark Whalon, as published in a *Yankee* magazine article back in 1937:

March 15, 1758: Invented combined boot-jack, apple parer, and wife paddle. Tried contraption—works perfect in all three.

January 1, 1759: Found that barn swallow's nest and live green leaping woodfrog pounded together to a paste and applied to horse's leg cured spavin.

June 10, 1761: Cut "X" hole in top of old felt hat; inverted and nailed over top of nail keg two-thirds filled with straw for hen's nest. Hen laid—egg fell through self-closing hole in hat—hen roosted on edge of nest—cackled—looked back—thought she'd been mistaken—got on—laid again—and so on all day. Hen died at 8 p.m. of exhaustion. Must perfect counterbalance control governor to prevent overproduction and stabilize market.

I personally ran into this type of humor one day when I was about ten years old and asked one of our farmhands as he was milking whether or not it was true that an owl can turn his head completely around as if it were rigged on a swivel.

The man continued his methodical milking, but he must have been pleased with the opening this question suddenly presented to him.

"No, that's not true at all, Jud," he replied seriously. "As a matter of fact, when I was a young boy your age, my brother and I killed many an owl simply by walking around the tree where they were perching until the bird broke his own neck trying to keep an eye on us."

The appalling part of this incident is that for several years thereafter, I believed him. Even tried out the theory on a little hoot owl. (He flew away before I could get completely around the tree in which he was perched.)

Along these lines, my father often talked about a river near Calais, maybe the St. Croix, that flowed so fast over the rocks that when it passed under a particular bridge, the heat from the friction would set the wooden supports of the bridge on fire. In fact, he would reveal without the hint of a smile, there was a saying thereabouts in the spring of the year that "if this warm spell keeps up, there will probably be a freshet that will burn out the bridge."

And he'd carry the whole thing even further, taking quite a

few of us youngsters right along with him down gullible trail, saying that he and his farm foreman, Russell, could not agree on the cause of these fires. Russell, he'd say, didn't think friction of the water caused the fires but rather the vibration of the bridge from the rushing waters, which caused the bridge timbers to rub together. But Father would convince us he was right by saying that the Massachusetts Institute of Technology had made experiments determining an increase in the temperature of water "put in rapid motion by stirring."

"It isn't that a Yankee will deliberately lie," my father told me some years later. "It is only that he has experiences that seem unique to others."

Well, I still believe, for instance, that the paint used on barns in the old days, mixed in a complicated formula involving skim milk and other natural elements, red in the north, colonial yellow farther south, and "dump cart blue" farther west, lasted a lot longer than any paint made today. In fact, the red paint on our old barn in Vanceboro, mixed in the old-fashioned natural way, is still standing today, although the barn itself collapsed back in 1947.

New England literature also includes many unannounced and unexplained gems of humor designed to trap the gullible. To be sure, just the fact of being in print strengthens the hand of the humorist. In February of 1981, for instance, we published in *Yankee* an article by Annie Proulx on collections of old-time New England recipes gathered and often published in "a motley assemblage of ladies' auxiliary cookbooks put out in small towns from Alburg, Vermont, to Edgartown, Massachusetts." The article ended with a few sample recipes, including "The True Pork Cake," "Scripture Cake," and "Popcorn Pudding," all of which were bona fide, legitimate recipes. Well, all of which except one. It was quoted from a Grafton, Vermont, cookbook and gave directions for "Field Mouse Pie." Here's how you make one:

5 fat field mice
1 medium can tomatoes
1 cup cracker crumbs
1 cup macaroni
1/2 medium onion, thinly sliced

Boil the macaroni 10 minutes. While it is cooking, fry field mice long enough to try out excess fat. Grease casserole with some of the fat and put a layer of macaroni in it. Add onion and tomatoes, then salt and pepper it well. Add field mice and cover with the remaining macaroni. Sprinkle the top with cracker crumbs seasoned with salt, pepper, and butter. Bake at 325F. for 20 minutes or until mice are well done.

A note to the directions added that in cold or rainy weather, when field mice are hard to find, the cook may substitute sausages.

The reaction by many readers was astounding. We received hundreds of letters, and I'd like to be able to say (although in all truth I cannot) that most were from outside New England. A few were protesting on the grounds of editorial bad taste, but most objected from a culinary point of view. "You should have included that the mice be gutted before frying," wrote a good number of readers.

As far as the gentle art of New England "tall tale" telling, or writing, is concerned, the whole affair was a wonderful success. From the point of view of *Yankee* magazine and public relations considerations, well, we probably shouldn't have printed it. Or we should have included some sort of explanation or disclaimer.

"Dirty jokes," so called, are not a big part of New England regional humor. And those jokes New Englanders do consider to be risqué are very tame compared to other humor standards. A number of years ago, George Kendall, a very erudite, cultured New England gentleman who sat on *Yankee's* editorial board and was for years the director of the MacDowell Colony in Peterborough, New Hampshire, handed me a number of "New England jokes" he'd handwritten for me when he'd heard I was writing this book.

"There's a couple in there that I'm afraid are a little too hot to handle," he told me with a mischievous twinkle in his eye, "but maybe you'll find a use for one or two of the others."

Here's the "hottest" one of them all:

It seems a certain young man was interested in the new, pretty young schoolteacher, and he asked her to go with him on a sleigh ride. Later, he was quizzed about his experience by the boys at the country store.

"Hear you took that new schoolmarm on a sleigh ride Friday night."

"Yep, I guess I did."

"You musta got a thrill out of that."

"Yep, guess I would have if I hadn't forgot to take my mittens off."

Thanks, George.

Explicit sexual descriptions are simply nonexistent in New England humor. And other than a certain amount of "courting" jokes, as above, the only other subject of a sexual nature that appears with any prevalence is that involving, strangely enough, illegitimacy. Of course, illegitimacy has always been part of country life, and while it's not spoken about all that much in public, there's a sort of quiet acceptance of it that renders it less of a taboo subject than some things one might expect to be of a milder nature.

"It's easier to have ten illegitimate children in New England than to paint a nude there," said the late Waldo Peirce, known nationwide for his paintings depicting New England, particularly Maine.

Many of the old favorites in the illegitimacy area of New England stories are similar to this one, which takes place at town meeting:

"Mr. Moderator," the story begins. "Is it true the town paid $500 for Ruthie Pratt's illegitimate child to be born?"

"That's correct, Mr. Hinckley."

"Well, is it also true the town collected $550 from the boy who was the father of the child?"

"Yes, that's also true, Mr. Hinckley."

"Then you might say the town made a profit of $50 on the deal?"

"Guess you could say that."

"Then, Mr. Moderator, I'd like to make the motion that we breed 'er again."

Like sex, use of a dialect is also not an essential ingredient of New England humor. It's used a lot, but misused far more often. After all, the word "ayuh" isn't particularly funny to someone who often says "ayuh." And unless you *do* say "ayuh" as part of your natural way of speaking, there is no possible way you can say "ayuh" and have it sound authentic. No possible way in the world. The sound of the word is far too subtle to be picked up. (For variations, see Chapter 7.)

However, dialect can be *written*. Many of the nineteenth-century New England humorists—such as Seba Smith, creator of "Major Jack Downing of Downingville, Way Down East," or Josh Billings, born and buried in Lanesborough, Massachusetts ("About the hardest thing a phellow kan do, iz tew spark two girls at onst, and preserve a good average"), or Charles Farrar Browne, otherwise known as Artemus Ward—many of these pioneer humorists wrote in heavy dialect. And while I believe the dialect used in even the written New England stories of today more often than not seriously obstructs the humor, the likes of Smith, Billings, and Artemus Ward made dialect work for them.

For example, in 1860, Artemus Ward, who once referred to Ralph Waldo Emerson as "a perpendicular coffin," described his experience as a census taker in characteristic fashion, even to his jumbled orthography:

> The Senses taker in our town being taken sick he deppertised me to go out for him one day, and as he was too ill to giv me informashun how to perceed, I was consekently compelled to go it blind. I drawd up the follerin list of questions which I proposed to ax the people I visited:
> "Wat's your age? Whar was you born? Air you marrid, and if so, how

do you like it? How many children have you . . .? Did you ever have the measels, and if so how many? Wat's your fitin wate? Air you trubeld with biles? Do you use boughten tobacker? Is Beans a regler article of diet in your family? Was you ever at Niagry Falls? How many chickens hav you, on foot and in the shell? Was you ever in the Penitentiary?"

But it didn't work. I got into a row at the fust house I stopt to, with some old maids. Disbelieven the ansers they giv in regard to their ages I endevered to look at their teeth, same as they do with hosses, but they floo into a violent rage and tackled me with brooms and sich. Takin the senses requires experiunse, like any other bizniss.

The line between successful and unsuccessful regional humor is, of course, infinitesimally narrow, depending on timing, voice inflection (if spoken), surprise, and the precise choice of words utilized. The latter is probably the most important. I remember a party my wife and I recently attended in which an elderly New Hampshire friend of mine had perhaps one more drink than he should have had. As we were leaving, he and his wife were just ahead of us and I could hear her gently admonishing him for "being drunk," although he seemed to be walking along all right. I really didn't mean to be eavesdropping, but on the other hand, I'm glad I caught his answer, because I consider it a classic.

"Betsy, a man ain't drunk," he said, "so long as he can lay down, hang on to the grass, and keep himself from rolling over."

Strangely enough, the humor here is enhanced by my *overhearing* it rather than having had it spoken to me directly. Successful humor is often puzzlingly subtle, be it the New England variety or that found anywhere in the world.

But as to actually demonstrating New England's own identifiable brand of humor, you're on the safest ground using those brief, understated, droll, devastatingly blunt one-liners typical of the "lost-tourist-asking-directions" and the "put-down" stories. Regional tall tales notwithstanding. The circulation manager of *Down East* magazine once sent a letter to Abner Mason of Damariscotta, Maine, notifying him that his subscription had expired. The notice came back a few days later with a scrawled message: "So's Abner." Nothing complicated there. Its simplicity and frugal choice of words is its key to modest success.

That and many other favorite Maine stories are recorded by Jim Brunelle in *Over to Home and From Away.* However, Jim starts out with a puzzling story about a lost tourist asking a Maine farmer if he knows the way to the town hall.

" 'Ayuh,' the farmer replies, setting up his victim for some crushing Down Eastism. But the tourist sees it coming and neatly dodges.

" 'Just checking!' he cries and drives off."

What's so funny about that?

4

THE WEATHER AND THE SEASONS

Most People Die on the Ebb Tide

Weather conversations ❧ what Mark Twain really said ❧ snow in July, the "Dark Day," and other weird phenomena ❧ New England's worst snowstorm ever ❧ why an artifact from the Portland is better than a spike made by Paul Revere ❧ a certain blockbuster of a hurricane ❧ accurately forecasting weather and the sex of babies ❧ how a sick squirrel can warp a winter forecast ❧ the secret of The Old Farmer's Almanac weather forecasts ❧ a woolly worm named Garth ❧ predicting by the numbers ❧ when it's Indian summer and when it isn't ❧ exploring old cellar holes ❧ first frost ❧ first snowstorm—a "sort of liberation" ❧ ice-in and what it takes to drive a car out on the lake ❧ the season called "March" ❧ what it means when the road agent waves ❧ ice-out ❧ a uniquely Boston sign of spring ❧ "Have you heard the peepehs yet?" ❧ when to plant peas ❧ the season that's never mentioned to outsiders ❧ exactly where the sun shines first each morning ❧ the date of Easter ❧ and the seasons of the mind

I DON'T LIE ABOUT A WINTER TEMPERATURE I've seen on the thermometer outside my bedroom window, when I report it at the office later in the morning. But if it is a very low reading, I don't announce it right away either. I wait for others to report the readings on *their* thermometers. Then, if the reports are higher than mine, I weigh my timing carefully, and at what I consider to be an appropriate moment, play my own reading.

"It was six below at your house?" I might say. "Well, that's really getting down there. At six o'clock, it was nine below at my place."

A brief but satisfying victory is mine if there follows nothing but some wows, no-kiddings, and is-that-rights. Often, however, someone will have waited even longer to play an even lower temperature. The victory is then his, or hers. Of course, my day is by no means ruined. It's a small matter. Nonetheless, no one enjoys beginning the day on a slightly sour note. That's the risk one must be willing to take if one decides to play the New England weather game in a competitive fashion.

The same rule—i.e., no lying—and procedures apply to the amount of snow in inches on one's driveway after a night storm and to the temperature during very hot weather, when one's reported high can conceivably lose to a temperature that is a degree or two lower in the shade.

Most of our weather conversation, however, is not of the competitive variety but is, rather, bland in the extreme. A cliché question is given a cliché answer, which is followed by a cliché summary beginning with the word "Well."

For example:

"Hot enough for you?"

"How do you like this rain?"

"Beautiful day, isn't it?"

"Is it gonna snow?"

Then:

"Supposed to get worse tomorrow."

"Good for the garden [or ducks], I guess."

"It just couldn't be nicer."

"Smells a little like it."

Finally, the summary:

"Well, I'll never complain about winter again."

"Well, hope we're not all washed away."

"Well, we better enjoy it while it lasts."

Occasionally, someone will inadvertently say something original. Stopping for gas at a general store just outside Laconia, New Hampshire, one extremely humid day last summer, I said to the elderly attendant, "Sultry, isn't it?"

"Doubt that," he replied slowly. "We don't have 'sultry' hereabouts."

And one day in the spring of 1978, I overheard a newly arrived summer person asking a Dublin townsperson how the winter had been in New Hampshire that year.

"Perfectly cussed," the townsperson replied. "In fact, it was a damn sight worse than we expected, and we expected it would be."

Often, the only way a little life is injected into a weather conversation is to exaggerate. (And incidentally, exaggerating is not lying.)

For instance: "Snowed? I guess it snowed. It took me two days to sweep out what blew through the keyhole."

"We've had so damn little moisture that me peas and me beans have gone right back into the ground."

Weather conversations are not meant to be amusing, informative, or inspirational. They serve as either a brief form of "touching" or as a preliminary communications contact necessary before the real portion of a conversation can commence.

"Weather is the leavening by which all great conversations rise," says writer John Baskin. While I do agree with John, I would also love to be able to outlaw certain New England weather sayings which, rather than being presented openly as communication clichés, masquerade as being original and/or clever. Worse, they are always preceded by the question "You know what they say?" For example:

"In New England, we have nine months of winter and three months of damn poor sledding." "We have two seasons here— winter and the Fourth of July." "If you don't like the weather here in New England, just wait a minute and it will change."

This last was originally said about New England by Mark Twain, but it has been claimed by every other region in the country. On a publicity tour for the 1982 *Old Farmer's Almanac*, I asked a cabdriver about the recent local weather conditions as we were driving from the airport into the city of Houston, Texas. He reviewed the preceding few weeks of local weather and then summarized with: "Well, as Mark Twain always said, if you don't like the weather in Texas, just wait a minute." I was speechless.

Mark Twain is quoted, or misquoted, more in New England weather books and articles than any other literary figure, including Ben Franklin. (Ben's best: "Some are weatherwise, some are otherwise . . ." to which someone once added, "Those who are weatherwise are seldom otherwise.") Almost every piece of literature on the subject of New England weather that I have read, for instance, begins with Mark Twain saying, "There are one hundred and thirty-six different kinds of weather in New England." That's a mild misquote, actually, because what he really said, originally as part of a speech he gave to a dinner gathering of the New England Society in New York City, was even more extreme. "In the spring," begins the proper direct quote from the speech, "I have counted one hundred and thirty-six different kinds of weather [in New England] inside of four-and-twenty hours."

New England's always extremely changeable, often odd, and occasionally catastrophic weather has indeed provided writers with plenty of material—all the way back to the time of the first settlers and right up to the present moment. (As I write these lines, I can see through the driving snow outside my Dublin, New Hampshire, office window a long line of stopped cars and trucks heading east on Route 101. They have been there for over half an hour. There are flashing lights, so our harried town cop is out there somewhere. No cars are on the road heading west. That means everyone on our hill leading up to the village is stuck there. Or a few are, and the rest can't get by. I may have to sleep here tonight, but it wouldn't be the first time.)

Some of the comparatively "minor" New England weather extremes that crop up in literature again and again include such as the July of 1816, during which it snowed for several days in New England, as predicted (due to a printer's error) in the 1816 *Old Farmer's Almanac*; the well-known "Dark Day of May 1780," when the sun was blotted out by "a mysterious strange darkness" that extended from New Jersey all the way across New England into Maine, prompting the Connecticut State Legislature to adjourn, believing the end of the world was at hand; the second "highest wind ever recorded," 231 miles per hour atop Mount Washington on April 12, 1934; and the disastrous Worcester, Massachusetts, tornado of June 9, 1953, which killed ninety people and was also forecast quite precisely by *The Old Farmer's Almanac* ("A squall and that's not all").

There is also the 1851 gale that destroyed Boston's Minot Lighthouse; the winter of 1868, when there were twelve consecutive weeks of sleighing before March; the Carol and Diane hurricanes of 1954 and 1955 and the 1967 and 1978 blizzards; the 1936 flood that raised the Connecticut River exactly 37.6 feet at Hartford; the disastrous ice storm of 2008 that left thousands of New Hampshire and Massachusetts residents without power for several weeks; and the February day in 1861 when the temperature in West Cummington, Massachusetts, went from forty-eight degrees above zero to thirty-two below in a matter of a few hours.

Three events in New England's weather life, however, tower above all the others. Not only are they remembered; they're celebrated. I know of no other weather phenomena so honored. These are the Blizzard of 1888, the Portland Gale, and the Hurricane of 1938.

In his capacity as editor and publisher of *The Old Farmers Almanac*, Uncle Robb Sagendorph was one of the speakers in 1960 at a dinner of the Blizzard of '88 Society, held annually in New York City. He told me afterward that he had had a wonderful time, that his speech on New England weather was well received, but that he had never met in one place so many elderly people whose apparently only crystal-clear memory was of a certain snowstorm. Witness after witness rose to the podium before and after Robb's speech to recount his or her own personal reminiscences of those three March days back in the year 1888.

"I happened to look out my kitchen window on Sunday morning—that would have been March 12—and noticed a few heavy, wet snowflakes were beginning to fall. I didn't think much of it at the time, but . . ."

As most of us know from reading about it many times, it was still snowing all over New England three days later. In some areas of Massachusetts, the official reports recorded the snowfall as from forty-eight to fifty inches. Drifts were ten to fourteen feet deep. While it didn't set records in all categories, the Blizzard of '88 is still considered New England's worst snowstorm ever.

> And when the second morning shone,
> We looked upon a world unknown,
> On nothing we could call our own.
> —John Greenleaf Whittier

The Portland Gale ranks as one of the three New England weather giants for a different reason. Certainly, it was a severe weather event—in fact, never before or since has so much snow fallen in the Boston area during a single November storm. But its lofty literary place is really due more to a mystery—a mystery involving a certain paddle-wheel steamer, named, of course, the *Portland*, and the 190 people who were aboard her out in Massachusetts Bay on the night of the storm, November 26, 1898. There was no radio or wireless then and none of the crew or passengers survived, so while many writers, including Edward Rowe Snow, have come up with plausible answers to some of the many questions that make this calamity so intriguing, no one can be absolutely sure what happened during those last hours. For instance, why did the *Portland* leave Boston for Portland, Maine, that evening when all the weather reports were particularly ominous? Why didn't she turn into the safety of Gloucester when she ran into the teeth of that eighty-mile-an-hour wind outside Boston Harbor? Why did she eventually end up only four and a half miles off the tip of Cape Cod? Did she, in fact, collide with the granite schooner *Addie E. Snow*, which was found by divers many years later in 144 feet of water not far from the sunken hulk of the *Portland* and which was one of many other ships that went down with no survivors during the Portland Gale?

Wonderful questions. No sure answers. Thus the fascination. A few people in the Truro area of Cape Cod still possess various cabin posts, stanchions, pieces of lumber, and other *Portland* souvenirs that washed ashore for several days after she went down. In fact, I once attempted to purchase a *Portland* stateroom door number for my small museum, known as Jud's Museum (described by a recent visitor as "a miserable, wretched little collection of junk"), located in my Dublin office. The door number is owned by a man whose parents summered not far from my aunt's summer house in Truro. It was originally taken from an entire *Portland* stateroom door retrieved on the beach by his grandfather, who then broke it up into a number of mementos. But *Portland* memorabilia, handed down from one generation to the next, is highly valued and not for sale. His reaction to my ten-dollar offer was a blank stare. Obviously, mentioning money was an error. So I proposed swapping his *Portland* stateroom door number for my copper spike made by Paul Revere. His answer: "Paul Revere made thousands of those spikes."

Relatives of the *Portland* victims formed what they called the *Portland Associates*, and every anniversary of the storm they went out to what they thought to be the approximate location of the *Portland*'s grave and flung flowers into the ocean. When they grew too old to carry on, a new association was formed, called the *Sons and Daughters of the Portland Association*, which continued the tradition until about 1956, when a permanent commemorative tablet was erected at the Race Point Coast Guard Station. It may be that the *Grandsons and Granddaughters of the Sons and*

Daughters of the Portland Association are still active. But in any case, the Portland gale will live forever.

Finally, there's the '38 Hurricane. We've had severe, damaging hurricanes galore during the years since 1938, but unlike the others, the '38 Hurricane is an integral part of New England *today.* Not just in literature either. Walk through a New England forest and note the sudden departure from tall pines to hardwood just as you crest a ridge and start down in a southerly direction. That's because so many huge evergreens on those southern New England hillsides blew down in the '38 Hurricane.

"Built with hurricane lumber" is still a common term, in reference to houses constructed of wood taken from trees downed by gusts reported to be as high as 186 miles per hour and regular wind that averaged 75 miles per hour. High-river markers all over New England have a notch or a notation for '38 Hurricane floods. Historical societies in hundreds of New England towns still display framed photographs of flooded, tree-strewn main streets. In vestibules and vestries of churches are photographs taken a few days after their steeples were blown down. Some, as in Dublin, show the steeple sticking upside down out of the church roof. Commemorative plaques at the sites of once-beloved trees, victims of the storm, can be found in many cities and towns. Along rivers, one can occasionally find a plaque indicating the site of a historic covered bridge that was washed out in '38. Many New England natives have family photo albums with a page or two filled with September 1938 newspaper clippings and snapshots.

In short, there's hardly a New England town in existence today that does not possess, in some form or another, tangible, physical proof that a certain blockbuster of a hurricane came roaring through New England one September day many long years ago. No other hurricane can claim the same.

Forecasting New England's weather is simple. Doing it accurately is impossible.

One of the problems is that, unlike forecasting in general, weather forecasting is denied the one and only surefire method of being one hundred percent accurate—that is, personally taking it upon oneself to *make* one's forecast come true. In the 1600s, for instance, two English almanac makers predicted the Great London Fire. Then they set it. They were both arrested and eventually hanged, but their prediction was accurate.

I once knew a man who successfully utilized this method of forecasting time and time again. He was the only doctor within a thirty-five-mile radius of Vanceboro, Maine, when I was growing up there in the 1930s and '40s, and he had his office in McAdam, Canada, just a few miles over the border from Vanceboro. He was famous for accurately predicting the sex of a baby before the baby was born. In fact, he was never known to be wrong. One night, over a few Scotch-and-sodas, he revealed his secret to my father.

After informing a mother-to-be that she was pregnant, he would add that it was going to be a boy. Then, in front of the woman, he would haul a black book from his desk drawer and write down the mother's name, followed by the word "girl."

If, some months later, his verbal prediction turned out to be true, the mother would simply marvel, "Oh, Doctor, you were right again." On the other hand, she might say, "Well, since it was a girl and you predicted it would be a boy, guess you were wrong, Doctor." In that case, the doctor would again haul out the black book, saying, "No, I don't believe I was wrong, and as you'll recall, I wrote down my prediction in this black book," which he would then show her. After the mother's name would be, of course, the word "girl." Right again.

A clever person can occasionally adopt this principle to improve his percentage of success, but on the whole, amateur New England weather forecasters (and every resident is one) must rely a good deal on intuition and instinct, attributes possessed in abundance particularly by our region's elderly seafaring and country people. As Samuel Adams Drake wrote in *The Pine Tree Coast* in 1890: "I speak of pilots who know the wind by its scent, and the wave by its taste, and could steer to any port between Boston and Mount Desert simply by listening to the peculiar sound of the surf on each island, beach and line of rocks along the coast."

James B. Connolly, in *The Book of the Gloucester Fisherman*, says there is "an intuition or instinct. . . in sea-born men which makes it safe for them to do the thing that other men say cannot be done."

The late Hal Borland put his sensitive finger on it best. In speaking of the old-time weather prophet in an editorial for *The New York Times*, Borland ended by saying:

> He lives with the moon's phases and knows that weather often changes with the moon. He is suspicious of a gaudy sunrise and a flaming red sunset. He takes warning when sun or moon wears a halo. He watches the birds, which sense weather even better than he does and feed heavily before a storm. He knows the likely meaning of sun dogs and mares' tails and clear dawns.
>
> He doesn't think of himself as a prophet, but he has lived with the weather every day of his life. It's in his bones, and when his joints ache he suspects something more than rheumatism. His weather sense is built in, like his stubborn love for the land. But prophet? No! He's just a cautious countryman who doesn't like to be taken by surprise.

My uncle called it "a subtle artistic something that cannot be easily defined." Whatever it is, it is essential if one is to achieve any accuracy in the utilization of nature's signs. And "going by the signs" is the most popular method of individual weather forecasting here in New England, other than simply hearing the weather reports through the media. The signs are everywhere all the time, and they unquestionably could have significance in the overall weather scheme of things. But interpreting them is something else.

If, in a given fall, a group of wasps build their nest very high off the ground, then we're apt to expect a heavy, snowy winter. The wasps, we figure, don't wish to have their nest buried by all the snow they know will be coming. On the other hand, if the wasps build their nest low to the ground, some of us will also expect a heavy, snowy, cold winter. Wasps may well be aware of the insulating value of snow and may therefore instinctively want their nest located down in it for that purpose. No doubt, most wasps know what they're doing, but . . .

The number of nuts gathered by squirrels in the fall is a commonly used winter indicator. Many nuts, tough winter. The problem, of course, has always been to count the nuts gathered by an individual squirrel and to judge that amount in comparison with the number of nuts gathered by the same squirrel during the previous fall. Latch onto a lazy or sick squirrel in either year, for instance, and the entire forecast is warped.

On my television appearances for *The Old Farmers Almanac* each fall, I often carry around a woolly worm in a jar. I don't really believe the width of the woolly worm's two black stripes indicates the severity of the beginning and end of winter, nor do I think the area between the stripes has anything to do with the middle of the forthcoming winter. It doesn't make sense. For the woolly worm or for anybody. And most signs of nature *do* make some sort of subtle sense. (As to *The Old Farmer's Almanac*, we base our annual weather forecasts for the entire United States and most of Canada on the many and complex cycles of the sun, as determined by solar scientists.)

Nonetheless, I carry along my woolly worm because all the television people want that sort of thing on their shows. Anyway, the woolly worm, or woolly bear, is an interesting little creature (the only worm I know that actually hibernates for the winter, just like a bear) with centuries of winter-forecasting tradition associated with it. It's also good company. One year, my woolly worm's name was Garth. Garth and I appeared on over a dozen television shows—in Montreal, Toronto, Detroit, Chicago, Cincinnati, St. Louis, Houston, Minneapolis, and Boston. What the television producers, interviewers, audiences, and I didn't realize was that Garth was dead. Died somewhere along the line, and I sincerely thought he had merely begun to hibernate.

I made the discovery after a television show on which the first guest was the tallest woman in the entire world, the second guest a man who could play "America the Beautiful" and several other patriotic songs by squeaking his armpit next to a microphone, and coming on third, myself. Somehow I felt inclined to display a little dignity for a change, and I therefore declined to take Garth on the air with me on this particular occasion.

After the interview, I returned to the waiting room to pick up Garth and found him out of his jar and in the hand of a small child who was scheduled to tap-dance on a skateboard later in the show. Poor Garth was upside down, with his little feet in the air. He was also as hard as a rock. He'd been dead, I'd guess, about a week. Since then I've given Garth's understudies a thorough physical each morning of the tour.

We all know innumerable signs of weather to come. "Signs! Signs everywhere for the man who knew his acres and their heavens, and one must learn to read them all aright," said writer Marion Nicholl Rawson as quoted in B. A. Botkin's *A Treasury of New England Folklore.* For instance, if ants go inside their nests in massive numbers, a storm is coming; if several frogs begin harumphing during a cold rain, warm weather will soon follow; if a codfish's eyes are bloated, a strong wind is on the way; if you notice rats moving shavings from the windward side of your house, expect rain; when pigs continually squeal loudly in the winter, there'll be a blizzard; and so on.

Without a strong sense of intuition, the correct interpretation of these signs is usually a hopeless undertaking. Not so with some, however. For example, it is unusual to see birds sitting quietly in their nests in the middle of a day. Birds are normally flying around during the day. Upon observing this natural phenomenon, we predict a storm will soon be upon us—and rightly so. Low-pressure air usually precedes a storm and low-pressure air, science informs us, makes flying more difficult. Also, many birds' nests are so flimsy that it's a good idea for birds to be in them to hold them together during stormy weather. In other words, nature has programmed storm sensitivity into many of her birds for a good reason, and that sensitivity manifests itself in a manner objective enough for us to interpret it accurately. Common sense coupled with experience is behind such doomsday, weather-related sayings as "If a man makes it through the winter, he'll make it through the summer." Open, snowless winters are justifiably considered to be unhealthy: "A green Christmas, a fat cemetery." And some of the moon sayings, like "a full moon brings a change in the weather," are not difficult to believe. After all, the moon dramatically changes the level of the Atlantic Ocean off our coasts twice a day. Our atmosphere is full of water, and so are we human beings. Many coastal people are convinced that if a person is dying and survives the turn of the tide, he'll make it to the next tide. Most people, they say, die on the ebb tide. New England weather sayings that seem to me to be totally meaningless are those created simply because they rhyme:

"When the cat lies on its brain,

Then it's surely going to rain."

. . . those that rely on nature's inherent fairness and short-term balance:

"If a month comes in good, it goes out bad." "A warm Christmas, a cold Easter."

. . . and sayings that depend upon a haphazard arrangement of numbers:

"As many days old as is the moon at the first snow, there will be that many snows before crop planting time again."

This last is at least based on what I consider to be the correct assumption that the universe is orderly. That every phenomenon has a cause and an effect. That nothing, including weather, occurs randomly. We learn, for instance, that the earth will take precisely 365 days, 5 hours, 48 minutes, and 46 seconds to travel millions of miles around the sun this year. We're told by astronomers that one hundred years from now, that same circular voyage will take one second less. It is a fact that at any given moment we are spinning around at speeds up to 1,000 miles per hour on our earth which is flying at 66,000 miles per hour around a sun that is traveling 481,000 miles per hour around a Milky Way that is rocketing at 1,350,000 miles per hour around a supercluster of galaxies. And all this in a pattern of cycles so exact that it is possible to accurately predict our position in the universe, relative to all these heavenly bodies, a thousand years into the future.

How frustrating that this obvious precision in our universe cannot translate reasonably into the assumption that the age of the moon at the date of an autumn's first snowstorm will indicate the number of additional snowstorms that will occur between then and the following spring! To be sure, the obvious flaw is that the numbers linked in the saying have no business being linked.

I was attempting to explain this in a little talk I was giving to a women's club in Montpelier, Vermont, a week after a severe snowstorm hit New England unusually early that year, on October 10, 1979. It was, naturally, the season's first snowstorm, and it so happened that on that date the moon was two days old. A perfect example, I thought, of how these numerological weather sayings simply do not work.

"So as you can see," I went on (interminably, no doubt), "if this moon-age theory were to be applied to the coming winter of 1979-80 in New England, the early snowstorm we just had a few days ago would be the second-to-last major snowstorm of the entire winter!"

General laughter all around. How silly. But, of course, it was.

The Seasons

Many of our New England seasons are secrets. I mean, we don't mention them all in our tourist brochures. Like for instance, there's Mud Season and Bug Season and . . . well, I'm getting too far ahead.

The year actually begins sometime after Labor Day when the summer people have left and the kids are back in school. It is then that a New England community pulls itself together for the new year. Town organizations become active again, the church makes plans for various regular activities, cultural events such as the Boston Symphony commence—in short, year-round life in New England begins in the early fall. And ends in June. July and August are more or less a pleasant never-never land.

The first seasonal milestone of the new year is the first day of the new year. That is the day that follows the night of the first frost. Not a "kitten frost," as writer Castle Freeman described it in the 1982 *Old Farmer's Almanac*. A kitten frost blackens only the tips of the leaves of some of the sensitive plants in the garden. It takes a killing frost, the "tiger frost" that devastates a garden, to turn us away from the year past and forward to a new cycle of the seasons. This doesn't always happen to everyone at once. Sometimes those living in the valleys begin the new year before those living on hillsides. Or vice versa. Seasons can be fickle that way.

It's not unusual to have plenty of warm weather after the first tiger frost. "Indian summer," people will say. But it isn't Indian summer. Indian summer arrives only after many cold days, when the trees are bare, after we've already had a good sample spoonful of the winter just ahead. Then it turns warm for a few days, maybe for even a week. That was a time our early settlers learned to dread. They would welcome the arrival of cold, wintry weather because then they could finally leave their stockades without worry and prepare their fields for the next spring. Native Americans didn't like to attack in cold weather. But if it suddenly turned warm and summery again, the Indians would often decide to have one more go at the settlers even though it was no longer their normal raiding season. "Indian summer," the settlers called it.

Exploring old cellar foundations hidden deep in the woods is my favorite Indian summer pastime. The trees are bare for good visibility, the temperature is balmy, there are no bugs, and the quiet, reflective atmosphere of a calm November day is perfect for walking through the woods in search of solitary millstones, winding stone walls, burial lots, and other fascinating (to me) lonely, hidden reminders of long-ago human life. Several years ago, I came across a rusted cook stove with good-sized trees growing up through the holes where the stove lids used to go. I sat on the bent portion of the trunk of a nearby apple tree and stared at that stove. Visions of pancakes, boiled dinners, doughnuts, and hot soups on cold winter nights blurred through my mind. By studying the nearby walls, a thin line of alders, several apple trees, two cellar holes (one evidently the sunken first floor of a large barn), and a barely discernible pile of cinders, I tried to imagine the layout of the farm for which this stove was the central focus three times each day, until . . . what? Where did they all go?

Another time I found a scythe embedded in a tree in the woods a few hundred yards from my house. Someone probably hung it there, intending to return for it within a few days. But he never did. And over the years, the tree actually grew around it. Same with a cork stopple that suddenly revealed itself about six inches from the outer bark of a maple log I was splitting for firewood (another good Indian summer activity). The remains of a boring around it were plainly visible too. Obviously, someone tapped that maple many years ago and afterward inserted the stopple in the boring to keep the sap from dripping out. For some reason we'll never know, he never returned to tap the tree again.

M. E. Baker, a friend of Uncle Robb Sagendorph, wrote a poem about all this back in 1941. It's still my favorite Indian summer cellar-hole poem. He called it "Yankee Revenants."

> They will come back, the men who plowed these hillsides,
> And look across deep valleys burnt by frost;
> To see the granite walls about hid meadows
> Fallen—their steadfast work of rearing lost.
>
> Seeking old houses their sad souls remember,
> Where love, birth, tireless thrift and death were known;
> Finding what drew them from beyond sky barriers,
> Bleak cellar holes, red sumac overgrown.
>
> We may not see them as they walk beside us,
> Along blurred logging tracks that still remain;
> But we shall hear them in the muted questing
> Whisper of leaves and sigh of autumn rain.

Sometime after Indian summer (and quite often before), we

all awaken one morning and sense from our bed an unusual quiet. Something is different. We rise and go to the window, where the explanation is there for all to see. Snow. There have been dustings here and there before that, but the first big snowstorm of the year, like the first tiger frost, is another of the year's important milestones. As nature writer Roger Swain wrote to me, it is also "a sort of liberation. The outdoor projects that didn't get done, now can't be done, and there's no longer any reason to feel guilty about putting the work off. It's too late to bring the stacked bean poles into the barn, to sow winter rye as a cover crop, or do a final weeding. Knowing that you can't do these things is nearly as satisfying as having done them all."

The first major snow leads into the holiday season, after which we all say, "Thank God, it's over," and enter into the bitter-cold month of January—and ice-in. Sure, small ponds, shallow lakes, and swamps have been iced in for a number of weeks, but the large, deep New England lakes, like New Hampshire's twenty-six-mile-long Lake Winnipesaukee, do not freeze over solid until around New Year's or later. If we're lucky, that first ice will be "black ice"—so clear it's difficult to determine its thickness except by an occasional string of bubbles here and there on the underside. I once saw an animal, probably a muskrat, swimming beneath black ice.

Once the ice is solid, out come the skates, the iceboats, the icehouses—even cars and snowmobiles—even cars, snowmobiles and ATVs. Small, crudely painted road signs appear, saying simply, "Shiners." That's enough information for ice fishermen seeking live bait.

"What does it take to drive a car out on this lake?" a man asked Bill ("The Barber") Austin and me one January day as we stopped the car in a parking lot after having driven back over the ice from my island cottage on Lake Winnipesaukee.

"Oh, usually just one, but sometimes two, shots of vodka," Bill replied, and he was only half joking. Even though I've been assured by New Hampshire Fish and Game authorities and others that the lake is as safe as Interstate 95, the very *first* drive out on the ice to my cottage each winter is done at close to full speed—and with my left arm holding the car door open.

Bitter cold, the January thaw, more cold—and then there's Groundhog Day, which is a national media event rather than a New England seasonal milestone. (If he emerges from his hibernating hole and sees his shadow, then he'll return whence he came to sleep out six more weeks of winter. If he does not see his shadow, then winter is over. Obviously, the legend originated somewhere other than in New England.) Snowy February, however, with its various winter carnivals throughout the region, precedes a season uniquely New England, and within New England, a season totally unto itself: the season called "March."

"What may happen in New England in any month of March," a Hardwick, Vermont, acquaintance told me one winter day when I was up that way, "is one of the things which God don't know. Along with how a jury will decide and a few more things like that."

Nineteenth-century humorist Josh Billings wrote that New England's March "derives her pedigree from the Danish verb, 'Whizz,' which means to blow, to wheeze, to snort, to pitch in endways and crossways, to shake window blinds, to smash barn doors, to scare pigs, to break clothes lines, to make men swear and women balky."

March is maple syrup month, the landscape changing to include silver pails (or miles of tubing) on thousands of trees along country roads and even on isolated groups of maples in front lawns. March is "mud season," our dirt roads turning to mud roads and our hardtop roads becoming a roller coaster of frost heaves. The few comparatively smooth stretches of road between heaves are identified by the always misplaced "bump" signs. March is the month that always, without fail, comes in like a lion and goes out like a lamb. Or vice versa.

But above all, March is town meeting month. As the various social levels (see Chapter 1) draw back together behind their own battle lines, as they do in the early part of March, life actually changes in New England. First of all, the town road agent, annually elected in many towns on town meeting day, begins to wave to everyone as he passes by in his truck. Then one notices that the daily social gatherings around coffeepots at the drugstore before it opens for the day, at the general store, at the diner, at the garage, and at the firehouse on Sunday mornings, are much larger than at any other time of year. More vociferous too. Some of the liveliest are the all-day beer-sipping and sap-boiling sessions at local sugarhouses.

* "I don't know where they're gonna get the money."
* "Damn fools."
* "Now, you can't tell a man how he's gonna make a living."
* "This town is just going money crazy."
* "Who the hell do they think they are?"
* "Those regulations don't make no goddam sense."
* "It just ain't right."
* "I don't know what this town is coming to."

. . . are among commonly expressed sentiments at every social gathering on each of the days leading up to town meeting. The late Ben Rice, an apple grower in Peterborough, New Hampshire, and a *Yankee* writer and editor for over forty years, once described the denouement of this massive emotional buildup.

"Town meeting will be about the same as usual," he wrote in a little essay entitled "March Tonic." "But say what you will, it does perk a man up to hear old John rant and spiel out all the figures he's been working on since last March to show that education costs more 'n it used to and don't give half as much as it used to.

"General feeling will be the town is gone to hell, and there's nothing to be done about it. This is the best tonic a man can have in March, and Ma and I will drive home as sweet as doves."

After the various initial signals of spring—the Boston Flower

Show, spotting a robin among snow patches on the lawn, and gathering pussy willows for the dining room table—there comes the next major seasonal milestone. Ice-out. During the latter part of March and into April, the ice, now deserted of all human activity, has been turning dark gray, almost black. Not the shiny, crystal-clear black ice of late December and early January. This is the dull, rotting gray-black ice of April. Coves and shorelines become free of it, but the main area of the big lakes remain locked in this gray mass—interminably.

Then, one late April or early May morning (later in northern sections, earlier in Connecticut, Rhode Island, and southern Massachusetts), someone who has passed the lake will announce, "The ice went out last night!"

The ice-out pool, in which bets are placed on the precise ice-out date, has a winner, and I make a special point of driving to the lake sometime that day to see for myself, firsthand. Like the marvel of autumn foliage, the first sight of open water in a big lake each spring is thrilling. The wind that helped bring about the ice's disappearance is often whipping up whitecaps, and I stand there on the shore amazed—always amazed—that a landscape so entrenched for so many months could change so dramatically in a matter of a few hours. If the day is calm and ice-out coincides with or follows "opening day," the lake will be full of boats and sections of the shore will be lined with fishermen. In any case, the annual ritual of personally looking at the ice-free lake is my own private signal to myself that another New England spring has arrived.

A number of years ago, I was in Boston the day the ice went out of many of the big lakes in New Hampshire, and I thought my own spring would have to be delayed. But by fortunate circumstance, I was witness that year to a uniquely Boston seasonal milestone. It happened as I was walking along Commonwealth Avenue. Suddenly I was aware that some of the people on both sides of the avenue were beginning to clap and cheer and smile at one another. There, moving slowly in traffic down toward the Public Garden, was a huge trailer truck. On board were six swan boats! They're stored all winter under cover and right around Patriot's Day, April 19, they're transported back to the Lagoon, the little lake in the Public Garden, for another season. You have to be in the right place at the right time to see the swan boats on this little overland voyage, but if you are, it's as good as ice-out.

Then there are the peepers (little frogs, actually): pronounced *peepehs* even by those who ordinarily utilize their r's. To be the one to hear the first-of-the-season "cheeps" of one or two peepehs on an April evening is a great honor. The trouble is that no one will acknowledge anybody else as being the first.

"Heard a few peepehs this evening in the swamp back of my house here in Spofford," a voice called into WKNE radio in Keene, New Hampshire, one early April evening as I was returning home from a trip, listening to the car radio.

"We have peepehs over here in Westmoreland this evening too," another man telephoned several minutes later.

"Out here in Acworth," a woman's voice came on the air, "we heard peepehs last Sunday."

The announcer then invited anyone who'd heard peepehs earlier than *that* to give a call—and some half-dozen listeners did. Quite an argument ensued when someone said that the peepehs in his town had been in full swing "for over a week." Finally, the original caller from Spofford telephoned back to say that the peepehs he was hearing there that evening were the first "group" of peepehs he'd heard that season, but that he "thought" he'd heard a "single peepeh" one evening almost two weeks before. At that point, the announcer began to play some music.

During this same time in April, there's a great deal of private, anguished deliberation over whether or whether not to plant the peas. "In by Patriot's Day, out by the Fourth of July," is the saying. Actually, it doesn't matter when they are planted just as long as they're ready to pick for the Fourth of July dinner. That *is* important. If they are ready even earlier than the Fourth, well, then that's to one's added credit. A number of New England newspapers annually have features on growers of the first peas.

But to not have one's peas in time for the holiday is to virtually eliminate an essential qualification for participating in gardening conversations that year. So the decision isn't taken lightly—and it's delicate. Plant them too early and the seeds will just rot in the too-cold ground. A late snowstorm—"poor man's fertilizer"—will not necessarily hurt them. But a lengthy cold rainy spell will. On the other hand, if one becomes overly cautious and waits too long, there'll be canned or frozen peas with the salmon that Fourth of July, and those can never, ever, be passed off as "fresh."

The last major New England season of the year is not ever mentioned in regional or resort promotional material. Never. But all of us New Englanders are very familiar indeed with "Bug Season." It really starts out with the black fly season—at least in the northern half of New England—and then expands into what's ordinarily labeled the summer season, which in turn can be broken down into a haying season, a corn-on-the-cob season, and "August." August is the month the young summer workers in the large resort areas discover it is either difficult or impossible to maintain a pleasant front to the tourists. "Bug Season" encompasses all of these New England mini-seasons simply because there are bugs swarming around all during these months. Not that they bother most of us all that much. There are many ways to cope with them, the best being to ignore them. But I personally have briefly known several couples who have moved to New England, discovered to their total surprise the existence of "Bug Season," and moved away because of it.

Possibly the black flies are the most difficult to tolerate, even though, thank goodness, they set with the sun. By the time the mosquitoes, who do not, the no-see-ums, who don't either, and the assorted deer flies are geared up to seasonal capacity, we're pretty much over our annual early-spring notion, fleeting as it is, that things in the country can be perfect.

Some years ago the town of Harrisville, New Hampshire, dealt with its abundance of black flies by actually celebrating them. Each spring there was a Black Flies Ball, to which residents came dressed up in black fly costumes. There were black fly T-shirts for sale in town and the Harrisville softball team was called—you guessed it—the "Black Flies."

Henry David Thoreau used to rub all over the exposed areas of his body a concoction "composed of sweet oil of spearmint and camphor." However, as most of us discover early in life, he concluded that "the remedy was worse than the disease."

Other unsatisfactory "remedies" include wrapping oneself up like a mummy so that not one square inch of skin is exposed, smearing on commercial fly dope, which enters one's eyes with the sweat from one's brow and renders one temporarily blind, and standing in either campfire or cigarette smoke or in a good ocean breeze. I find it helpful to remind myself that whenever I'm with bugs, I'm either picnicking, fishing, camping, working in the garden, or otherwise engaged in a pleasant, warm activity. In theory, therefore, one is programmed to automatically associate *pleasure* with voracious black flies that swarm into one's nostrils and mouth.

Ignoring our bugs requires an extreme form of mental concentration on things like the blossoming lilac bushes and fruit trees, the sound of birds in the early morning, the greening of the countryside, the full brooks and rivers, the blooming of the Indian turnip (or jack-in-the-pulpit), and those wonderfully long hours of daylight.

Because it varies so significantly in New England, the length of daylight at certain times is good fodder for weather conversations and can even be included in our list of seasonal "firsts." Noted are the longest and shortest days and, particularly, that first day in late January when someone says, "Hey, it's still light outside!" at five o'clock in the afternoon. However, I've found that even more interesting to *Yankee* readers is the question of where in New England—exactly where—the sun shines first each morning. In answer to the letters requesting that information, I would always reply that the sun first hits West Quoddy Head, Maine, which is New England's easternmost point of mainland. So many people argued with me that in 1971 we decided to undertake an exhaustive study of the matter with the help of our *Old Farmer's Almanac* puzzle editor, the late Blanton C. Wiggin.

Our findings: Between January 11 and March 6 and between October 7 and November 29, the hills of Grand Manan Island, New Brunswick, block the sun from West Quoddy Head for up to five minutes, thus giving most of those mornings to Cadillac Mountain on the island of Mount Desert. The only times that West Quoddy Head wins are mornings from March 7 to March 24 and from September 19 to October 6. For much of the remaining time, we discovered the winner to be a dark-horse candidate, Mars Hill, 1,660 feet high, located on the New Brunswick line north of Maine's Washington County, which proudly claims to be "The Sunrise County of the U.S.A." However, even during the comparatively long Mars Hill periods of the year, we discovered exceptions. For instance, sometimes the high hills of Carleton County, New Brunswick, block the Mars Hill sunrise for a few minutes, giving an occasional morning to the top of Mount Katahdin in central Maine.

We published these fairly complicated results in the January 1972 *Yankee*, but it only seemed to intensify the arguments. Residents of Washington County were particularly upset, although I recall that we received only about three subscription cancellations from that area. At least everyone concerned seemed to agree that the one and only place in New England where one can stand on the mainland and watch the sun go *down* over the Atlantic Ocean is at Race Point, Provincetown, Cape Cod.

I should add here that the only seasonal event on which we all invariably have *no* opinion is the date of Easter. For the record: It's the first Sunday following the full moon on or after the vernal equinox. With some exceptions!

⤨

So it is that our weather and seasonal conversations and controversies happily continue year in, year out—and we'll never tire of them. First frost, first snow, ice-in, ice-out, woolly worms, when did you hear peepehs, got your peas in yet, how cold was it at your house, this snow is nothing compared to . . . well, you know what they say. . . .

We utilize our weather to communicate. We utilize our annual controversies to somewhat relieve the mental pressures brought about by the real hardships imposed upon us by our unsympathetic and unforgiving New England climate. After all, we know deep down that our own "seasons" are really seasons of the mind. Hal Borland, in the final essay of his posthumously published book, *Twelve Moons of the Year*, called them "arbitrary divisions" that the real seasons inevitably and always overlap.

"The year's end," he wrote, "is neither an end nor a beginning but a part of the infinite whole. The most we can do is say, 'Up till now,' knowing that now itself has no meaning without a yesterday and a tomorrow. Any year is a vast procession of nows, which add up to the continuity of foreverness."

5

THE LEGENDS

Please—Anyone Know the Real Name of Paul Revere's Horse?

The following New England legends are explained, verified, exploded, corrected, or otherwise dealt with: hippopotamus teeth on the Maine shore ❧ incorrect time of the Pearl Harbor announcement ❧ the real beginning of the Revolution ❧ why Priscilla married John Alden ❧ the midnight ride of Paul Revere, the name of his horse— and who hung the lanterns ❧ the Old North Church confusion ❧ Connecticut's Israel Bissell ❧ America's first dentist; the Cradle of American Liberty—Lexington or Concord ❧ The Minuteman—both of them ❧ the Palatine; the Countess's mutilated gravestone ❧ the Old Oaken Bucket ❧ the House by the Side of the Road; the riddle of Mother Goose ❧ Moby Dick ❧ "Kilroy Was Here" ❧ Uncle Sam ❧ what Ethan Allen once said ❧ Nathan Hale ❧ Molly Stark ❧ "Go West, young man, go West" ❧ Daniel Webster ❧ Howard Blackburn ❧ Hannah Dustin ❧ the Great Molasses Flood ❧ the sinking of the Essex and its gruesome aftermath ❧ widows walks ❧ origin of the Nutmeg State ❧ Who in Sam Hill was Sam Hill ❧ the first "I pledge allegiance" ❧ where "Down East" begins ❧ why covered bridges were covered ❧ spring dance floors ❧ Marie Antoinette and her house in Maine ❧ Thunderbolt and Lightfoot ❧ American Stonehenge and other strange rock piles ❧ who posed for the Fisherman of Gloucester statue ❧ the birthplace of the American Navy ঙ the crate that carried Lindbergh's plane ঙ the beer bottle church ঙ the "Church with the Hand on Top" ঙ the bullet-hole house ঙ Newport's perplexing Old Stone Mill ঙ the Wedding Cake House ঙ why no one should visit the Ocean-Born-Mary House ঙ and who actually landed on Plymouth Rock ঙ

"THERE'S A PUTTY CONSID'ABLE SIGHT O' THINGS in this world that's true; and then ag'in there's a sight o' things that ain't true," said Sam Lawson in *Oldtown Fireside Stories* by Harriet Beecher Stowe. "Now my old gran'ther used to say, 'Boys . . . if ye want to lead a pleasant and prosperous life, ye must contrive allers to keep just the *happy* medium between truth and falsehood.' "

Although none of us would ordinarily care to admit it, our New England legends often straddle that delicate line. The truth means the historic facts—which, in some cases, no one knows or ever will know. The falsehoods are exaggerations, embellishments, just plain errors, lies, and perfectly honest misinterpretations. Of course, just the truth and nothing but is often good enough. Back at the turn of the century, for instance, a certain Mr. Roy Coombs of Vinalhaven, Maine, picked up some odd-looking smooth white stones, four to five inches long, that he found lying on the beach. Curious, he wrapped his discoveries in a candy box that he mailed to the geology department at Harvard University for identification.

A few weeks later, the package was returned with a letter that said: "The specimens you sent are teeth from a hippopotamus."

Coombs figured that either some wag at the university was playing a joke on him or the geology department there was on the decline. At any rate, he kept the teeth on display in his living room, carved the largest into a knife handle, and often amused visitors with the fact that Harvard University had identified some stones found along the Vinalhaven beach as hippopotamus teeth.

"Well, they probably *are* hippopotamus teeth!" an old-timer down at the Vinalhaven town wharf told Coombs some years later. "Back when I was a young fella, I found something about a mile from here that turned out to be a bone from an elephant's leg. I still got it."

True enough. In fact, two elephant legs were found on Vinalhaven Island in the mid nineteenth century. I've seen one of them myself. It was owned by the late Alton H. Blackington, a New England newspaper writer and radio broadcaster, whose widow sold many of his photographs and radio scripts to my uncle Robb Sagendorph when Alton died in 1962. I assume the Blackington family still has the bone that was once within the leg of Mogul, an elephant aboard the circus ship *Royal Tar*, which, back in 1836, burned and went down with all hooves near Vinalhaven on a voyage from St. John to Portland.

A bona fide legend, whether it is based on fact or a combination of fact and fancy, possesses intriguing, horrendous, mysterious, historically significant, informative, human, or otherwise attractive elements that somehow render it a story worth repeating—and repeating—and repeating. Most legends require considerable time to develop fully. They also need "a people" with both "a tradition of historical continuity . . . and a sense of group identity" (as expressed by folklore expert B. A. Botkin in his *Treasury of New England Folklore*).

In other words, legends need "regions" in order to exist and perpetuate themselves—regions like the Deep South, Texas, Appalachia, perhaps the upper Midwest, Oklahoma, the West (meaning, mostly, Montana, Wyoming, and part of Colorado), the Far West (particularly California and, as a different region, Oregon), and New England. Especially New England. New England possesses the three requirements—time, historical continuity, and group identity—to a greater degree than other American regions do. And unlike most legends of other regions, New England legends have come to belong to all Americans.

We New Englanders, for example, cannot lay exclusive claim to such legends as those surrounding the battles of Lexington and Concord on April 19, 1775. We concede that the Revolution belongs to all Americans, but we do feel particularly responsible for the safekeeping of these legends.

This feeling of responsibility makes us inordinately concerned about minute details. As all America knows, for instance, at exactly 2:23 p.m. on Sunday, December 7, 1941, Franklin Roosevelt officially announced from the White House that the Japanese had bombed Pearl Harbor. The precise time of the announcement was first printed by the nation's only Sunday afternoon newspaper, the *Westerly (Rhode Island) Sun*. The *Sun* scooped the nation that day, and all the rest of the media automatically repeated the 2:23 p.m. figure. But it was wrong. The actual time was 2:22 p.m. It so happens that the *Sun* did not have three 2's in that large-sized headline font, so the editors in charge that afternoon simply changed the time by one minute. For all of history, it became 2:23 p.m.

Somehow, this tiny historical inaccuracy became known to many New Englanders, particularly Rhode Islanders. Whenever we publish something about Pearl Harbor Day in *Yankee*, I receive a few letters asking us to "correct the history of Pearl Harbor Day" by printing the 2:22 p.m. figure. And we have. But nobody really cares, except some of us in New England.

So it is that the stuff of many a New England legend is our very obsession with the truth—the *exact* truth in *precise* detail. Our joining fancy to fact in spite of ourselves is due to our somewhat stubborn nature, which keeps us from agreeing (or admitting) what the truth really is!

Why New Englanders Are Annoyed with Longfellow

Those who usually add fancy to historical facts are poets, writers, and artists. "Artistic license" has a way of converting straight history into legend. Yet many New Englanders prefer the straight historical facts, as each person perceives them, to the so-called legendary version of an event. It's a form of insidemanship. "Here's what *really* happened," we're fond of pointing out, if we can find an outsider patient enough to listen. The only problem is that no amount of facts will change most people's fundamental perception of a historic event that has been already described by a noted poet, writer, or artist.

For instance, history buffs in New Hampshire—and only in New Hampshire—have always believed that the colonists' attack on Fort William and Mary in New Castle, New Hampshire, four months before the Battle of Lexington was, in fact, the beginning of the American Revolution. They feel that the only reason America doesn't have the same perception is because Henry Wadsworth Longfellow didn't happen to write a poem about Fort William and Mary.

Longfellow did indeed reveal how John and Priscilla Alden came to be married. "Why don't you speak for yourself, John?" beautiful Priscilla said to John in a "tremulous voice" after John had obediently sung the praises of Priscilla's potential suitor, Miles Standish. And the rest is history even more than poetry! "The Song of Hiawatha" merged Native American legends into our perception of American legends. But perhaps Longfellow's most important poem in terms of historical impact is found among his *Tales of a Wayside Inn*, based on real characters of the Red Horse Inn (known today as the Wayside Inn) in Sudbury, Massachusetts. Every New Englander, and probably every American, can recite at least the first two lines:

> Listen, my children, and you shall hear
> Of the midnight ride of Paul Revere.

The poem is actually called "The Landlord's Tale," and although published eighty-eight years after the events it described, it left an indelible stamp on certain historical facts.

New Englanders have always been a little annoyed with Longfellow's account. For instance, why didn't he include the name of Paul Revere's horse? Every horse has a name. What a silly oversight! This particular horse was called Brown Beauty . . . or Brown Betty . . . or Minuteman . . . or . . .

Opinions vary, with the vast majority favoring a mare (though some argue a gelding and others a stallion) called Brown Beauty, which Revere supposedly never returned to her owner, Samuel Larkin, after he'd borrowed her for his famous ride. Many hold she was a Narragansett Pacer, a breed popular before the Revolution (George Washington owned two Narragansett Pacers) but which no longer existed after about 1800. Surely Longfellow should have included some of those things.

As to the *real* name, well, the late Joseph C. Allen, known throughout New England for his wonderful flair and humor rather than any strict allegiance to accuracy, strongly favored Minuteman.

"Sounds reasonable," he explained to me once, "things being as they were."

Also somewhat irritating is the fact that Longfellow omitted the name of the man who hung the two lanterns in the steeple of the Old North Church. He simply referred to him as Revere's "friend" who "climbed the tower of the Old North Church,/ By the wooden stairs, with stealthy tread,/ To the belfry-chamber overhead."

Most believe it was the sexton of the Old North Church, Robert Newman, who climbed those 154 steps with the lanterns. Others vehemently support a Captain John Pulling, who was Revere's good "friend" and shared the same political beliefs. Pulling advocates, comprising principally the captain's descendants, argue that Revere would not have entrusted the mission to anyone but a valued and courageous friend such as Pulling. But there's not enough hard evidence to dissuade either side.

Even the Old North Church itself has, over the years, been involved in controversy. In 1979 I received an impressive collection of data from a small group of amateur historians who feel strongly that Paul Revere's lanterns didn't hang in the Old North Church at all. They maintain the lanterns were hung in what history today refers to as the Second Church, but which was known in 1775 as "Old North." Second Church was situated across the street from Paul Revere's house in North Square, its steeple also had a clear view of the harbor, and it was the only Boston church demolished by the British after the lantern episode. Second Church advocates point adamantly to a letter Revere wrote twenty-three years later, recalling that "if the British went by water we would show two lanterns in the North Church steeple." They say that if Revere had meant the present-day Old North Church, he would have said "Christ Church," as it was known at that time. Longfellow avoided that particular little hornet's nest by omitting the street address of the Old North Church.

Connecticut Yankees have a special problem with Longfellow. They wish he'd seen fit to mention one Israel Bissell of East Windsor, Connecticut, who left Watertown, Massachusetts, on the afternoon of April 19, 1775, calling men to arms in town after town all through the state of Connecticut and down as far as Philadelphia. It is said he rode 345 miles in five days, and that at one stop along the way he didn't even have to rein in his exhausted horse. It simply dropped dead. That's the stuff of poetry, but because a poem was never written about it, say Connecticut Bissell fans, the heroic ride of *their* man has been virtually forgotten.

There are other bones of contention, but as far as I'm concerned, one thing is certain. During Hurricane Carol in 1954, the entire steeple of the present Old North Church blew over, hung there for a while, and then fell down into the street. I know because I walked right up and examined it after the storm. Later that evening, I happened to reach into my pants pocket for something and discovered a six-inch-long piece of wood from the historic Old North Church steeple! Several years ago, thinking silently to myself that possibly the lanterns didn't hang in that particular steeple anyway, I traded my piece of wood for a hand-wrought copper spike fashioned by Paul Revere and salvaged from the battleship *New Hampshire* sunk off Graves Light, Manchester, Massachusetts, in 1922. I still have it.

Paul Revere, like Ben Franklin (who discovered that the world's first water beds were used in Babylonia before the birth of Christ), was so incredibly versatile that some of his previously unpublicized accomplishments continue to crop up from time to time. One of my favorite pieces of "inside" Revere information is that he was this country's very first professional dentist. Many know he is alleged to have furnished George Washington with a set of badly fitting teeth. But I only recently ran across the text of his advertisements and his office sign. The ads read: "He fixes teeth in such a manner that they are not only an ornament but a real use in speaking and eating."

Lexington Versus Concord

The official first battle of the American Revolution is often referred to as "The Battle of Lexington and Concord, April 19, 1775." That doesn't set particularly well with either Lexington or Concord. Both Massachusetts towns consider themselves alone to be the *specific* cradle of American liberty. But in the minds and imaginations of Americans in general, Concord has the edge, thanks in large part to Ralph Waldo Emerson.

> By the rude bridge that arched the flood,
> Their flag to April's breeze unfurled,
> Here once the embattled farmers stood
> And fired the shot heard 'round the world.

That first stanza of Emerson's "Concord Hymn" is carved (without credit to Emerson) on one side of the pedestal of the Daniel Chester French statue, *The Minuteman*, which stands near the "rude bridge" in Concord where the three-minute battle occurred. Robb Sagendorph used to recall the writer Martha Taylor Howard's telling him that her father, Samuel Taylor, was present at the unveiling of the Concord Minuteman statue on April 19, 1875. President Ulysses S. Grant, his cabinet, Longfellow, Lowell, and scores of other notables were there on that raw, windy April day at which a number of chilled spectators "got their never-get-overs," as Sam Taylor told his daughter.

Emerson's stirring lines, as Nathaniel Hawthorne wrote, "made Concord's reputation."

However, Lexington has a *Minuteman* statue too! Its version, sculpted by H. H. Kitson, was dedicated in 1900 and was, ironically enough, modeled after an Englishman. (His name was Arthur A.

Mather, who later became a U.S. citizen, settled down in Medford, Massachusetts, and was the national heavyweight wrestling champion and the national canoe paddling champion.) At the base of a flagpole near Lexington's Minuteman is an engraved line proclaiming Lexington the "Birthplace of American Liberty." Nice ... but it lacks that special ring.

Several artists have contributed to the somewhat inaccurate "legendary" impression of the Lexington battle. The first drawing of it, by artist Amos Doolittle, is probably pretty accurate, because Doolittle sketched it only a few days after the battle occurred. If "battle" is the right word. It shows well-organized British soldiers lined up in combat formation, firing a volley at a motley group of scattered colonials, who are not firing back. Those not already lying dead or wounded on the ground are hightailing it—a perception of that particular historic event not compatible with popular legend. By 1830, artistic renditions of the Lexington battle show a few Minutemen firing at the British, with the others just standing around watching. A Hammett Billings painting of 1868 depicts almost all the Minutemen engaged in battle. However, it is the heroic 1886 Henry Sandham oil painting that forms the basis for the modern version of the Battle of Lexington, April 19, 1775. The Minutemen and the British are all toe to toe, blasting away at each other.

All these shenanigans point up the important element of time in the making of legends. The first, small battle monument at Concord wasn't dedicated until 1837 (at which Emerson's "Concord Hymn" was first sung—to the tune of "Old Hundred"—by a local chorus), and most of the impressive memorials standing today in Lexington and Concord were never viewed by anyone who was alive in 1775. I might add that it's not only New Englanders who are apt to allow legends to develop for years before officially recognizing their historical (and tourist) value. For instance, Texans let the Alamo remain in a heap of rubble for almost eighty years after it fell to Santa Anna in 1836.

A Flaming Ship

Sometime in the 1700s, a ship called the *Palatine* sailed from a German port, bound for Philadelphia. The captain died or was killed en route; the remaining officers and crew robbed the German and Dutch passengers before leaving them on the *Palatine* and taking off for land in lifeboats. That much is fairly well recorded in history. Now legend takes over. . . . The *Palatine* then drifted or was sailed onto the shores of Block Island, Rhode Island, where greedy islanders plundered and killed the passengers and then fired the ship and set it adrift, with one live, screaming woman still on board. *Or* (and this is the much-preferred Block Island version today) the islanders heroically rescued the passengers when the *Palatine* hit the Block Island shore and, according to an island historian, the Reverend S. T. Livermore, "tenderly nursed" the survivors back to health while burying the others in "Palatine graves." I have personally seen four little "Palatine" gravestones on the island, so labeled by a historical monument.

Dr. Grace M. Sherwood of the Providence State Record Commission told *Yankee* writer Dan Paonessa in 1972 that the actual ship was the *Princess Augusta*, which was carrying German passengers from the Palatinate, then a division of Bavaria. She put the blame for all the *Palatine* fuss on poet John Greenleaf Whittier.

I don't think Dr. Sherwood was being fair. After all, what poet could possibly resist writing about a burning ship returning to a certain island year after year to remind its present-day inhabitants of their wicked, wicked ancestors? Certainly John Greenleaf Whittier couldn't. However, I'm sure he never imagined the long-term effect a particular six-line section of his poem "The Palatine" would have on future generations of New Englanders.

> For still, on many a moonless night,
> From Kingston Head and from Montauk light
> The spectre kindles and burns in sight.
> Now low and dim, now clear and higher,
> Leaps up the terrible ghost of fire,
> Then, slowly sinking, the flames expire.

Since Whittier wrote those lines, witness after witness has actually seen the burning *Palatine!*

"I was walking home on a night late in November," Mrs. Venetia Rountree, a former business manager of one of Block Island's summer hotels and a graduate of Brown University, told our Dan Paonessa. "It was moonless and windy and we were busy getting ready for a storm the Coast Guard station on Mohegan Bluff told us to expect. Then I happened to glance out to the sound and saw a flickering glow. The light grew bigger as it approached the shore—and I recognized it. It was the *Palatine.*"

I recall another Block Island native visiting our *Yankee* office in 1958 and earnestly describing to my uncle how, as a young girl living on the north shore of the island, she was awakened one night by her parents and saw, for several awestruck moments, a flaming ship that "rounded the point" and then disappeared beneath the waves.

Walter Johnson of the United States Geological Bureau once tried to calm everyone down with a scientific explanation for all these *Palatine* sightings. He suggested that they are actually clouds of gas, which, after escaping from vast deposits below the ocean floor and reaching the surface, can actually ignite into flames. I think Whittier's poetic version is downright tame compared to *that.*

Whittier caused a different sort of reaction with his poem "The Countess," which "legendized" a Massachusetts servant girl's one-year marriage (at which point she died of tuberculosis) to a wealthy French count.

> The Gascon lord, the village maid,
> In death still clasp their hands;
> The love that levels rank and grade
> Unites their severed lands.
>
> What matter whose the hillside grave,
> Or whose the 'blazoned stone?

Well, as it turned out, it mattered to hundreds of souvenir hunters, who, for years after the poem was published, flocked to the girl's forsaken grave site in the Greenwood Cemetery just outside Haverhill, Massachusetts, and chipped off pieces of slate from "the 'blazoned stone." Caretakers of the cemetery finally had to put an iron fence around it, but visitors continued to chip away by reaching through the bars. The stone was later completely covered with an iron-mesh frame.

Samuel Woodworth's poem "The Old Oaken Bucket" is more or less a New England legend unto itself; one can still drive down Old Oaken Bucket Road in Scituate, Massachusetts, and see the homestead, the well, the bucket, and farther on, the "wide spreading pond and the mill that stood by it." No controversy there. But New Englanders persist in arguing about which is the *real* "House by the Side of the Road," as featured in Sam Walter Foss's poem of that title. We don't seem to be content with even the *possibility* that it might be imaginary. From time to time, candidates have included houses in Portsmouth and Tilton, New Hampshire, as well as Lynn and Somerville, Massachusetts.

> Let me live in my house by the
>   side of the road,
> And be a friend of man.

Fine. But *which* house? I met Foss's daughter, Mary (Molly) L. Foss, by correspondence in 1968 and she said it's definitely the little farmhouse on Pancake Lane in Candia, New Hampshire, Foss's birthplace—and she ought to know.

Poems, songs, and ditties traditionally claimed by New England but most assuredly having their origin in England during the 1600s are the "Mother Goose" nursery rhymes. The New England connection stems back to an Elizabeth Foster of Charlestown, Massachusetts, who married one Isaac Goose of Boston and then, as the legend goes, eventually recited these nursery rhymes to her grandchildren so often that one of her sons-in-law, Thomas Fleet, a printer, decided to put them in book form about 1719, under the title "Songs for the Nursery" or "Tales from Mother Goose" or "Mother Goose's Melodies for Children" or *something*. The reason it's difficult to pinpoint the title is that no one has ever come forth with the legendary little book, even though it's often listed under that 1719 date in American bibliographies. Listed in Boston tourist brochures is the tombstone of "The Original Mother Goose," located near the Paul Revere monument in the Old Granary Burying Ground on Tremont Street. I've walked through the Old Granary many times and noted all the Gooses (Geese?) buried there, including "Mary Goose, wife to Isaac." Mary was Isaac's first wife. I've never found Elizabeth. Oh, well . . .

> For every riddle under the sun,
> There is an answer or there is none.
> If there be one, try and find it;
> If there be none, never mind it.
>
> (—MOTHER GOOSE (WHOEVER SHE / HE WAS)

New Englanders will abide fanciful legends about Humpty Dumpty or Little Bo-Peep, but we cannot seem to forgive artistic license in literature on matters pertaining to common sense. For instance, a number of fishermen and seafaring New Englanders I've spoken with have no use for Herman Melville and his book *Moby Dick*. Too many nautical inaccuracies in it. They always point out that no whaling captain would ever have allowed his ship's tiller to be made from a whale's jawbone.

"Too damn brittle," a Martha's Vineyard old-timer once fairly shouted at me. "They never would have trusted it. It might have snapped like a pipestem in a big sea and then the *Pequod* would have been without steering gear. No, sir. They never, never would have done it!"

So much for *Moby Dick*.

Kilroy and Uncle Sam . . .

A series of small historical circumstances, each triggering the next in just the right sequence, is often responsible for the creation of a legend. It's similar to a long winding row of dominoes toppling over one after the other. For every existing legend, there must be thousands of potential legends that never found their way into our collective imagination, having failed to pass through a certain go-or-no-go circumstantial checkpoint. Indeed, we New Englanders are often more interested in those checkpoints than in the legend itself.

Kilroy is a good case in point. To those of us who were around during the Second World War, the name Kilroy is as familiar as MacArthur, Roosevelt, or Betty Grable. The words "Kilroy Was Here" were penciled on rest room walls, carved on picnic tables, painted on bridges—you name it.

Everyone knew his name, but no one seemed to know *who* Kilroy really was or *if* he really was. No one, that is, except the workers at the Fore River Shipyard in Quincy, Massachusetts. They knew he was James J. Kilroy, born September 26, 1902, in Boston's South End. He attended Commerce High School, served briefly as a state representative and a Boston city councilor from Roxbury, and when the war started, became a rate setter or "checker" at the Fore River Shipyard, working on the battleship *Massachusetts*, the heavy cruiser *Baltimore*, the carrier *Lexington*, and numerous troop carriers.

"It was Jim's job to go around and count the number of holes a riveter had filled," explained his widow, Mrs. Margaret Kilroy of Halifax, Massachusetts, to *Yankee* writer Robert W. Cubie, whom we sent to Quincy in 1970 to find out how this American legend came to be, and if New England could truly claim responsibility for it. "The riveters were on piecework and got paid so much for each rivet. After Jim had counted the rivets put in by a certain worker, he'd put a checkmark next to them so that they wouldn't be counted twice.

"A few dishonest men," Mrs. Kilroy continued, "would know when Jim was going off duty, and they would sometimes erase his checkmark. The checker on the next shift would come through and count the rivets again, which meant those riveters would get paid twice.

"One day, just before he was going off duty, Jim heard his foreman ask one of these dishonest riveters if Kilroy had been there. When the man said no, my husband was furious, because he knew he'd already checked that man's rivets. So he took his chalk and wrote 'Kilroy Was Here' in letters too large and too bold to erase."

So far so good. But there were two more circumstantial checkpoints to pass through. The first was Kilroy's decision to write "Kilroy Was Here" next to all his check marks from that time forward. The second was a higher-up decision, made in the interest of speed, not to put the usual second coat of paint on the ships' hulls, which would, under ordinary circumstances, have covered up Kilroy's chalk markings. As a result, "Kilroy Was Here" miraculously appeared over sailors' hammocks, along ships' corridors, on flight decks, and in heads. And when these ships were later stripped for repairs or damaged in battle, puzzled workmen found the same chalked message inside boilers and bulkheads.

After the war, Jim Kilroy entered a nationwide contest, sponsored by the American Transit Association through its radio program *Speak to America*, for the best letter explaining the origin of "Kilroy Was Here." He won. His prize was a 22-ton 1910 trolley car. Since the Kilroys had nine children, they used it as a playhouse. In 1956, when the children were grown and no museum would pick it up, it was hauled off to the town dump.

There are others today who claim "Kilroy" originated with an Irish-American RAF pilot shot down over France, who left his Kilroy calling card along his escape route. An Albany, New York, steeplejack, also a James Kilroy, claimed he was the originator. The United States Army officially labeled Kilroy "a mythical character." But New Englanders have no doubt whatsoever who Kilroy really was.

We know who Uncle Sam was too. Sure, people in the states of Delaware and Indiana still think it was a Sam Wilson, born in Wilmington, Delaware, and buried in Merriam, Indiana. But in the 1960s, even the United States Congress recognized the New England-born Samuel Wilson as *the* Uncle Sam. And just as in the case of Jim Kilroy, a series of minor historical circumstances had to follow one after another until, presto, a legend! Here are the principal ingredients of this particular one:

1. The Wilson family, who moved in 1780 from what is now Arlington, Massachusetts, to Mason, New Hampshire, had to decide to name one of their eleven children Samuel. That was an essential first step.

2. Sam had somehow to get to Troy, New York, or at least to a place accessible to oceangoing ships. As it happened, Sam and his brother Eben walked to Troy in order to seek their fortunes. If they had walked to Worcester, Massachusetts, for instance, everything would have been different.

3. Sam had to become involved in a meat-packing business in Troy and the word "uncle" had to be a common word of endearment in that area at that time. In fact, "Uncle" Sam and "Uncle" Eben eventually employed over a hundred men and slaughtered a thousand head of cattle weekly.

4. The United States had to go to war. It did. We call it the War of 1812.

5. The government had to give E. & S. Wilson Company a contract to supply meat to the United States Army. It saw fit to do so.

6. "Uncle" Sam Wilson had to be appointed government inspector of meat. Because he was in the right place at the right time, he was appointed.

7. Part of his job as government inspector had to be to brand his own white oak barrels containing his own meat with the initials of the United States. It was.

8. Barrels of meat so branded had to be piled up on the dock where passenger ships also landed. They were indeed placed precisely there.

9. A debarking or embarking passenger had to be curious enough (or dumb enough) to ask someone on the dock, preferably a Wilson employee, why the meat barrels were all labeled with the initials "U.S." It happened (the

passenger was one of many disembarking from Robert Fulton's *Firefly*). And the person asked *was* an employee of the Wilson Company.

10. The person asked had to reply: "Those initials mean 'Uncle Sam'—he owns everything around here and he's even feeding the whole army!"

Well, there are a few more steps that had to occur, and they all did. Including the circumstance that our country at that time seemed to need a personification of the American character.

Naturally, not everyone agrees with everything anyone says on the subject. Some maintain, for instance, that it was New York Governor George D. Tompkins who asked about the initials, not a passenger disembarking from the *Firefly*. (Legends certainly evoke our extreme interest in detail.) At any rate, long before Uncle Sam Wilson of Massachusetts, New Hampshire, and New York passed away in 1854, everyone was saying "Uncle Sam" and meaning our country. A legend was made.

Incidentally, the legendary *appearance* of Uncle Sam can be traced back to an 1851 parade in Amesbury, Massachusetts, in which a Scottish-born man with white chin whiskers, one George Buchanan, of Woburn, Massachusetts, appeared wearing a high hat with immense white buttons sewn around the band and stripes fastened to his white trousers. An artist from *Leslie's Illustrated New York News* was present at the parade and the next issue of the magazine featured a drawing of Mr. Buchanan in his costume, over the caption "Uncle Sam." Obviously, the costume struck the public's fancy, the white hat buttons were soon replaced by stars, and . . . well, one thing just naturally led to another.

The "I Wish I'd Said That" Variety

There are certain legends that seem to evolve out of no logical sequence of events at all. Merely a little something someone said can catch our imagination, be repeated, perhaps somewhat embellished, and eventually take its place among our well-known

New England legends. The original statement is always of the "I wish I'd said that" variety, although we are inclined to do a little editing over the years to make it more appropriate for historical consumption. For instance, Ethan Allen allegedly demanded from the British commander the surrender of Fort Ticonderoga, "in the name of the Great Jehovah and the Continental Congress." However, Israel Harris, the grandfather of the late Professor James D. Butler of Madison, Wisconsin, was present and often told his grandson (as reported by historian and folklorist B. A. Botkin) that Ethan Allen's real words were: "Come out of there, you goddam old rat."

On the other hand, Captain Nathan Hale may have been a poor spy, but he is more than redeemed in history and legend by his heroic final words, words that, as far as historians can determine, he really did say: "I only regret that I have but one life to lose for my country." No amount of editing could improve that.

Perhaps the most puzzling New England legend that originated simply by a statement is the legend of Molly Stark. Puzzling, because Molly never said anything that's recorded or did anything of note. However, her husband, New Hampshire General John Stark, said and did a lot of things. It was just before the Revolutionary War battle of Bennington, Vermont—fought just over the Vermont line in New York State by mostly New Hampshire soldiers—that John Stark unknowingly made Molly into a legend. "There are the Red Coats," was his battle cry, "and they are ours, or this night Molly Stark sleeps a widow."

Then, along with Vermont's Seth Warner and Samuel Herrick, he went on to a decisive victory over the British, a victory that contributed significantly to Burgoyne's subsequent surrender at Saratoga two months later. Stark was also a hero at the Battle of Bunker Hill and is said to be the originator of New Hampshire's state motto, "Live Free or Die."

But no one remembers poor John Stark for any of that. Sure, Manchester, New Hampshire, has preserved his boyhood home, but it now serves as the meeting place of the Molly Stark Chapter of the DAR. A small fort in New Castle is named for him and there's a statue of him in Manchester and another in Concord, New Hampshire, which served as the model for a John Stark commemorative bottle of bourbon several years ago. However, because the figure in which the bottle was molded depicted Stark in full military uniform, with his hand shoved inside his coat, everyone thought it was Napoleon.

Now, Molly is something else again. For reasons never fully explained by anyone, Molly Stark is really big in New England today. The road between Brattleboro and Bennington, Vermont, once called the Molly Stark Trail, is now known as the Molly Stark Byway. There used to be several state markers along it, which showed a female figure standing beside a cannon (these are nown updated there as a series of eight obelisks with pertinent local history.) Probably someone somewhere along the line confused Molly Stark, who never fired a cannon, with Molly Pitcher, heroine of the Battle of Monmouth in New Jersey, who did. (Or perhaps even with Deborah Bradford Sampson of Plympton, Massachusetts, who fought in the Revolution disguised as a man.) In New Boston, New Hampshire, a brass cannon used at the Battle of Bennington and fired each July 4 is known as the Molly Stark Cannon. A Bennington school bears Molly's name. There is a Molly Stark State Park, a Molly Stark Hospital, Molly Stark gift shops and restaurants and streets and motels and almost every commercial venture you can think of, all named Molly Stark.

The people working at the Bennington Museum have told me that tourists are constantly asking, "Who *was* this Molly Stark?" There's not really much to tell. She was born Elizabeth Page in 1737 in Haverhill, Massachusetts; she married John in 1758; they had eleven children; she was a good, courageous pioneer farm wife; and in 1814, she finally turned the tables on that stirring battle cry that made her a legend, and John Stark sadly slept a widower.

Also engendering a legendary effect seemingly out of proportion to its original intent is Horace Greeley's simply stated advice to Josiah Bushnell Grinnell during a time when Grinnell, then a clergyman, had lost his voice. After all, Horace Greeley, born in Amherst, New Hampshire, was the founder of the *New York Tribune*, a strong antislavery voice before the Civil War, an influential advocate of universal amnesty and universal suffrage after the Civil War, and a member of Congress. In 1872 he even ran for President. But how is he remembered? As we all know, by his offhand remark to Grinnell that he ought to "Go West, young man, go West." Well, at least he's remembered for *something*.

Legends in Their Own Time

Unlike Molly Stark's, Greeley's, et al., the reason for the continued existence of a few New England legends is abundantly clear. These develop relatively quickly from particular people and events that appear bigger than life. *Much* bigger than life. The truth requires no embellishments because it already is extraordinary. These are, literally, "legends in their own time."

Daniel Webster was one. History records his stunning achievements, including, as many say, preserving a Union to pass on to Abraham Lincoln to save. Legend established him during his lifetime as a man who could do anything. Why, he even broke the established rule of grammar that dictated that plural nouns should take plural verbs. After Daniel Webster's time, people said the United States *is* and not the United States *are*. "Webster country" isn't just around the Marshfield area of Massachusetts —where his homestead is open sporadically to the public during summers— but everywhere in New England. His portrait is in Faneuil Hall and in hundreds of New England town halls, libraries, and schools. On Webster Hall at Dartmouth College a tablet says: "Founded by Eleazar Wheelock; Refounded by Daniel Webster." If history records he once stopped at a certain place for a cup of water from a well, that cup is on permanent display at the local historical society. Where he spent the night is usually stated on a little sign outside the building. His legend is the New England–wide reflection of the true man.

However, it isn't necessary to be a dominant historical figure.

Fisherman Howard Blackburn of Gloucester became an instant legend merely by surviving five days in a dory off Newfoundland's Grand Banks during the month of January 1883. He and his partner had become separated from their fishing ship, the *Grace L. Fears*, in a blinding snowstorm. Of course, many people, now forgotten, have survived for days in an open boat. What made Blackburn a legend in his own time was the *way* he survived. After his partner had frozen to death on the third day, Blackburn knew his own hands and feet would soon be frozen too, and that he would then no longer be able to row toward the Newfoundland coast.

"So I made up my mind that if my fingers were bound to freeze," Blackburn later explained, as quoted in a number of old newspaper clippings I have squirreled away in my office, "I'd make 'em freeze in such a shape as to be of some use to me. So I curled 'em around the handles of the oars while yet they wa'nt too stiff to do so. Then I sat there without moving while they froze in that shape around the handles of my oars."

Once frozen solid to his oars, Blackburn rowed for several more days, with the body of his shipmate rolling about stiffly in the bottom of his dory. Finally, he reached the small Newfoundland hamlet of Three Rivers, was saved, and eventually returned to Gloucester. He had lost all his fingers and most of both feet, but he owned and operated a successful saloon in town for a number of years and enjoyed his colorful reputation. In 1899, crippled as he was, he actually crossed the Atlantic to England alone in a light sailing dory. Two years later, he did it again—this time to Portugal, in the twenty-five-foot sloop *Great Republic*, which has been restored and enshrined by the Gloucester Historical Commission. Living legends, it seems, just naturally do that sort of thing.

Hannah Dustin of Haverhill, Massachusetts, also rapidly achieved legendary status by surviving an ordeal. Only she survived it in a rather bloodcurdling manner. After being captured by Native Americans on March 15, 1697, one night about two months later she and two other captives drove tomahawks into the heads of ten sleeping Native Americans at a camp in Boscawen, New

Hampshire. Before setting out for freedom, however, Hannah performed an additional little horror that truly ensured her place in New England history and legend. She scalped all ten Native Americans (I've actually seen her "scalping knife"—it's on display at the Buttonwood's Museum, Haverhill, along with the ax she used) and brought these grisly bits of evidence back to the home folks in Haverhill. Of course, everyone was delighted and, I'm led to believe, no one was known to give her any hassle throughout the remainder of her life.

A bizarre and comparatively recent occurrence that became another instant New England legend is the Great Molasses Flood of January 15, 1919, when a fifty-eight-foot-high tank full of molasses, located on Commercial Street in Boston, suddenly burst and poured two and a half million gallons of the sticky stuff all over the place, drowning or otherwise killing twenty-one people. In 1965 I talked to a man who knew the owner of a small Boston welding company that had submitted the lowest bid for cutting up the ruptured tank and cleaning up the mess. He deeply regretted winning the job. Not only did he lose money, but the work was a nightmare. Clothes, gloves, torches, hoses, any sort of equipment, was coated with a layer of sticky molasses within minutes of being on the job. Inside the broken tank, molasses had crystallized into a four-inch layer of sugar, which burned with a thick, choking smoke when contacted by acetylene torches. In the spring, flies swarmed to the area, getting inside workers' helmets and goggles. In short, two and a half million gallons of spilled molasses created a legendary mess.

The only good to come out of the Molasses Flood, as far as I can determine, was that it did settle once and for all exactly how slow molasses is in January. One of those injured in the disaster, a William Ryan, was working across the street from the tank when it collapsed. When he saw the heavy brown wave approaching, he tried to outrun it to safety, but it caught up with him and dragged him down into the ooze. I'm told that the fastest sprinters barely exceed twenty-five mph and Ryan, even in his fear, was not likely to be faster. So I think we can assume molasses runs somewhere around twenty-five to thirty mph in January.

The bizarre sinking of the Nantucket whaleship *Essex* in November of 1820, and its gruesome aftermath, must take its place with "instant legends" too. Not only was the *Essex* rammed and sunk by a huge bull whale, a historical event well noted by Herman Melville thirty years later, but during the quarter of a year the crew drifted about the Pacific in lifeboats before eight of the original twenty were rescued, they ate each other. In fact, a member of the prominent Nantucket Coffin family, Owen Coffin, was eaten. Owen lost a drawing and then very willingly and bravely allowed himself to be shot by Charles Ramsdell, after which his body was shared by the others. These details are only vaguely referred to in nineteenth-century descriptions, and even the survivors were reluctant to discuss it. There is the story of the Nantucket lady who asked a survivor's daughter about the vessel. "Miss Mollie," she was told, "here we never mention the *Essex*."

The captain of the *Essex*, George Pollard, one of the survivors, went to sea again, was wrecked again (but not by a whale), drifted for days in an open boat again, but did not resort to cannibalism. He wound up being rescued on an island near Tahiti, and there, for the first time, officially divulged all the details of the *Essex* episode to two missionaries. But in the meantime, because of the whisperings of those close to the survivors, a full-blown legend was already entrenched.

In his old age, Captain Pollard became a fire-watcher on Nantucket, and islanders relating the story today say his mind slipped a little. A reporter from Boston once asked him, shortly before he died, if he could remember Samuel Reed, who had been in one of the *Essex* lifeboats.

"Remember him?" the old captain is said to have replied. "Hell, son, I ate him!"

Twelve Most Often Asked Questions

In our obsession with the exact truth in every last detail, we

New Englanders particularly want to know the origin of things: old house features like widow's walks and spring dance floors, names, expressions, holidays, customs, certain objects, and on and on. Each morning of every working day at *Yankee*, the mail includes a number of letters from New Englanders or descendants of New Englanders living all over the country, asking for *origins*—the *real* true story in detail, exactly *how* it came about. The answers, in many cases, are legends. Not that we don't wish to provide the true answers. However, there are often *several* "true answers" that have been handed down from one generation to the next, and perhaps none is entirely true. Or there are several *conflicting* versions, each one of which is entirely true! The question of the real birthplace of the American Navy is a good example of that, and so I'll include it in the following dozen "most asked" *Yankee* reader questions over the years. Although I believe each of our answers was correct, at least as far as it went, each could very well have been prefaced by the phrase, "As the legend goes . . ."

Were widows walks on New England houses originally built for the wives of seafarers so they could watch for the return of their husbands' ships?

No, but closed-in cupolas with windows, such as on the Dr. Daniel Fisher House in Edgartown, Massachusetts, were built for that purpose. "Widow's walks" or "captain's walks" or "whale walks" or "captain's lookouts" are found on old houses hundreds of miles from the ocean. They provided a protected platform on which to stow buckets of sand and water to put out the frequent chimney fires. The term was erroneously applied by some romantic writer way back when, and like so many instances of "poetic license," it caught on far better than the cold, hard truth.

Please tell me the origin of wooden nutmegs in Connecticut and how that state became known for years as the Nutmeg State.

Sometime in the early 1800s, in the town of Waterford, Connecticut, the minister there, a Reverend Jacob B. Spofford, was invited to tea one day by a rather wealthy lady by the name of Mrs. Eliza Peterson, who, knowing the reverend was fond of boiled rice sprinkled with sugar and nutmeg, asked her servant to prepare it. Her servant replied there was no nutmeg, so Mrs. Spofford suggested she borrow some from a neighbor. The rice, liberally sprinkled with nutmeg, was greatly enjoyed by the reverend, and after he'd left, Mrs. Spofford complimented the servant and reminded her to return the borrowed nutmeg. The servant informed her she hadn't borrowed any, because none of the neighbors had nutmeg either.

"What did you use, then?" demanded Mrs. Spofford.

"Well," replied the servant, "I didn't want to ruin your party, so I just grated the handle of a button hook."

The amused Mrs. Spofford evidently circulated the story and thus eventually Connecticut became the Nutmeg State. In order to fill in a rather large gap in that particular sequence of events, it is also often told that certain people in Connecticut used to sell nutmegs carved from New England trees rather than the seed of a true nutmeg tree, which had to be imported from somewhere in Indonesia.

At any rate, it all grew so confusing that back in the 1960s the Connecticut Legislature officially changed the Nutmeg State to the Constitution State. Didn't do any good. One mustn't tamper with legends. We all still know Connecticut as the Nutmeg State.

Was there really a Sam Hill, and if so, who in Sam Hill was he?

He was Colonel Samuel Hill, 1678-1752, of Gilford, Connecticut, where he was town clerk for thirty-five years, judge of the probate court for twelve, and deputy to the general court for twenty-two or more sessions. In fact, he ran for so many offices so many times that "running like Sam Hill" became an expression denoting outstanding persistence and endurance. From there, Sam just sort of worked his way into being a generally used old-time expression, as in "Who in Sam Hill truly cares?"

What is the origin of the Pledge of Allegiance?

A young editor by the name of Francis M. Bellamy, in the Boston office of *The Youth's Companion*, wrote it one August evening in 1892 at the direction of the *Companion's* editor, James Bailey Upham, who had just persuaded President Benjamin Harrison to ask Congress to sanction Columbus Day as a national holiday—which they did. Bellamy's first draft of the Pledge read: "I pledge allegiance to my flag and to the Republic for which it stands, one nation indivisible, with liberty and justice for all," and that's how it was first printed in the September 8, 1892, edition of *The Youth's Companion*.

One of *Yankee's* freelance designers, Jill Shaffer, told me once that as a little girl, she thought it began: "I led the pigeons to the flag . . ." Fortunately for us all, the legend fairy failed to take it from there.

I know the nautical term "down east" refers to sailing with the wind or downwind, which ships usually do when traveling northeast along Maine's shore, but where exactly does the area of "Down East" begin?

A few people, mostly summer people, equate Down East with the entire coast of Maine. They maintain it begins the second you cross the Piscataqua Bridge at Portsmouth, New Hampshire, going north. The majority of New Englanders would say Portland is the very southernmost town or city Down East. Purists argue that Camden or even Penobscot Bay is the starting point, but I'd call that area "way Down East." Then, of course, Nova Scotia would become "way, way, way Down East."

Why were covered bridges covered? To keep the snow off? And why were some so high?

Joe Allen of Vineyard Haven, Massachusetts, who answered reader questions in *Yankee* magazine for over thirty-five years in his "Sayings of the Oracle" column, grew really sick of questions like this. Because he'd grown old enough to speak or write exactly what was on his mind, and because I had pledged to him that while I might not use all his answers I would never *edit* a published answer, there were many things Joe wrote in his final years that I could not use. I was afraid of massive subscription cancellations.

Here is his last reply to the covered bridge question, written about a month before he suffered the stroke that eventually proved fatal at age eighty-nine. It's heretofore unpublished (I just didn't have the guts) and it's quoted verbatim—forgive me, Joe:

> Jesus for Guard Almighty, we thought all hands knew by this time. Bridges were covered, damn fool, for the same reason women used to wear petticoats—to protect their underpinnings. Ever hear that wood rots when it gets wet? Your asinine suggestion that they were covered to keep the snow off the road is dead wrong. In fact, I recollect throwing snow inside the bridges after a snowstorm so our sleighs wouldn't grind on the wood. As to the height of covered bridges, any simpleton would know it took some height to get a full hay wagon through.

Were spring dance floors in New England made "springy" deliberately, or were they just the result of weak construction?

Many years ago I had a conversation with Philip W. Baker on this subject. Phil, a noted expert on historic-building restoration, had personally studied spring dance floor construction details during some of his company's projects. His conclusion: some were made deliberately and some were that way by accident. He says the actual springing quality was created by the lack of supports beneath the ballroom floor and/or the use of particularly springy timbers for floor joists. He told me that the Jones Tavern in Weston, Massachusetts, had one of the very best spring dance floors, but like so many of them, it didn't conform to present-day legal specifications and had to be reinforced, which removed the spring. The original Jones Tavern floor joists were made of three-by-ten-inch spruce—"a real whippy wood," Phil said. Certainly that had to be deliberate. Phil and his fellow workers were amazed at how easily they could make the floor "pick up a lively rhythm."

I've walked and bounced (but not danced) in the ballroom of the historic Hamilton House on 9 Chestnut Street in Salem,

Massachusetts, and I'm convinced that the considerable spring of that floor in such an otherwise solidly constructed house was no accident.

I've seen what's called the Marie Antoinette House listed on tourist brochures as being in North Edgecomb, Maine. Why in the world was the queen of France living in Maine?

Well, Marie Antoinette had her head chopped off (October 16, 1793) before she had a chance to be rescued by Lafayette and others, who had planned to send her to America on the brig *Sally* of Wiscasset. She was to have been harbored in what now is called the Marie Antoinette House (then located on, and later moved from, Westport Island, a stone's throw from Wiscasset).

However, her furniture, *just* her beautiful furniture, came to Maine on the *Sally*, and much of it is still around. A gorgeous mirror-fronted bookcase of hers is on display at the reconstructed General Henry Knox residence (open summers) in Thomaston. Other pieces are in Wiscasset, Rockland, and scattered about the country. Of course, hundreds of pieces of French furniture are *said* to be Marie Antoinette's but are not. In the year 1795 alone, for instance, a Colonel James Swan of Dorchester, Massachusetts, principal owner of the *Sally*, arranged to have over one hundred shiploads of furniture belonging to French nobility (on the "outs" during the French Revolution) brought to America. Only *one* shipload contained the Marie Antoinette pieces.

There was a movie several years back about two Western cowboys, called Thunderbolt and Lightfoot. Wasn't that originally a New England legend?

The movie departed from history and New England legend a split second after the title flashed on the screen. The real story goes back to 1818, when a Dr. John Wilson arrived in Dummerston, Vermont, and began practicing medicine. No one knew Dr. Wilson's background. He always wore a scarf around his neck, he was known to indulge himself with a wee toddy now and then and then and now, he enjoyed the company of ladies, and he often fell flat on his face at the town contradances. However, there were those who trusted Dr. Wilson drunk more than any other doctor sober. He eventually moved to Newfane, then to Brattleboro, married, had a son, was either separated or divorced, and then, in 1847, contracted an unrecorded disease and died.

Just before he died, he summoned several friends and said he had a last request. He wanted to be buried with all his clothes on. Even the neck scarf. They agreed, but as soon as he'd passed away, they whipped them off. Well, actually the undertaker removed them, prior to washing and embalming the body, while the friends observed. On Dr. Wilson's neck was a long, ugly scar, apparently from a sword or knife. In the calf of one leg was what appeared to be an old bullet wound. That leg was withered and shorter than the other, a fact he'd covered up by inserting a thick wedge of cork in his shoe and refusing to limp. (So perhaps it was more than the toddies that sometimes influenced his equilibrium.)

All this got around rapidly, including to the sheriff's office. The sheriff studied his list of wanted men and found that one John Doherty, who had escaped the law in Ireland in 1818 and was known to be living somewhere in America, exactly fit Dr. Wilson's description, even to the scars and the cork heel.

So it would appear that Doc Wilson practiced medicine in Vermont for twenty-nine years without a license and under an alias. He was actually John Doherty, one of the most feared highwaymen in Britain during the early nineteenth century. Because of his lightning raids, in which he was always courteous, never robbed women, and so on, he became known as Captain Thunderbolt. He liked the name and usually told his victims that they had the distinction of being robbed "by none other than Captain Thunderbolt."

When he teamed up with a Michael Martin, a young thug from Kilkenny, he named him Captain Lightfoot. Martin escaped to America at about the same time as "Doc Wilson" did, but one version of the legend says they never got together in this country. Another says they both taught school in the Round Schoolhouse in

Brookline, Vermont. In 1965 a *Yankee* subscriber, Carl Hardwood of Baldwinville, Massachusetts, wrote me that his mother remembered "two men teachers who taught at the Round Schoolhouse who came over to the United States from England to escape prosecution for some crimes." He went on to say that one had the nickname "Thunderbolt" and the other stayed only a few weeks.

At any rate, Martin returned to a life of crime, was arrested in Springfield, Massachusetts, was tried, convicted, and hanged about 1821. It was Martin who, just before his execution, gave the full description of his former partner, Captain Thunderbolt, who by then was a simple, kindly, somewhat overdressed country doctor quietly practicing his medicine in Dummerston and falling down on his face at the Saturday night dances.

I understand there's a four-and-a-half-ton flat stone somewhere in New Hampshire with a groove all around the outside of it, carved thousands of years ago, for the purpose of catching the blood of human sacrifices. True?

There is such a stone in North Salem, New Hampshire, supposedly carved for that purpose, and there are lots of peculiar dry-stone "beehive" constructions, as they're called, all around New England. The people who own the properties on which these mysterious things can be viewed usually ask me not to publish the exact locations. They don't want tourists inundating the area.

In the November 1971 *Yankee*, however, we made the mistake of describing exactly how to find a certain perplexing underground stone structure in the vicinity of Goshen, Massachusetts.

"Tarnation!" the property owner wrote me within three days after the issue came out. "Just when I thought things had quieted down you go out and print that danged old legend about 'the Goshen Stone Mystery' again." He went on to say that "hordes" of people had already arrived and that he was afraid someone would fall down into this particular legend and then sue him. "Please, please, please," he implored, "tell your readers in the next issue that it's nowhere near this town or else say I've filled that blasted tunnel up with broken glass. Which I may do!"

The most famous bunch of stones was once called Mystery Hill and is now called America's Stonehenge. Here, in North Salem, New Hampshire, one finds the so-called sacrificial stone so many of our readers inquire about. Incidentally, America's Stonehenge is in all the New Hampshire tourist brochures and is open to the public. It seems to me that a new theory of the origin of America's Stonehenge is put forth every ten years or so. During the 1960s, a number of the archaeologists some of our writers interviewed seemed to conclude they were the work of Bronze Age people from the British Isles who crossed the Atlantic about 1200 B.C. and established a short-lived colony here in New England.

Then in 1975, my neighbor, the late Andrew E. Rothovius, a fine author in the field of archaeology and meteorology, looked into it again and reported that the scientific community now felt it might be the other way around. In other words, they decided that maybe Europe's stone-building culture, so strongly oriented to the heavens, as at Stonehenge, actually moved from west to east and originated over here—in North Salem, New Hampshire—about four thousand years ago.

In 1959 I struck up a conversation with an old country gentleman during the only tour I've ever taken of the America's Stonehenge site. I remember his telling me earnestly that it was the early colonists who built these stone structures and that they built them to winter-store their turnips. I pointed out that his theory in no way addressed itself to the carved groove all around the huge sacrificial stone, but he chose to ignore that point.

I've also seen the strange carvings—letters, crude figures, and symbols—emblazoned on rocks lying about what they call Round Swamp, near Sandwich, Cape Cod, on what is now Otis Air Force Base property. I was told by local residents that they were carved in the late 1700s by one Charles Nye, who courted a Sal Pry out in Round Swamp (except during bug season), then went to sea for almost four years, returned to find Sal married to someone else, and withdrew to a small cabin in the swamp, where he spent the rest of his life carving on rocks and old tree stumps.

"Suppose old Charlie Nye could have at one time wandered out of the swamp as far as North Salem, New Hampshire?" a Pennsylvania man wrote after *Yankee* had published a number of these rock legends in the May 1964 issue. I replied that it seemed he was really stretching believability, but . . .

Who really posed for the famous Fisherman of Gloucester statue in Gloucester, Massachusetts?

I remember that we once came right out and said flatly that it was Captain Clayton Morrissey, a Gloucester fisherman. The reasoning was that when sculptor Leonard Craske was commissioned in 1923 by a committee of "Master Mariners" to create a memorial to all Gloucester fishermen, it was Captain Morrissey who took Craske out for a day's sail on the schooner *Elizabeth Nunan* after the committee had rejected Craske's initial clay model. It seems Craske had his fisherman *sitting* at the wheel. The committee members, horrified, recommended that Captain Morrissey take Craske out for a sail in order to implant firmly in the artist's mind that no one, but no one (except a yachtsman), would ever steer a boat from a sitting position. During this demonstration sail, Craske is said to have made many sketches of Captain Morrissey *standing* at the wheel.

We published the article in August 1964, and the barrage of letters from Gloucester and surrounding communities commenced.

"Anyone who knew Charles Newell of West Newbury knows he was the one who posed for the *Fisherman of Gloucester*. The statue looks exactly like him." (This from many West Newbury residents.)

"It was around 1923 that Leonard Craske asked me to pose for him at the St. Botolph Studios in Boston for the *Fisherman of Gloucester* statue. The studio was set with a ship's wheel, which I held on to in various poses in the nude. The nude pose was necessary to have all the muscle structure in proper proportion, and only later were clothes added." (Louis J. Andrews, in a letter

I published in November 1964, when he was wrestling coach at Milton Academy.)

"Leonard Craske used my husband, Colin Campbell Clements (1894-1948) as the model for his *Fisherman* statue. However, when the committee of Master Mariners viewed the original efforts, they judged Colin to be too 'romantic looking,' not enough weathered by the sea, so they insisted the face be redone and it was." (Mrs. Colin Clements, Hampton Falls, New Hampshire.)

Probably the *real* story is that Craske used all four men at one time or another during the creation of the sculpture, but letters still trickle in supporting Morrissey, Newell, Andrews, or Clements. Some also say the fisherman is standing on the wrong (right) side of the wheel, but the Master Mariners passed judgment on that question long ago, saying it didn't matter "one spit in the ocean which side of the wheel a man stood on."

As long as he stood.

What is the true birthplace of the American Navy?

The two Massachusetts towns that have argued with each other for years over this question are Marblehead and Beverly. And certainly here is a fine example of an instance in which no one can agree and yet everyone is correct.

Marblehead's claim: On September 2, 1775, George Washington commissioned a Marblehead man, Captain Nicholas Broughton, a Marblehead ship, the *Hannah*, and a Marblehead crew into the service of the United Colonies of North America.

Beverly's claim: When George Washington's order came through, the *Hannah* was tied up in Beverly harbor. She therefore sallied forth from Beverly on her first mission as a U.S. Navy ship.

In order to settle the argument in time for a Navy Day celebration planned by the two towns in October 1935, the U.S. Secretary of the Navy, Claude Swanson, was called in and asked to investigate and decide, once and for all, which town should rightfully claim to be the birthplace of the American Navy. Secretary Swanson, obviously not experienced in New England ways, innocently accepted what he considered to be merely a simple matter of looking up a few historical facts.

He came to Massachusetts from Washington and first investigated Marblehead's claim. He found it to be true. Then he looked into Beverly's. Also true.

About this time, word of the Secretary's investigation began to get around, and within a few days he received a letter from the governors of South Carolina and Georgia, saying that as early as July in that same year of 1775, naval forces created by both those states had jointly captured a British supply ship carrying powder and had then delivered this powder to the Continental Congress for the use of the United Colonies. Both claimed to be the birthplace of the American Navy.

Then he discovered that on August 1, 1775, by order of Major General Schuyler, Commodore James Smith had taken command of the sloop *Enterprise* at Crown Point, Lake Champlain, "for the service of the United Colonies." All of us today who have traveled through Whitehall, New York, on Lake Champlain, have seen the large sign still proclaiming Whitehall, New York, as the birthplace of the American Navy.

Rhode Island inserted its oar too. On August 4, 1775, General Washington had requested the governor of that state to send ships to Bermuda to capture British powder stored there. The Rhode Island sloop *Katy* did just that, a group of Rhode Islanders told Secretary Swanson in no uncertain terms, and therefore established Little Rhody as the birthplace of the American Navy.

Finally, the now harried Secretary learned that five days before the Battle of Bunker Hill, a Captain Jerry O'Brien had sailed out of Machias, Maine, and with a crew of farmers armed with pitchforks, sabers, and axes, had attacked and boarded a British naval sloop of four guns, the *Margaretta*, and forced its surrender. Machias, Maine, strongly claims to this day that it is the true birthplace of the American Navy.

It was at that point that the Secretary was heard to say to one of his aides, "Oh, to hell with it!" That evening, he boarded a train and returned to Washington.

His subsequent "official" report was more diplomatic. "Whereas the relative claims of . . . places to be considered as the birthplace of the Navy rest upon one of (several) sets of circumstances which might be considered as constituting a birth of a navy, I find it impossible to decide . . ."

And so the hassle continues here in New England, even as I write these lines.

Living in a Legend

I couldn't begin to mention all the physical manifestations of famous legends that can be viewed in New England today. They're everywhere. My favorites, however, are those with which I've had some personal connection. For instance, I've snooped around a certain abandoned little house nestled in some pines on the shores of a river in Hopkinton, New Hampshire—a little house made from the crate used to ship Lindbergh's Spirit of St. Louis back to America on board the U.S.S. Memphis after his historic Atlantic flight. Legend has it that an officer aboard the Memphis, who happened to be a native of Hopkinton, made a deal with Lindbergh en route to acquire the crate, which he eventually turned into the small house. The crate/house ended up finally at a small private museum in Canaan, Maine after having been moved to Deerfield, New Hampshire where it housed a flute player and her daughter for many years. The quiet, secluded setting of this now forlorn structure juxtaposed in my mind with the worldwide Lindbergh hoopla of years ago created for me one of those fleetingly special moments during which everything seems pleasantly sad.

I've studied the top of the steeple on the First Baptist Church in Hampton Falls, New Hampshire, through binoculars to determine whether or not there's really a five-and-a-half-foot-high beer bottle up there. It's up there, all right. The most popular of several explanations is that during the 1850s a brewery in Portsmouth offered to donate the money necessary for a brand-new steeple, if the symbol of their product was placed at the top for all the world to see.

"Smacks a little of soul-selling," the pastor, Reverend R. Scruton, told me, "but that was our only offer at the time." Hampton Falls residents are thankful that the Trueform Brassiere and Corset Company, for instance, didn't decide to make a better offer.

I didn't need binoculars to see plainly the large pointing hand on top of the steeple of the Methodist Church in Milton Mills, New Hampshire, when I was investigating the "Church with the Hand on Top" one beautiful fall day in 1966. It was made of a solid block of wood and had been carried to that dizzy height in a half-bushel wicker basket by Aratus Shaw, who, with others, built the church as a labor of love in 1871, utilizing only donated materials.

It makes history real for me to see and touch and ponder the perfectly preserved bullet hole in the shed wall of the Elisha Jones house (not open to the public) in Concord, Massachusetts, a British soldier's parting shot as his regiment was retreating following the Concord fight on April 19, 1775. It's almost as if it happened yesterday or last week. Same with the plainly visible tomahawk marks on a door at Old Deerfield Village.

And yet the squat twenty-six-foot-high fieldstone tower with its semicircular arches between chunky columns, located in a small park in Newport, Rhode Island, seems to me to be somehow unreal. It's known as the Old Stone Mill, or sometimes the Norse Tower. Labeled "the most controversial building in America," it's been there longer than anyone can remember, but no one knows how or why it came to be built. Theories name the colonists of the 1600s, who were real enough, but also people like Eric Gnupsson, bishop of the Greenlanders in 1112, or the Scandinavian Paul Knutsun around 1355, and others of a similar ilk. I find it difficult to relate to Eric and Paul.

Most of these Norse theories were discredited anyway when an archaeological dig around and under the tower, begun in 1948, unearthed only colonial artifacts. Nonetheless, the librarian in the historical society said to me, "Local people don't like to spoil a legend." A Newport real estate man echoed that same feeling:

"I don't think there's a chance it's Norse, but as long as it's talked about, that's the main thing." He wanted a colorful tourist sign erected, illustrated with a Norseman in full twelfth-century getup, to direct people to the tower, but the more conservative Newport element squashed that idea.

Some people actually *live* in a New England legend, and that's not always so easy. I've met and talked with the owners of two of New England's most famous legendary houses, the Wedding Cake House in Kennebunk, Maine, and the Ocean-Born-Mary House in Henniker, New Hampshire ("The Only Henniker on Earth"). Although both are private residences, both are also nationally known tourist attractions—unofficially.

The Wedding Cake House was built in 1826 by a shipbuilder who loved to carve, George W. Bourne, and then, thirty years later, adorned by Bourne with so much elaborately carved wooden fretwork that it really does resemble a wedding cake. Its legends include a new bride committing suicide by throwing herself down the stairs, several ghosts, and a few murders. The remarkable appearance of the place just seems to invite legends.

Mrs. Harold Lord, widow of the great-great-grandson of the original George W. Bourne and owner of the house when I first began researching this book, told me that *none* of the legends are true. Not a single one! "But people's imaginations sure go wild when it comes to the house," she said. She also told me she sometimes awakened in the morning to find people wandering around her house. Just tourists. During warm summer nights, she was often startled by small explosions and brilliant flashes of light. Amateur photographers were out there on the lawn taking night pictures. Strangers would continually ring the doorbell and ask for a tour. Sunday dinners were complete with strange faces pressed against the living room window.

"Why don't you sell?" I asked Harold Lord a few years before he died in 1977. He replied that this was his ancestral home, where his roots were, and that he just couldn't bring himself to leave. Mrs. Lord felt the same way.

In July of 1972, I featured the famous Ocean-Born-Mary House in *Yankee's* "House for Sale" column, in which we editorialize each month about various unusual properties available in New England. I remember how strongly the owner emphasized to me that she wanted every potential buyer to telephone for an appointment. No casual visitors. I wrote in strong language that if people stopped by unannounced, they would really be sorry, but I understand some foolish readers did anyway. So now, to add to the old one, there's a silly *new* legend that these particular people were torn to ribbons by man-eating guard woodchucks. I'm sure that's not true, although I am certain they were not received with open arms. The house did eventually sell, but I pledged to the new owners that I would not write anything about its *current* status. They are vainly hoping that the old legend will simply fade away. It never will, of course. Legends in New England *never* fade away.

The Ocean-Born-Mary House legend goes back to the year 1720, when a baby girl was born to James and Elizabeth Wilson, (or perhaps Miss Elizabeth Fulton) aboard the ship *Wolf* sailing from Londonderry, Ireland, with immigrants intending to settle in Londonderry, New Hampshire. Within hours or days of this seagoing birth, a pirate, or privateer, by the name of Don Pedro, and his band of men boarded the *Wolf*. When Don Pedro saw Mrs. Wilson (or Miss Fulton) with her newborn child, he said he would spare the lives of everyone aboard if the child was named Mary, after his dear mother. Mrs. Wilson (or Miss Fulton) agreed, the sentimental Don Pedro allowed the *Wolf* to continue her voyage, and he even gave little Mary some green silk to be used for her future wedding dress.

Well, Mary grew up in a Londonderry house (later torn down and reassembled in Little Compton, Rhode Island, where it is known today as the Sea-Born-Mary House), married, had four sons, and in 1742 was widowed. The legend then splits apart:

Version One says Don Pedro eventually retired from the sea, built the Ocean-Born-Mary House in Henniker, invited Mary and her sons to come live with him, which they did, and buried somewhere on the property a treasure chest (for which people with metal detectors have searched in vain). He then was murdered in the orchard and his body placed under the three-ton fireplace hearthstone, where it remains to this day.

Version Two says one of Mary's sons built the Ocean-Born-Mary House in 1780, that Mary and all her sons then lived there, but that Don Pedro had nothing to do with the actual house at all. No buried treasure and nobody under the hearthstone.

Whatever. What's certain is that the Ocean-Born-Mary House will be a legend at least as long as there remains a New England.

Remembering Details

There are, of course, legends that reflect a rather dark side of our New England psyche, concerning murders, monsters, ghosts, curses, and certain other horrors, but I'll tremulously examine those in a subsequent chapter. Also, my apologies to a certain few for not delving deeply, due to space limitations, into other stories such as the one about the mountain in Sebago Lake, Maine, which in the last hundred years has moved about one mile to the south; the obsession of Hiram Marble and his son, Edwin, who devoted most of their lives to digging, at the rate of one foot a month, some two hundred feet down into rock near their Lynn, Massachusetts, home; the last pregnant woman to be hanged in the state of Massachusetts (her name was Bathsheba Spooner); and the ten-acre plot of land in Worcester, Massachusetts, that was legally willed to God.

Nor will I dwell on the fact that the submarine G1, which sank in 105 feet of water in Narragansett Bay in 1900, had wheels for running on the bottom; that Rudyard Kipling became deathly seasick doing research for his *Captains Courageous*; that Eli Whitney, inventor of the cotton gin, was reported to be the first person in America to use a bathtub; that the snowmobile was invented in 1913 by Virgil D. White, a West Ossipee, New Hampshire, Ford dealer; that the Shakers also made Victorian furniture; that a Damariscotta, Maine, man, Harold Castner, did not write "Sweet Adeline" but was the very first person in the world to *sing* it; that a newspaper used to be published regularly on the top of Mount Washington, until the delivery boys, who slid down the mountain railroad tracks on specially designed boards, were mostly all killed; that the yo-yo was first manufactured in Gloucester, Massachusetts; and that, according to several New Englanders present, Teddy Roosevelt rode a mule, not a horse, up San Juan Hill.

To admit, as I must, that each of the preceding has constituted a major editorial feature in *Yankee* magazine sometime over the years is to give the somewhat erroneous impression that *Yankee* and New England are obsessed with trivia. Not so. Well . . . not *excessively* so. But as I've said before, we New Englanders, on the whole, do not consider historical details to be trivial.

Remembering "details," it seems to me, is simply an effort to remember, period. An accurate memory preserves past history, which in turn supports the present—from which we launch into the future. In light of mankind's rapidly increasing volume of knowledge that most of us do not understand, remembering, for instance, that "O Little Town of Bethlehem" was written by a Bostonian, Philips Brooks, in 1874, is at least *something* to hang on to! It's a touchstone with reality, trivial as it may also be.

Yet frail memory plays tricks with us or fails, which is probably another reason we sometimes become obsessed with it. The last time I leaned over the railing and looked down at Plymouth Rock, enshrined there in Plymouth, Massachusetts, a father and his daughter of about eight years were beside me.

"Do you know what happened here?" I overheard the father asking.

"Oh, yes, Daddy," the girl replied. "This was the place the penguins landed."

Last spring at a dinner party I was attending in New York, I told this story to the group at my table. Everyone chuckled and then, a moment later, an elderly lady next to me turned and said in a low, confidential tone, "You know, my niece is at Skidmore College and they're teaching her that Columbus never landed on Plymouth Rock after all."

Is there nothing sacred anymore?

6

GENEALOGY
(AND OTHER FORMS OF ONE-UPMANSHIP)

Where Lowells Speak Only to Cabots

How to be snobbish without appearing so ෙ three kinds of yacht clubs ෙ island and native snobbery ෙ how snuffboxes were used ෙ purple glass on Beacon Hill ෙ the Chosen City of the Universe ෙ the Athenaeum, a cultural phenomenon ෙ the ultimate definition of a Boston Brahmin ෙ snobbism of the Yard ෙ who are you, really? ෙ First Families and why ෙ the difference between the Pilgrims and the Puritans ෙ Mayflower ancestry and why it's second best ෙ the Pilgrim who fell off the Mayflower ෙ putting Virginia in perspective ෙ good ancestors and bad ancestors ෙ New England across America ෙ Daughters of the American Revolution and other hereditary societies ෙ the man who sired three children after age 100—maybe ෙ illegitimate and executed ancestors ෙ coats of arms and who is eligible ෙ looking up one's own family tree ෙ the correct places to be buried ෙ the world's ugliest monuments ෙ and how today Mayflower descendants are related to the Chinese

A S YOU ENTER OR LEAVE THE OLD SHIP-BUILDING TOWN of Thomaston, Maine, you'll see a small sign. It reads: "Thomaston, 1605." Simple. No need to explain that a certain George Weymouth of England founded the town fifteen years before the Pilgrims landed at Plymouth. In fact, if such an explanation were included, the sign would lose its effect. In other words, by becoming informative, it would no longer demonstrate that specific brand of one-upmanship peculiar to New England snobbism.

Maine explorer Sir Ferdinando Gorges had the right idea. "We might have had ye Pilgrims in Mayne," he wrote, "but we didn't want them."

New England snobbism is based on a regional reverence for that which is old. And as the late Maine author John Gould once wrote, "It takes considerable art to be snobbish without appearing so." Thus the perfection of Thomaston's devastating little sign.

Naturally, pride in one's history has many wonderful attributes, and as so many boring speakers (including myself) have said at historical society meetings around New England, "A sense of the past is essential for a ripe culture." However, it is also essential, particularly in New England, for snobbery.

I haven't been in any of the three yacht clubs in Marblehead, Massachusetts, for some years, but I remember how each used to demonstrate physically its place on the New England social ladder. Out on Marblehead Neck, where all the summer people have their places, are the Eastern Yacht Club and the Corinthian Yacht Club. Old families with old money—that is, families that have been in the area (including the Boston area) for a number of generations—belonged to the Eastern Yacht Club. No one else was allowed to join. The clubhouse itself always looked to me as if it might collapse. It needed stain or paint, there always seemed to be a loose board or two out on the porch, and the dining and other facilities were modest, though with a certain quiet, *old* charm. However, belonging to the Eastern meant you were "in." If you didn't belong, you were "out"—and might just as well join the Corinthian Yacht Club.

The Corinthian accepted new people with new money, and its clubhouse and docks were new, meticulously maintained, modern, and posh. To a Texan or anyone else not knowledgeable in New England ways, inspection of the physical facilities of the Eastern and the Corinthian back in those days would have caused the Corinthian to be the immediate and obvious choice. From the New England point of view, that would be all well and good. As my aunt on my father's side once told me, "A Texan may be a braggart, but he can never be a snob."

Then there was the Boston Yacht Club, located across the harbor from "the Neck," in the town of Marblehead. It was always considered the place for those not in any way interested, or able to be interested, in social considerations. It was for townspeople. So its clubhouse was neither run down nor posh. It was straightforward, perfectly comfortable, practical. Of course, some members of old area families, particularly the young ones with old money, deliberately chose the Boston Yacht Club over the Eastern. That's a related but slightly different form of snobbery, which was negated completely if you belong to both, as some did.

I don't mean to imply that townspeople, or natives, aren't willing and able to play the game of one-upmanship.

"Did you come from the mainland?" islanders will ask pleasantly as you arrive by boat on Martha's Vineyard, Matinicus Island, or wherever, knowing full well the only other place to come from is the open ocean. The snobbery of being an islander is gently there.

In the same way, I often overhear natives greeting old-time summer people arriving in Dublin, New Hampshire, where I live, with the question: "Are you here for the season?" They're not intending (usually) a put-down, but it nonetheless remains a beautifully subtle reminder that the summer person does not belong and will never belong.

Old houses are better than new houses. Old companies are better to work for than new companies. Better to own an old barn than to build a brand-new one. Old wooden boats are wonderful. New fiberglass boats, particularly fiberglass *motorboats,* are not. "Do you charter?" is a rather cruel question sometimes used by wooden-sailboat owners to gain an additional increment of one-upmanship. The only way you can outsnob someone like that is to have your boat documented.

Real New Englanders, as we all know, do not wear showy new clothes. As the late writer Cleveland Amory liked to point out, "For a woman to dress too smartly . . . is to open herself to the charge that she is a social climber." A typical expression of New England contempt is: "She has everything she owns on her back." Like the run-down Eastern Yacht Club, slightly threadbare clothing that has been owned for years is a sign of gentility. It's an indication that you feel there are far more important things in life than mundane concern for physical appearance.

Of course, New Englanders *are* concerned with physical appearance. My father always wore a flannel shirt, tweed jacket, and bow tie—even when he was fishing. But the coat had a few holes in it. (Incidentally, holes are fine. Stains, no—except on your hat.)

New Englanders also take pride in their knowledge of old *things*. Knowledge of even a minor esoteric detail concerning an old New England object demonstrates one's linkage with the past and thus becomes a possible move in the game of one-upmanship. Several years ago, I was examining an antique snuffbox owned by a college friend of mine and his wife, who had just moved into an old town house on Beacon Hill.

"Do you know why New England snuffboxes, like this one, are so worn in the middle of the cover?" he asked. I felt that perhaps the editor of *Yankee* magazine *ought* to know, but I didn't.

"In the old days, snuffboxes in New England were passed from one person to the next with a little ceremony to ensure good luck," my friend explained, a bit smugly, I thought. "Holding the box unopened in his left hand, a man would strike the cover with his right elbow. Then he would strike it with the knuckles of his right hand before passing it along to the next person, still in the left hand. That's why."

"Interesting," is what I recall responding, before I launched into a tedious explanation, as a way of recouping, of why the window glass in his newly acquired old town house was purple. I explained how totally purple glass was ordered from Hamburg,

Germany, for new houses being built on Beacon Hill from 1816 to 1824, because it was thought at the time that sunlight shining through purple glass was beneficial in treating rheumatism.

"That's one of several marvelous theories," my friend said. "But of course, the truth is that the glass in the old windows here on Beacon Hill was *not* originally purple. Rather, it was made in a glass factory on Essex Street and that particular then-white window glass contained, either by accident or by design, an excessive amount of manganese, which, when acted upon by sun and time, has produced the lavender and purple hues."

He'd made his point, but then, to be sure I was aware of my error, he actually removed one small pane of purple glass. Around the edge, where the broad band of protecting putty had kept off the sun, there was plain white glass.

I haven't been able to get together with this particular friend since then. Must give him a call sometime.

Old cities are, naturally, better than new cities, and Boston and environs, being the oldest, enjoys a very special place indeed in the reality, both past and present, of New England snobbery. And while the many and often-told stories about Bostonians and their engagingly snobby ways and attitudes can sometimes be amusing, it remains a fact that most are true.

"My goodness," said a Boston woman when the *Boston Transcript* announced it was going out of business. "Whatever shall the country do now for a newspaper?"

That same particular woman was known to have said, when her husband was in the Antarctic for a six-year scientific expedition, that he was "out of town."

I remember a brief cocktail party discussion in a house on Commonwealth Avenue on the subject of the desirability of extensive travel.

"Why should I travel," one elderly matron interjected, "when I'm already here."

James T. Fields, a great supporter of the "Chosen City of the Universe," as he called Boston, used to delight in telling the story of a Boston man he personally knew who, after viewing a production of *Hamlet*, was expressing his wonder at the genius of William Shakespeare. Finally, he was moved to the ultimate praise. "There are not a dozen men in Boston," he said, "who could have written that play."

Boston and its suburbs (to which a lot of the "old money" has moved) really *is* the center of New England culture and social life. Not because culture and social life in other parts of New England are not as good. In many cases, they are. They're just not as *old*. I mean, formal dinner dances in Springfield, Massachusetts, for instance, are very fine, but as the participants themselves say frankly, they're "not Boston." The Boston Symphony Orchestra travels to the Berkshires every summer, but when it returns to the "Hub" in the fall, Berkshire County, as writer Tim Clark says, "hangs up its tuxedo and pulls on the long underwear and overalls."

One of many uniquely Boston cultural phenomena, if I may call them that, is that housed in the five-story building at 10½ Beacon Street, a building unmarked except for the street number. As any but first-time visitors to Boston would know, however, the Athenaeum has for years been one of the world's finest private libraries and remains today a wonderful "retreat for those who would enjoy the humanity of books," as is graven on the brass plaque just inside the huge entrance doors. The Athenaeum has been frequented by the likes of Nathaniel Hawthorne, Daniel Webster, Louisa May Alcott, Dr. Oliver Wendell Holmes, and Ralph Waldo Emerson, and for years its director and librarian was the late Walter Muir Whitehall, a Boston Brahmin if ever there was one. To be sure, the Athenaeum has also been called a "shrine whose primary purpose is to preside over the last rites of Brahminism." Election to its board of trustees has been traditionally (although softened somewhat now) a First Family monopoly and an honor in Boston society second only to membership in the Harvard Corporation. Yet I don't know of any other place in New England where a scholar would rather go for serious research.

Incidentally, it *is* true that the Athenaeum contains a book bound with human skin. It also owns George Washington's private library. The fact that both are in the same room may have led one confused newspaper reporter to write some years ago that in the Athenaeum one could see "the diary of George Washington, bound in his own skin." That is not the case. The actual "skin book" is the deathbed confession of one George Walton, and the skin that of a Jamaican.

Even though the dictionary broadens "Brahmin" to include all New Englanders of "a cultured, long-established, upper-class family," it seems to me that the two words "Boston" and "Brahmin" are inexorably linked.

The best image of a Boston Brahmin, in my opinion, is to be found in a certain anecdote told by Cleveland Amory, in his book *The Proper Bostonians*, about the late Wendell Barrett of Boston, known during his lifetime as "the Brahmin of Brahmins." It seems that on one of his trips to Ireland, Barrett visited the famous Blarney stone. However, he did not, as most every other visitor does, lie on his back and kiss it. Instead, he touched it with his umbrella and kissed that.

Down through the years, one's place in Boston, at least insofar as the Brahmin world is concerned, has been defined by one's class at the "Family Seminary," as the Adamses called the nation's oldest college, known to my father (class of '23) and just about everyone else as "Hahvad." E. Digby Baltzell, in *Puritan Boston and Quaker Philadelphia* (this book makes Boston out to be the very clear winner insofar as citizen achievement is concerned), writes about a distinguished newcomer to Boston being considered for the presidency of a local bank.

"What was his class?" a board member asked casually in the due course of the discussion.

"He had no class," another replied. "He went to Yale."

There are countless such stories about Harvard. And those who enjoy them most and tell them most often are the very Brahmin types who went to Harvard and who are, in fact, the characters in the stories. There is a devastating element of extra one-upmanship here. In other words, one can appear to be telling a silly story about the snobbism of the "Yard" at the same time one is clearly, though with acceptable subtlety, reminding one's listeners that Harvard is the *only* college in New England or anywhere about which such stories could possibly be told.

One evening in 1947, my father was reading *The Proper Bostonians*, which had just been published. Laughing uproariously, he read aloud to my sister and me an anecdote concerning Elizabeth Dwight Cabot. (I remember that I didn't get it. That, in itself, is somewhat revealing.) At any rate, the anecdote related that one day in September 1881, Harvard began its sixth regular football season with a loss. That same day also witnessed the death of President Garfield. In her diary, Elizabeth Dwight Cabot wrote feelingly of the assassination, closing her entry with the line: "Of course, I could think of little else and, coming on top of the Harvard defeat, I went blundering around doing my shopping and found myself so tired that I had to stop and go for some dinner."

New Englanders are inclined to differentiate between good and bad by determining whether it's old or new. Frugality, reluctance to change, reliance on the "tried and true," abhorrence of all things showy or gaudy, pride in the past, a strong need for tradition and continuity—all these natural inclinations in our personalities result, not surprisingly, in our wearing slightly threadbare old clothes, joining old, comfortable-not-posh social clubs, owning old boats, attending old schools and colleges, living in old houses, marrying into old families, and so forth.

But of all the tangible things involved in one's true social place and social identity in New England, ancestry seems most important. Whereas in other regions of the country, people are interested in who your parents are, in New England we seem equally interested in who your grandparents were—and your great- and great-great grandparents! I mean, who *are* you, *really?*

The old New England stories about having to be born here in order to be native to the area are partially true. But more is required.

"I know I'll never be considered a native here in Vermont, because I wasn't born here," said my sister to her "native" neighbor after she had lived in Putney for fifteen years. "But my three children were all born right here in Putney, so they can certainly be called Vermonters, right?"

"Well," began the slow rejoinder, now often told in speeches around New England (particularly by me), "if your cat had kittens in the oven, would you call them biscuits?"

To be sure, my sister never raised the subject of "natives" again.

Joseph P. Kennedy, father of the president, was frustrated all his life by always being referred to in the press as "an Irishman."

"I was born here," he used to say, "my children were born here. What the hell do I have to do to be an American?" Well . . . perhaps not *quite* as much as he would have had to do to be a New Englander!

If, however, you're firm enough in your long New England ancestry, then you can disdain all the other accouterments of regional gentility. Might be risky, but the one-upmanship potential in the apparent contempt for socially acceptable New England behavior is enormous. Not caring is, of course, the ultimate snobbery. But if—and only if—your ancestry equipment is in good shape, then buy a new fiberglass motorboat, live in a modern house, wear a loud tie, say you don't play tennis, go to Dartmouth instead of Harvard, own a snowmobile, refrain from participating in the activities of your town's very old and "in" social club (although you must, in any case, belong), marry an outsider . . .

Proper ancestry starts with New England's First Families. According to Oliver Wendell Holmes, the requirements for a First Family were "four or more generations of gentlemen and gentlewomen; among them a member of his Majesty's Council for the Provinces, a Governor or so, one or two Doctors of Divinity, or a member of Congress not later than the time of long boots with tassels."

First Families include the Cabots, who, as the saying goes, speak only to God; the Lowells, who speak to the Cabots; the Adamses, acknowledged by most to be the foremost of all First Families; the Forbeses, perhaps the wealthiest; the Appletons, who made a fortune, as so many First Families did, in the textile industry after coming to Boston from their native New Hampshire; the Saltonstalls, who have sent sons to Harvard in every generation since Nathaniel Saltonstall graduated in 1659; the Peabodys, whose family fortune was founded by Joseph Peabody of Salem—a privateer during the Revolution; the Winthrops, who helped found the Massachusetts Historical Society (right up there with the Athenaeum in social status); the Putnams, who, along with the Jacksons, Bowditches, and Warrens, headed the Harvard Medical School throughout the nineteenth century; the Quincys, who include a president of Harvard; the Phillipses, who founded both Andover and Exeter; the Lodges, who have been senators as well as nearly every other good position in the world including Harvard overseer; the Emersons, whose scion Ralph Waldo did quite well in the writing field; the Eliots, who include presidents of both Trinity and Harvard . . . and on and on.

Though not forever. While you're not beginning to "slum" after naming the first fifty or sixty, you *are* beginning to water the soup. The number of First Family members didn't increase throughout the years as much as one might expect, because they all hung around with each other and intermarried. Thus you have a Cabot Lodge, a Godfrey Cabot Lowell, a Peabody Gardner, an A. Lawrence Lowell, and others. As historian John Morse, Jr., writes in his *Memoir of Colonel Henry Lee*: "Lees, Cabots, Jacksons, and Higginsons knew each other well . . . and had a satisfying belief that New England morality and intellectuality had produced nothing better than they were; so they very contentedly made a little clique of themselves and intermarried very much, with a sure and cheerful faith that in such alliances there can be no blunder."

In New England today, First Family status still provides an important inside track insofar as obtaining an executive position is concerned. At least on the initial contacts. Outside New England is a different situation, of course—as exemplified by the often-told story of the young Bostonian who requested a family friend at the Old Colony Trust Company to write a letter of recommendation to a Chicago firm to which he was applying for a position.

"I can recommend him to you without the slightest reservation," wrote the family friend, saying that the young man's mother was a Cabot, his father was a Lowell, and his ancestors were all Peabodys, Appletons, Forbeses, and Saltonstalls. The Chicago firm replied that they really were looking for different information. "After all," they wrote, "we are not contemplating using the young man for breeding purposes."

Not every famous name from Revolutionary days necessarily founded a First Family, but it is of passing interest to note, as E. Digby Baltzell writes, that proportionately more New England or Boston men of national consequence founded First Families than did non-New England men, particularly Philadelphians. For instance, John Adams and Thomas Jefferson, though espousing quite different political philosophies during their lifetimes, were great friends in their last years and even died on the same day, July 4, 1826, exactly fifty years after the birth of the nation each helped found. Both were members of the upper class in their colonies; both were natural leaders. But only John Adams founded a First Family. (In fact, John Adams founded a *super* First Family—one with two presidents, two signers of the Declaration of Independence, three ministers to England—some 175 years without having ever failed, for even one generation, to produce somebody of national eminence.)

It was Baltzell's opinion that it was men of conservative, rather than liberal, temperaments who had been, for the most part, the First Family founders. And New England, as we know, has enjoyed an advantage in men of conservative temperaments. Thus John Winthrop founded a First Family. William Penn did not.

William Penn was a liberal thinker, a dreamer, a pacifist, a Quaker ("or some very melancholy thing," according to the seventeenth-century diary quoted by D. Elton Trueblood in his book *The People Called Quakers*). For the most part, the Pilgrims, who came over on the *Mayflower* and landed in Plymouth in 1620, were of that same gentle temperament. Brave and tough, to be sure, but certainly proud they had little Old English blue blood in their veins.

So, in keeping with Baltzell's theory, New England's First Families did not originate with the *Mayflower* group. Instead, most if not all New England First Families trace their American ancestors back to those of an upper-middle-class nature, who sailed over here from England in 1629 (and for a number of years thereafter) on the *Arbella* and fifteen other ships, to found the Massachusetts Bay Company. These people, including a Saltonstall, a Winthrop, a Phillips, a Bradstreet (but no Dun— although a Dunn came over on the *Mayflower*), a Quincy, and most of the other First Family ancestors, were conservative businessmen with a strictly puritanical outlook on work, religion, sex, death, and the hereafter. As we all know, they were Puritans.

However, while the descendants of both the Pilgrims and the Puritans followed different patterns, both most certainly constitute proper New England ancestry. To be sure, *Mayflower* ancestry doesn't have the truly substantial clout of First Family ancestry, due in no small measure to the fact that most *Mayflower* descendants do not have the financial and political power that is automatically associated with First Family names. But it's nonetheless very fine to be a member of the General Society of Mayflower Descendants. And if, for instance, you're a Chilton (the oldest passenger on board was James Chilton), or a More (Richard More was one of the children on the *Mayflower*), or a Rogers (Thomas Rogers signed the Mayflower Compact but did not survive the first winter, although, fortunately for some, his son did), or if you're descended from one of the other twenty families aboard the *Mayflower* who are now known to have present-day offspring, then you can join the society. You could, perhaps, also hang a huge print of the ship *Mayflower* in your living room, which might at times elicit enough conversation at social gatherings for you to mention your *Mayflower* ancestry without appearing overly forward about it.

But keep in mind that among the immigrants to Massachusetts between 1620 and 1650 were at least twenty-four named More and fifteen named Rogers. At least two immigrants to Virginia in the same period were named Chilton, according to *Mayflower Families Through Five Generations, Volume II*, published in 1978 by the General Society of Mayflower Descendants, Plymouth, Massachusetts. So a More, Rogers, or Chilton of today isn't necessarily of *the* More, Rogers, or Chilton family that sailed on the *Mayflower*.

As Vrest Orton wrote in his book *The Voice of the Green Mountains*: "If the good ship *Mayflower* . . . had taken aboard all the ancestors that are now claimed to have come over on that voyage, it would have been bigger than today's *Queen Elizabeth II*."

I regret I have no ancestors who came over on the *Mayflower*. I was, however introduced in the following manner: " And although our speaker claims no *Mayflower* descendance, he does have a relative who ran for the boat and missed it." (That particular relative then waited some eighteen years before catching a boat that subsequently landed in Newburyport, Massachusetts.)

If I could be a *Mayflower* descendant, I'd like to be a Howland. John Howland fell off the *Mayflower* as it was rounding the tip of Cape Cod. "But it pleased God he caught hould of ye top-saile halliards," wrote Governor Bradford about the incident in his *History of Plimouth Plantation*, ". . . held his hould (though he was sundrie fathoms under water). . . and then with a boat hooke and other means got into ye shipe againe." A few days later, John Howland was one of a small group of *Mayflower* men "sente oute" to discover a locality suitable for their future home. Thus it was that John Howland stood on "Forefathers' Rock," as Plymouth Rock is also called, five whole days before the rest of the *Mayflower* people landed on it. Now, *that's* one-upmanship.

If one possesses neither a First Family name nor a *Mayflower* connection, all is not lost. The basic need (in terms of genealogical snobbery—certainly nothing else) is merely a multi-generation New England ancestry. The further back, the better—but it doesn't *really* matter whether your people were distinguished scholars or horse thieves, intelligent or demented. Illegitimacy, incest, and executed ancestors (unless it was for stealing a horse) are exceptions to this broad-mindedness. Like everything else in our region, it's longevity that counts. Longevity in New England.

I must say that Virginians always seem to be yakking about how Jamestown was founded before Plymouth and that *they* produced the likes of Washington, Jefferson, Madison, Monroe, Chief Justice Marshall, and other such notables. It can be quite tedious to listen to all that sort of thing. We New Englanders are ready, willing, and able to be snobby ourselves, of course, and enjoy replying that of the fifty-six signers of the Declaration of Independence, sixteen were delegates from New England. Virginia had seven.

To have one of those sixteen in one's family tree is very much a plus. To a somewhat lesser extent, but still nice, is to be related to the likes of Rufus King, Nathaniel Gorham, or Caleb Strong, who helped frame the Constitution in 1787. Likewise, to have ancestors among the 119 people known to have dressed up as Native Americans for the Boston Tea Party is something of which a number of today's New Englanders are proud. But if anyone says he or she is related to Paul Revere, a Boston Tea Party participant among all his other historic achievements, don't believe it. Although Paul Revere had sixteen children by two wives, there are no known direct descendants of his today.

Rhode Islanders like being related to Roger Williams; Hartford, Connecticut, Hookers and Hayneses are proud that their ancestors Thomas Hooker and John Haynes founded their city; the Davenports have the edge in New Haven (their John Davenport first settled there); in Lawrence and Lowell, Massachusetts, there are a few Lawrences and Lowells descended from the original First Families who helped establish the textile mills there; Maine's Knoxes are aware that their Major General Henry Knox founded West Point and the National Guard before retiring in Thomaston; and on and on throughout New England.

Furthermore, in the genealogical sense, New England stretches right across America. The Mathers founded Cleveland, Ohio, and other Midwest towns; the Putnams are strongly associated with Buffalo, New York; the Perkinses with Cincinnati; William Greenleaf Eliot (grandfather of T. S. Eliot) established the public school system of St. Louis; the Eliot children went farther west and helped build Portland, Oregon; the Adamses helped develop Kansas City, Kansas, as well as Denver, San Antonio, and even Houston, Texas (!); Sherburne County, Minnesota, is named for Moses Sherburne of Mount Vernon, Maine, who helped write the Minnesota state constitution; Wisconsin's first, third, seventh, eleventh, twelfth, and eighteenth governors were New Englanders; in Michigan, the Sanfords, Fairfields, Martins, Mearses, Fullers, Tafts, Barbers, and many others have their ancestral roots in Vermont; Chicago, once called Fort Dearborn, was named after a New Hampshire general until they decided to name it after an onion; the man named Brigham Young, founder of Salt Lake City, Utah, hailed from Whitingham, Vermont.

The list could literally continue for hundreds of pages. As a result, there are millions of Americans living throughout the United States who consider themselves to be New Englanders— at least in part. As such, they have as much right to enjoy their indulgence in a little New England snobbery as any of us do.

The Daughters of the American Revolution, founded in Washington, D.C., but well established in New England, is very sensitive about being labeled snobbish. The DAR, 165,000 Daughters strong, is the largest patriotic-hereditary organization in the world, and its library in Washington, open to the public, is regarded as second only to that of the Mormon Church among genealogical archives. It is crammed to the roof with copies of marriage, birth, and death certificates, voting and property tax rolls, deeds, war records, and all the other public documents that establish a person's existence. The purpose of that is to prove each member's claim that one of her ancestors fought or had a big hand in the American Revolution. On *our* side. No Tories allowed. Only direct lineage is included—and excluded are descendants of illegitimate children and polygamous marriages.

"Most [members of the DAR] are too ignorant of American history and American ideals to know what they are doing," Dr. George S. Counts of Columbia Teachers' College once said. "Their patriotism is a combination of thinly veiled snobbery and the protection of privilege."

Another side to the subject is often expressed in the simple and sincere statement by a Daughter that it really is "an honor to have an ancestor who fought for the Revolution."

I have often been the speaker at meetings of New England chapters of the DAR and I've found the members, almost always on the elderly side, to be charming. And no *more* snobby than any of us New Englanders concerned with genealogy. Although the organization as a whole has been criticized over the years for taking stands opposing the likes of the United Nations, the Universal Declaration of Human Rights, federal aid to education, and so forth, its individual members often say they only want to preserve family history for their grandchildren.

One particular DAR dinner I attended, awhile ago, will always be vivid in my memory. The opening ceremonial procession was, as usual, complete with all sorts of flags and banners, and the marching Daughters, in beautiful formal gowns, were wearing the official ribbons, bands, gold bars, and pins that indicate ancestors, family ties, and positions in the local and national organizations.

An extremely elderly Daughter, dressed and decorated to the hilt, was at the piano, but I couldn't believe what she was doing. Perhaps, some years ago, she knew piano chords and could manage to play something. No longer. All she had left was a marching rhythm—and enthusiasm. *Pound pound* de *pound pound* de *pound,* is my recollection. Every pound was a discord.

I felt distinctly uncomfortable and embarrassed for everyone as I stood on the stage with the other chapter officers, facing the oncoming processional. However, no one seemed to mind. The ladies marched slowly down the aisle in time to this pounding, as if Van Cliburn himself were at the keys, and turning slowly in front of us, they took their seats. I began to notice one and then another of the ladies, ones I'd met before the meeting, subtly catch my eye as they turned and give me an almost imperceptible wink. They knew! They *all* knew. Their tolerance of the struggling but still game lady at the piano was a kindness—and since then my feelings for the DAR have been mixed with emotions that brought a lump to my throat that evening.

On that same occasion, while having dinner at the head table, I asked the ladies about other hereditary societies. Turned out that each one was active in at least five besides the DAR. One lady belonged to thirteen! And I don't mean their names are simply included on the membership rolls. They participate in the considerable activities of each and plan long tours around the country for the sole purpose of attending the meetings.

Here are a few—my table companions happily recited them to me as I jotted the names on the back of a napkin:

- Colonial Dames XVII Century
- Dames of the Court of Honor
- Daughters of the American Colonists
- Women Descendants of the Ancient and Honorable Artillery Company
- Sons and Daughters of the Pilgrims
- United States Daughters of 1812
- Colonial Dames of America

- United Daughters of the Confederacy
- Descendants of the Illegitimate Sons and Daughters of the Kings of Britain
- Society of the Descendants of the Colonial Clergy
- Americans of Royal Descent
- Flagon and Trencher (Descendants of Colonial Tavern Keepers)
- The Hereditary Order of the Descendants of Colonial Governors
- Daughters of Founders and Patriots of America
- Piscataqua Pioneers
- The National Society of Old Plymouth Colony Descendants
- Daughters of Union Veterans of the Civil War
- Order of the Crown of Charlemagne in the United States of America
- Order of Three Crusades
- Sons and Daughters of The First Settlers of Newbury, Massachusetts
- The Baronial Order of Magna Charta
- The National Huguenot Society

There's a tombstone in the cemetery of Cornwall, Connecticut, that reads as follows: "Here lies interred the body of Mr. John Sage who departed this life on January 22, 1750, in the 83rd year of his age. He left a virtuous and sorrowful wife with whom he lived 57 years and had fifteen children. Twelve of them married and increased the family by repeated marriages to the number of twenty-nine. He had 120 grandchildren, 40 great-grandchildren, 37 now living, which makes the number of offspring 189." John's descendants today could run in the millions!

Abaih Edgerton of Pawlet, Vermont, left 209 descendants when he died at age 85. Eight families in Clarendon Springs, Vermont, produced exactly 113 children, including only one pair of twins. And Nantucket's Tristram Coffin supposedly left even more descendants!

It's not always easy to keep the branches on the family tree untangled. A common complication arises from the fact that many New England men outlived several wives and then, after marrying again late in life, sired more children. A hundred-year-old Connecticut journal mentioned by genealogist Donald Lines Jacobus in his book *Genealogy as Pastime and Profession* says: "Died, of physical exhaustion, Lieut. John Brandon of Saybrook at the age of no years. He left him a young widow and three children, the latter all under 110 years of age." I'm not at all sure I believe that.

I do know for a fact, however, that one Thomas William, second earl of Leicester, England, sired a son at a time when one of his daughters was already a grandmother. And from the records of the New England Historical and Genealogical Society, going strong in Boston since 1845, I note that a certain Colonel William Webster, age sixty-seven, married a Martha Winslow of Kingston, New Hampshire, who was nineteen. She also happened to be the colonel's sister's granddaughter. Martha, then, was wife to her great-uncle, sister-in-law to her grandfather and grandmother, aunt to her mother and father, and great-aunt to her brothers and sisters. She was also stepmother to five children, fourteen grandchildren, and one great-grandchild.

Illegitimacy is another problem—not only because the records of illegitimate children are vague, but also because a professional genealogist will sometimes ignore a discovery of illegitimacy in order to spare his client any possible distress. The same holds true for ancestors who were hanged or otherwise executed. The late Donald Jacobus, a noted genealogist, knew of just such a case. It seems the history of a certain New England family published in the 1960s (for which Jacobus did not do the research) correctly states the date and place of a family member's death without revealing that, under an assumed name, said family member was executed on the date specified, for being "the greatest mass murderer known to American criminal history."

One method of spotting an illegitimate girl in a New England family tree is by the actual name. It was sometimes considered appropriate to call girls born out of wedlock such names as Lament and Trial. Boys born out of wedlock were usually given the name of the reputed father, if known, so those are more difficult for a genealogist to identify.

There are circumstances when illegitimacy is considered acceptable. Even somehow desirable. Those are cases of tracing royal European ancestry in order to qualify for a family coat of arms, still a status symbol if properly researched. So in the event a real bastard is the necessary link in establishing the royal line necessary for one to be able, legitimately, to hang a beautifully framed family crest in one's den, fine. In fact, it's a convenient conversation point.

"My family goes back to the royal house of Orange. Of course, I really don't care about that sort of thing, but the prince of Orange had no *legitimate* children, so . . ." (Ha-ha-ha-ha all around, thus softening to an acceptable level the fact that the subject was brought up in the first place. But it *was* brought up.)

As most of us know, many companies who make and sell family coats of arms don't bother with research. They are, to put it bluntly, frauds. Charles Francis Adams, of the First Family Adamses, once declared that only two families in all New England, the Winthrops and the Saltonstalls, were worthy of the honor of arms-bearing. An article in *Yankee* back in 1971 by a former employee of the English College of Heralds added the names of non-New Englanders George Washington, Walt Disney, and Douglas Fairbanks, and then offered, at the end of the article, to undertake research into "armigerous" (arms-bearing, but not necessarily royal) ancestry for our subscribers—for a modest fee. Quite a few subscribers from around the country sent him the modest fee, but they would have done as well throwing their money into the Atlantic Ocean. We hassled over that fiasco for well over a year.

Professional genealogists, however, seem to me to be hardworking, honest, and genuinely interested in their specialty.

Of course, many New Englanders trace their family history themselves, without the help of professionals. They say it's fun if you have the time to wander around old cemeteries, check records in various towns and cities, visit libraries, write letters of inquiry to relatives you've never met, separate tons of relevant material from the irrelevant, answer and place genealogical advertisements, and so on. Writer Eben W. Keyes II was just such an amateur genealogist. He truly enjoyed adding twigs to his New England family tree. He told me he used to, on occasion, telephone town halls for information, although he later found that a written request for data was more rewarding. One of his last such telephone inquiries, exemplifying the problems one can encounter in the pursuit of ancestors here in New England, was to the town clerk of a small northern New Hampshire town. The conversation went approximately like this:

KEYES: "Hello. I'm interested in any records you have of an Ezra Snow who was born in your town about 1750. Can you tell me who his parents were, and if he had any brothers and sisters?"

VOICE (*pause, as records are consulted*): "Yes. Ezra Snow was born here in 1748, son of John and Rachel Snow. He had two brothers, John and Amos."

KEYES: "Thank you! Do you have any records of his marriage? Or of any children?"

VOICE (*pause*): "Yes. Ezra Snow married Elizabeth Caldwell in 1774. Seems they had two children, Ezra, born 1776, and Sarah, born 1779. He died in 1820."

KEYES: "You've been very helpful. May I have your name in case I need more assistance later on?"

VOICE (*pause*): "Ezra Snow." (*Click*)

One-upmanship, that often sad little game we humans must play in one form or another, doesn't stop with death. Not at all. Just as interest in our ancestry can, for some, extend the game backward into our past, so monuments and cemeteries continue it forward into the future. For years, the Old Granary burial ground, now in the shadow of the Boston Athenaeum and across from the ancient Park Street Church, was the proper place for New Englanders to spend eternity. Here First Family dead lie buried four deep, including Benjamin Franklin's mother and father, Paul Revere, Samuel Adams, and John Hancock. In more recent years, Forest Hills, on the road to Milton, Massachusetts, and Mount Auburn, the "Gateway to Heaven" that happens to be located in Cambridge, Massachusetts, are thought of as acceptable places to be.

I walked through Mount Auburn recently and had to marvel at the size and elaborateness of some of the larger mausoleums. The sculptures are quite something too—including weeping maidens, life-size sculptures of dead children, tons of cherubs, urns, and weeping willows. It wasn't so long ago that what is considered extravagantly maudlin today was very much "in." My grandmother, for instance, displayed in her house a wreath made from the hair of a dead relative. On the mantelpiece in the same house was my grandfather's appendix, pickled in a jar. Whenever we visited "Pop" and Grandma when I was a boy, that particular fireplace mantel was where I'd head first. And I'd stare, always fascinated.

Absent for the most part in Mount Auburn cemetery are the memorable epitaphs one sometimes finds in the older graveyards around New England. Mount Auburn was, and still is, too proper for any but the most dignified memorials.

Dignity is an important requirement of most any stone reminder of a onetime presence here on earth. But the most dignified and elaborate of memorials are not *always* an indication of great wealth and New England social position. There have been many people who decided to save for years in order to have a superfancy remembrance. For example, a man named Lucas Douglass died, apparently penniless and alone, on the streets of Ashford, Connecticut, one cold December night in 1895. He'd never married and had few relatives. Shortly after his death, it was discovered he had a will that left enough money—thousands of dollars—to erect, as he had stipulated, a 34-foot-high monument of Italian marble complete with headstone, urns, and a 140-foot stone wall surrounding the plot. It's there to be seen in the Westford Hills cemetery today. It includes epitaphs ("I have heard Thy call"), a portrait of Douglass in a circular medallion, and all manner of various inscriptions. Since he ordered all this before he died, at least he had some satisfaction from it. However, the most common reaction of the several hundred tourists who come to view it each year is one of wonder and pity, neither of which is particularly germane to the one-upmanship game.

Henry Daniel Cogswell, a wealthy Rhode Island doctor of the nineteenth century, encountered far worse reactions to his efforts at self-perpetuation. In fact, his major contribution to the world may have been the regulations of today's fine arts commissions relative to suitability and good taste of monuments in public places. Not that Dr. Cogswell initiated such rules. Rather, it was his memorials that vividly demonstrated the *need* for them! It seems the good doctor donated large stone monuments doubling as drinking fountains (he was a teetotaler) to Boston, Fall River, Pawtucket, Rockville, and over a dozen other American cities, each topped by a statue of himself and, unfortunately, as described in a New Haven newspaper of the day, "outlandishly ugly."

One of the few remaining Cogswell fountains stands today in Central Park, Rockville, Connecticut. Years ago, it had been thrown into a nearby lake, as many of Cogswell's memorials were, but it was retrieved in 1969 and erected in its present location without many of its original ornaments and with a flower pot substituting for the statue of Dr. Cogswell. There's another at the entrance to Slater Park in Pawtucket, Rhode Island.

New England, of course, abounds with memorials, historic markers, plaques, and monuments. Each celebrates an event or a person from New England's past, of which we are so proud. And all of them, when considered together, emphasize New England's continuing stability, continuity, and the fact that it was here, the state of Virginia notwithstanding, that *everything* began. Why, in Little Compton, Rhode Island, there is even a monument commemorating the birthplace of a chicken. Contributions from around New England and beyond, plus land donated by one Deborah Manchester, made it possible to so honor the first Rhode Island Red hen.

I know of no one who can better place us humans and our mannerisms in perspective than my late friend Guy Murchie. Author of *The Seven Mysteries of Life*, *Song of the Sky*, and other books, Guy addressed the subject of genealogy by pointing out that no human being of any race can be less closely related to any other human than approximately fiftieth cousin, and most of us are a lot closer. This is simple arithmetic. If we double the number of our ancestors for each generation as we reckon backward, our personal pedigree would cover all of mankind before the thirtieth generation. But then you must allow for inbreeding; perhaps a better term would be "shared ancestry." Even so, fifty generations still very easily covers the planet.

"Even such a well-publicized line as the *Mayflower* descendants," Guy wrote, "can hardly begin to track down all their relatives of 350 years, and a little knowledge of early Yankee seamanship and fecundity in the tea and slave ports of Asia and Africa, plus mathematics, will show that their ranks probably now include more than a million Chinese in China, a comparable number of Hindus in India and blacks in Africa—not to mention several million Americans and Europeans."

Well, perhaps we can console ourselves by saying our New England genealogical activities involve *direct* lineage. Except they usually don't, especially if there's a good reason not to. We'll deviate as far off the direct line as necessary in order to link up with a famous person.

In July 1937, we published in *Yankee* a letter from a subscriber who sent us the ancestral lineage of Franklin Delano Roosevelt, of which she was a peripheral member, after he had announced on a political tour of New England that he was "glad to be in New England, from which have come most of my forebears."

The reader response can be best exemplified by this one-sentence letter sent to us by a Hardwick, Vermont, gentleman: "The only names I didn't notice in the Roosevelt genealogy," he wrote, "were Nebuchadnezzar, Columbus, and Adam and Eve."

I have in my personal files, for instance, a genealogical chart prepared by my mother's brother that meanders sideways through marriage after marriage until it connects, ever so fleetingly, with the Samuel Lincolns of Hingham, Massachusetts, who are— just incidentally, of course—in the main trunk of the Abraham Lincoln family tree.

I should point out at this juncture the fact that I include the above Lincoln tidbit in a vaguely disparaging context, thus relieving it somewhat of its potentially boastful overtones. (Even *I* am sometimes amazed at the subtlety of our New England snobbery.)

It's possible that snobbery is sometimes too harsh a word. Not altogether unsuitable, but just too harsh. As I wrote in the beginning of this chapter, a sense of the past is essential not only for snobbery but also for the existence of a ripe culture. And as we proceed along through our lives, our growing interest in our ancestors is probably somehow linked to the fact that it won't be long before we join them.

> Consider, friends, as you pass by,
> As you are now, so once was I.
> As I am now, so you shall be.
> Prepare for death and follow me.
> —*Common New England epitaph of the early 1700s*

At the end of the lifelong game of one-upmanship, the score is usually tied. While I truly marvel at the superior technique of some—Maine writer John Gould, for instance, in his lengthy biography in *Who's Who in America*, lists himself as "farmer"—I think most New Englanders simply want to be remembered in a good light. Our affection for all things old is the affection with which we would someday like to be remembered ourselves.

The late Joe Allen told me once of the time when he was asked to compose a tombstone epitaph. It seems a neighboring family on Martha's Vineyard decided to include in their family burial plot a memorial to a certain Uncle Mathew who had gone to sea and been captured by cannibals. According to the story the family had preserved for several generations, Uncle Mathew had been cruelly cut apart, cooked in several different horrible manners, and eaten completely up. The family had the correct name and dates on the memorial stone, as well as an engraved drawing of Uncle Mathew's ship. But they now wanted to include an appropriate tribute and asked Joe, being the writer he was, for help. Joe's suggestion: "Tried; and found good in many ways."

7

LANGUAGE

All Those in Favor Say "Ayuh"

Proper use of the "a" and the "r" ❧ the one word that can identify an outlander ❧ the nine definitions of "ayuh" ❧ tos, ups, downs, overs, and outs ❧ when to add an "on" ❧ some uniquely New England words ❧ using words incorrectly for clarification ❧ throwing up a road and subject to gates and bars ❧ commonly used phrases from the sea ❧ language that leaves a way out ❧ the cleanest of all clean jokes ❧ cutting the devil's throat ❧ how to correctly mispronounce Bangor, Berlin, Worcester, Concord, Sudbury, Swampscott, and Gloucester ❧ platitudes, profanity, and medical reports—who uses what, when, and how ❧ profanity substitutions ❧ what an angel says when someone takes his wings ❧ and a New England language test

ASK A WAITRESS IN MOST ANY AMERICAN restaurant if you can have a *poached* egg and she'll understand. Say you want it *porched* and she'll be with you if she originally lived in the Deep South. Ask for a *dropped* egg, and unless she's a New Englander, her face will remain blank. You'll need to explain that you'd like it *fried in water.*

The separating area in the middle of a four-lane road is a *mall* in New York, a *medial strip* in Pennsylvania, a *median strip* in parts of New England and in the Midwest, a *medium strip* in Kentucky, a *center line* in the West, a *center strip* in Ohio, and *neutral ground* in Louisiana and Mississippi. We New Englanders, particularly in the spring, sometimes feel *logy*. But in Indiana they are more apt to feel *dauncy*, while elsewhere they might be sort of *punk, puny,* or *draggy*.

There is little question that the language is markedly different from region to region across the United States. I *guess* (or if I were from the South, I *reckon*, or if from some of the New England offshore islands, I *presume likely*) the only argument is whether or not those differences are disappearing due to common exposure to the media and a more mobile population. Based on my admittedly unscientific observations over the years, I do not believe so. Regional accents, perhaps—to some extent. Regional language, no.

Words and expressions unique to individual regions remain in use not only because many are based on specific historical, geographical, or other attributes of their regions (i.e., "straight as a loon's leg" will never be an Oklahoma expression) but also because the utilization of regional language is a signal that one belongs. Or that at least one is making the attempt. And most everyone has, and will always have, an urge to belong. If a Texan suggests a swim in a *pond*, he or she is not a Texan. A pond is a *tank* in Texas because so many ponds are man-made. When outsiders who come to live in Texas learn that, they say "tank." In the same way, my camp on an island in New Hampshire's Lake Winnipesaukee is not a place for tenting. As outsiders are quick to learn, a *camp* in New England can be a pretty luxurious home if it's used for weekends and vacations. So can a *summer cottage*. Newcomers to South Carolina find that the natives prefer *splinters* to *kindling; battercakes* to *pancakes; streaked* meat to *bacon; wheelbaw* to *wheelbarrow; plunder room* to *attic*.

A North Dakota friend of mine told me when we first met that he never realized the word "summer" could be used as a verb.

In fact, he got quite a chuckle out of it. After he had moved to Vermont to take a job with *Vermont Life* magazine, however, I refrained from smiling when he informed me his parents were building a *camp* on Lake Winnipeg in Canada and were intending to *summer* there. Good, I thought. Good that regional language is perpetuated by both natives and newcomers.

Furthermore, since the nineteenth century, when so many thousands were heading out to settle the West, we New Englanders do not move from place to place all that much. The late Henry Beetle Hough, the distinguished editor and writer, lived on Martha's Vineyard all his life. He has visited the island of Nantucket, located only a few miles east of Martha's Vineyard, just once. That was in 1916 and, he told me, "I could only stay a few hours between boats." (He probably didn't wish to be called a "coof," an old Nantucket term for an off-islander.)

My aunt on my father's side lived in her West Newton, Massachusetts, home for nearly seventy years. The house in which she was born is five miles away. The old photographs in her family albums show my father and other relatives posing in a living room that looked much the same some fifty years later—in the same chairs, arranged in the same way, and with the same decorations on the fireplace mantel. "I worked out a good arrangement back then," she once told me, "so why change anything?" Her accent and use of what might be termed the New England language changed over the years just about as much as the inside of her house.

Even newcomers to New England eventually learn the region's expressions, names, and words, but what newcomers cannot learn is how to pronounce them. For instance, any outsider can come to understand all the subtle meanings of the New England word "ayuh" and when to say it. However, he cannot, in his lifetime, learn how.

There are probably more than a dozen New England accents. Each differs from the others in a number of subtle ways, but the uses of *a* and *r*, it seems to me, constitute the basic differences. There is the broad *a*, the lost *r*, the unbroad, nasal *a*, the misplaced *r*, the lost *a*, the regular *a* and *r*, and the misplaced *a*. New Englanders utilize these various *a*'s and *r*'s, or absences thereof, in various combinations.

Let's start with *r*. "We'll pa'k the ca' in Ha'vud Ya'd" is the well-worn example of the lost New England *r*. (And it can be pronounced with either the broad or the flat, nasal *a*.) However, consider "Yeste'day afte'noon, Mary sawr a man drawring ca'-toons." Here we have three lost *r*'s but the entire sentence is actually only minus one *r* since two *r*'s have been added. One *r*, in "Mary," is used normally. Incidentally, some New Englanders prefer "May-ree," but the *r* still remains in place. As for myself, I think that's a good *idear*.

The use of *a* is more complicated. Like the *r*, it can be added to words in which *a* normally does not belong. *Caow*, *naow*, and fish *ware* (for fish *weir*) would be examples. Also, in instances where *a* is ordinarily united with *o* to produce a long *o* sound, as in *load* or *boat*, the *a* is eliminated, resulting in *lo-d* and *bo-t*, both of which rhyme with *foot* or *toot*, *toot*, *tootsie*, *good-bye*. The *a* in *barn* is eliminated, along with the *r*, if the word is preceded by *cow*. The result here is *cow bn*, with the heavy accent on *cow*. In "*daown the ro-d a piece*," the *a* is both eliminated from the common *oa* sound and inserted where it doesn't ordinarily belong.

Some New Englanders utilize the broad *a*—*cahn't*, *tomahto*, etc.—while others prefer the flat, nasal-sounding *a* that, as writer Mary Louise Gilman, a Boston transplant from Kansas, pointed out in a 1973 article in *The National Shorthand Reporter*, renders the word *park*, for instance, into the word *pack*.

"Thus if your hostess suggests you *pa'k* your bags," she writes, "you'd better know whether you're coming or going."

The nasal sound so often associated with the flat *a* pronunciations, and which Walt Whitman, in *An American Primer*, found so offensive, is probably less pronounced today due to better health. Sickness and colds during bitter winters raised havoc with old-time New England noses. Although the nasal sound continues today to some extent, thank goodness there are no *heart* attacks among native New Englanders. None at all. Of course, some will suffer a *hat* attack and others perhaps a serious *hot* attack. And we all know that famine isn't necessarily one of the Four Horsemen of the Apocalypse. Rather, it's what a New England farmer does when he's working.

There's no denying that the various combinations of special New England *a*'s and *r*'s can occasionally retard effective communication. Gilman cites a classic example of the *r* problem: "Who can distinguish whether [a person] lives on *Western* or *Weston* Avenue when there is no distinction? Of the ninety cities and towns street-indexed in the *Atlas of Metropolitan Boston*, twenty-four have either a *Western* or *Weston* and two have both. Boston lists *Western* Avenue, *Western* Place, *Weston* Place and *Weston* Street. . . . My only recourse: spell it, please."

I find it difficult to tune my ear to some of the utilizations of *a* and *r* in specific geographical regions of New England. The *b*'s are all but impossible for me. However, better ears than mine hear an *h* in a western New England *wheelbarrow* but hear no *h* at all in *weelbarrows* along the coast. Linguists, in fact, usually do divide New England speech areas into coastal, central, and western. I do notice that the accent that differs most from, let's say, the English spoken on television is the coastal Maine accent. It is truly as exaggerated as that spoken by those sickening (with a few exceptions) imitators on media commercials. During my Maine childhood days, I remember we could immediately identify an outlander by the way he or she pronounced the word "spoon." Our rendering was somewhere between *spun* and *spawn*, but nobody from out of state could come close. A Maine friend tells me I can hit it correctly even today—but only after four or five rapid practice shots at it.

The word "ayuh" is very common in Down East areas today, but many people feel it's not utilized much in other parts of New England. Those people just aren't listening. New Englanders do not play it up in the heavy-handed, obvious way the imitators do. That would be embarrassing in light of the fun and jokes that have involved the word. But "ayuh" is very much a part of the New England language—a soft, sometimes hard, slurred, sometimes distinct, quiet, sometimes loud, unobtrusive, natural *ayuh*. Many outsiders are not aware it's being used. Perhaps they hear *yea* or some such casual, nonregional form of acquiescence. A fine ear for language sounds, however, not only hears *ayuh* but begins to decipher and interpret the many varying pronunciations of the word. In fact, as far as I can determine, "ayuh" has more meanings based purely on pronunciation than any New England word, and it's a word that isn't even in the dictionary!

For example (with apologies for the inadequacies of the spellings—some sounds just can't be spelled):

1. *Ay-uh* (second syllable a half note higher in pitch than the first) means "I heard what you said."

2. *Aaayyyeeeuuhh* (in more or less of a monotone, and lengthened out to four or more seconds) means "No," particularly in response to a question necessitating positive action of some sort.

3. *Eyuh* (very quick, almost a bark, with the *e* hardly pronounced at all) means "Yes, I'm ready to make the next move (or take the next step) in the task we're involved with."

4. *Eeeeyyaaooh* (slowly, but doesn't last as long as No. 2, with the middle section at a markedly higher pitch than either the back or the front end) means "I hear you but I really do not agree with you."

5. *Eeeeayuh!* (slow in the beginning but cut off abruptly at the end, which is at a slightly higher pitch; often repeated three or four times, with one of them ending at a slightly lower pitch) means "We've talked enough and I'm about to move on."

6. *Aaayuhh* (in a sort of nasal whine, the ending at a lower pitch, repeated over and over with both outgoing and intaken breaths, and continuing even while the other person is speaking) means "I really sympathize with you."

7. *A-yuh* (each of the two syllables pronounced distinctly, both

in the same rather low pitch) means "I agree with you."

8. *Eyuh! Eyuh! Eyuh!* (a short burst of three, rapidly, in a monotone, the accent on the second syllable, followed by a few seconds' pause and then, whether or not the other person is speaking, repeated) means "You are wasting your time and my time because you're telling me something I already know."

9. *Ayy-yuhh* (both syllables emphasized equally and in an exaggerated manner, the second syllable at a slightly lower pitch) means "I am an outsider trying to pass for a native," or (more likely) "I am making fun of those amusing old characters you find in New England."

The New England language is easier to learn than one of the various New England accents. But like English itself, there are few rules. As soon as you've identified a rule, you discover more exceptions than examples. For instance, you might hear a Maine man say he intends to go *gunnin'* for partridge that afternoon. You figure *gunnin'* is used instead of *huntin'*. But it isn't. If you're after deer instead of partridge, then you're *deer-huntin'*. We seldom eat *venison* either. Eat a lot of *deer meat*, though. Or take that simple little word "lot." There are, in New England, plenty of wood *lots*, four-acre *lots*, and even barn *lots*. However, there are no corn, potato, or oat *lots*. A pasture is generally considered to be a large, untilled area, often with several groupings of trees scattered here and there. But these trees do not constitute a wood *lot*. The *stand* of trees in a wood *lot* is bigger and thicker. A *field* of potatoes may be a *patch*, but you cannot describe a field of grain with that word.

The smallest of words may be the most difficult for outsiders to place correctly. In Maine, we used to have four principal directions: *up* river, *down* state, *over to* home, and *from away*. We went *up* to Boston and from Boston we went *out* to Prout's Neck (near Portland, Maine). But from Prout's Neck we went *up* to inland Vanceboro, whence we went *over* to McAdam, Canada, or *down* to Calais. St. Stephens is just across the international border from

Calais, but we went *to* St. Stephen*s*.

Every town in New England has its own set of *tos, ups, downs, overs, and outs* in relation to the rest of New England. And if you depend upon north-south logic, you'll be wrong about half the time. For instance, everyone knows one goes *down* the coast of Maine when one is sailing northeast, *up* the coast when sailing southwest. The term "Down East" obviously originates from sailing downwind with the prevailing westerlies when traveling from Massachusetts ports to those along the Maine coast. However, one can indeed go *up* to Bangor from Massachusetts. Correctly.

"Up" is a hard-working little word. It is added to *brought, banged, warmed, tumbled, let, picked, dressed, turned,* and countless others. Also, you find *up and did it, up and coming, up and around,* and even *what are you up to?* Banks in Maine have *drive-up* tellers. (Connecticut banks have *drive-in* tellers.) You can *shine up* to someone, but that isn't quite the same as *taking a shine to* that someone.

"Take" is used in many situations too. I can *take* another job, *take* after someone, or take sick, during which time I ought to *take* it easy. A person can *take* off another person, meaning mimic, or *take* him down a peg. "Take" can also be added for seemingly no reason at all—such as, "I'll take and give him a good lesson."

In the same way, "on" is added to statements for no apparent reason. My North Dakota friend asked me "On what?" when I happened to say our poetry editor was coming *on* from California for a month at the MacDowell Colony in Peterborough, New Hampshire. In fact, we endured a period of several minutes during which we were totally out of communication.

"Our poetry editor is coming on from California tomorrow."

"On what?"

"What do you mean, 'on what'? I said Jean Burden, our poetry editor, is coming on from California. Flying, as a matter of fact."

"Oh, you mean she's coming on a plane."

"Is there any other way?"

"No, I mean you must have been referring to the plane when

you said she was 'coming on.'"

"I wasn't referring to her mode of transportation at all."

"Well, why did you say she was coming *on* something?"

"I didn't. I just said . . ." and around and around we went.

Of course, no region in the United States can claim exclusive use of common English words. However, a regional flavor to our English language does emerge from the varying uses of common words and the unique combinations of those words utilized for specific subtle effects. That's not to say that every true region doesn't have a few words and expressions of its very own. For instance, there's the word "leanter," pronounced *leen-terr*, the accent on the first syllable and including a strong *r* at the finish. The *leanter* connected to our barn in Vanceboro was that section of the structure where the cows were kept. It's not in the dictionary and I've never seen references to a *leanter* in other parts of the United States. Plenty of *leanters* in New England. We had *sports* from Boston and other cities who would come to our area, hire local, licensed guides, and spend a week hunting or fishing. The huge old *churn tree* in my Dublin, New Hampshire, field is not found outside New England. Others refer to it as a maple tree, but they may not be acquainted with the fact that Native Americans once used large receptacles resembling wooden churns to tap New England maple trees.

Ask a New England lumberman if he'd like sugar and cream in his tea and he may answer, "I take my tea *barfoot*." If he is from Vermont, and only if he is from Vermont, he'll say he feels as *fine as a frog's hair*. Then there is a *muzzup* for a coffee break, a *honker* or *hunker* for a gale of wind, the *puckerbrush* for a thicket of young hardwood, *fudging* for fooling, to *pestle* around for a puttering activity—these are all New England terms. So is the word "heft." You *heft* something to test its weight. Before you do, however, you need to get *aholt* of it. Then you might *tunk* it. To *tunk* something is to give it a light tap, as in "Tunk it a mite. She needs to go just a whisker."

"Wicked" has been used a little differently in New England

for centuries (and nowadays, by teenagers in many areas of the country). A person is never characterized as *wicked*. However, the weather could be *wicked* hot or *wicked* cold, and a man could be *wicked* poor or even *wicked* rich. He might also be *miserable* poor.

I find that words are often used in a technically ungrammatical way in order to clarify, enhance, and simplify meanings. When my neighbor in Dublin during the 1960s, a well digger, said to me that his helper's fists were about the *bigness* of a cantaloupe, I received a very clear picture. Clearer than if he had used the neutral word "size." When the lady of the house says to a visitor, "Come and set while I *hot* up the coffee," the invitation is direct and descriptive.

One day, the writer Bill Conklin and I were standing around *gamming* in front of the small post office in Walpole, New Hampshire, when Bill attempted an introduction between a recent arrival to Walpole and a Walpole native.

"Hello, Hap," Bill said. "Have you met my new neighbor, John White?"

"We've *howdied*," Hap answered, "but we've never shook." After I remarked to Bill how simple and appropriate the verb *howdied* was in that situation, he proceeded to relate to me a true incident involving an innovative use of "thrown up" and "subject to gates and bars." (For those few who may not be familiar with the terms, let me preface by saying that when a town "throws up" a road, the road reverts permanently to the property owners on either side, along a line agreed upon. However, if the road is "thrown up, subject to gates and bars," then, while not having the responsibility to plow or maintain it, the town retains the right to reclaim it at a later date if it votes to do so.)

"A very beautiful young lady in Bellows Falls," Bill began, "was separated from her husband, a big, tough-looking truck-driver, last year and she moved into an apartment in Claremont. Although he pretends indifference, her estranged husband has remained possessive and jealous—to the point, some say, of parking outside her building in Claremont on Saturday nights with an old deer rifle on his lap.

"One evening a couple of weeks ago in a local hangout where I was having a beer, I heard a young man at the bar ask about the girl's whereabouts in most admiring terms. From down at the end of the bar came the answer, 'She's been thrown up, but she's still subject to gates and bars.' "

And, as Bill concluded, everyone in the place, including the young man, knew the situation.

Some of the most descriptive New England phrases originate from our nautical history. *Hanging in the wind, squared away, three sheets to the wind,* understood by *all hands, steady as you go, shipshape, riding it out, learning to luff and bear away* (or to give and take)—these old-time nautical expressions flavor our New England language to a far stronger degree than they do in, say, Texas or the Deep South.

Every region has certain words that reflect its history, its geography—and its personality. For instance, Southerners seem to me to be immediately open and friendly, even with total strangers. "Y'all come!" they'll say, which would appear to include humankind. We New Englanders are more reserved about extending invitations, or anything else, and our language reflects it. In fact, as far as I can ascertain, New England does not possess any word or expression that is the equivalent of "Y'all come." There are simply no circumstances imaginable in which it would be desirable to have everyone, particularly strangers and their uncles, included. Our tendency is to qualify our statements, minimize our emotional commitment, and reduce the chance of error. In short, we feel compelled to be careful.

In response to someone inquiring about our health, we're apt to reply with such phrases as "Fair to middlin'," "Makin' out," or "Guess I'll survive for another day." We might agree that it's a nice day, but "We'll pay for it tomorrow," or "It is unless it rains." A bumper crop season is "fair," an excellent job "will do," and "I might mosey on over to Juke's house by and by." We simply don't want to be trapped, or held to anything that can change due to circumstances beyond our control.

Also, we seem to have a revulsion for any use of language that slops over with emotion or sentimentality. One hears about the local youth who graduated cum laude from MIT as a *right smart* boy. That's enough. "Pretty as a picture" is about the ultimate in feminine personal appearance. Instead of utilizing adjectives to describe a situation, person, or thing, New Englanders feel more comfortable making simple, graphic comparisons. Somehow, that's less emotional.

It's as *black*, for instance, as a crow, ink, one's hat, or even the ace of spades.

It's as *clear* as a bell, crystal, noonday—or mud.

It's as *fresh* as a bird, a daisy, or paint.

It's as *clean* as a hound's tooth or a pig's whistle.

Actually, I know about a *clean* that's cleaner than even a hound's tooth or a pig's whistle. A while back I was having my hair cut. I asked my barber and friend, Bill Austin, if he knew a really *clean* joke I could tell during a talk I was scheduled to make that evening at the Peterborough Women's Club.

"Sure, I've got a clean one for you, Jud," Bill said with a twinkle in his eye.

"It's got to be really clean, though, Bill," I warned.

"Clean! Well, now, this joke is so clean, Jud, that you could tell it to your grandmother sitting on the john."

Now, that's *clean*!

Later, Bill and I went on to exchange a few other examples of typically New England descriptive phrases and expressions that exclude, for the most part, adjectives and adverbs. Here are a few from Bill's memory:

It stands out like a blackberry in a pan of milk.

You can trust him as far as you can throw a meeting house by the steeple.

She was dressed to death and drawers all empty.

Fog so thick you could cut it up into chunks with your jack-knife . . . you could hardly spit.

She was homely as a hedge fence . . . as hell is wicked . . . enough to stop a down train.

Her head looked like it had worn out two bodies.

Comparisons like these—and we all know hundreds of them—truly do communicate the desired image more quickly and cleanly than a number of descriptive adjectives could do. One of the very clearest in my mind is a certain phrase my father used when he, my sister, and I threw stones into the farm pond in front of our house. Once in a while, someone would throw one very high and it would enter the water without making a splash. "You cut the devil's throat," he would say. And that sound will be in our minds forever.

Morality is expressed in the form of maxims or "sayings" ("Haste makes waste"), but it seems to me that most of these are used universally, even though many are of New England origin. One in particular, however, may be exclusively New England's —at least, the outsiders I've told it to never heard it said in their native areas. And that's just as well, because like so many maxims, it can be a brutal conversation-stopper. I was last exposed to it several years ago in Weston, Vermont, while dining with *Yankee* editor, writer, and photographer the late Lawrence F. Willard (a true lover of fine food), his wife, Helen, and Helen's mother, the late Etta French, a native Vermonter, then quite elderly. It was time for dessert, and as a large bowl of homemade strawberry ice cream was being passed around, Larry said, "I'm not really supposed to eat ice cream, so I'll just take a very small helping."

At which point Etta French piped up, "You might as well eat the devil as sip his broth."

Poor Larry replaced the serving spoon that had been poised to take a modest scoop and silently passed the bowl along to me.

Summer people and townspeople do not always speak the same New England language or communicate in the same way. This is not surprising if one assumes that summer people tend to have gone further with their formal education. It would seem that the development of language has been brought about chiefly by people with less formal education. More concerned with communication than with speaking "correctly," they are more innovative with the language ("We've howdied but we haven't shook," and so on). Eventually, their innovations, if used by enough people, become "correct" enough for use by summer people!

Also, natives are inclined to deliberately exaggerate their regional accents in certain circumstances, particularly when among themselves. Charles Edward Crane, in his book *Let Me Show You Vermont*, points out that "vowel twisting," for instance, as in "he ken knock a haouse daoun," is a vaguely contemptuous effort to demonstrate that the speaker is not of the aristocracy but rather comes from good country stock. Common folk. In other parts of the country, he might be called a "good ol' boy." He should say *pint* for "point," too, and *airth* for "earth," *housen* for "houses," *rare* for "rear" (as in "the horse rares up"), *slick* for "sleek," *swarth* for "swath," *agen* for "against," and on and on.

That same vague contempt is turned on outsiders who have not learned how to pronounce certain New England geographical names. It's the basic I-belong-and-you-do-not-belong attitude of human beings everywhere. I try to be tolerant on this subject, but I really cannot seem to stop that slightly irritable feeling from creeping into my brain when I hear Bangor, Maine, being pronounced *Bangger* (correct: *Bang-gore*). Or Berlin, New Hampshire, pronounced as if it were the German capital (correct: *Burr-ln*); or Worcester, Massachusetts, rhyming with "rooster" (correct: *Wuss*, rhyming with "puss," followed by *ter*); or Concord, New Hampshire and Massachusetts, pronounced to rhyme with "discord" (correct: *Con-cd*), and so forth. New England radio and television announcers, at least those hired from away, are the worst offenders. They may learn a few of the common ones, including those I've just mentioned, but many never bother to master Sudbury, Swampscott, Norwood, and Gloucester. In each of these, the most common error is too much emphasis and clarity in the last syllable. And I've even heard some actually force the first syllable in Gloucester to rhyme with "cow"—aarrgh! (Correct: *Glàw-str.*)

I recently asked a lady who had moved to Massachusetts from Ohio how long she had been living here in New England. "Just long enough," she replied, "to learn to mispronounce the words and town names correctly." She's very happy here.

The most noticeable contrast in the communication techniques of summer people and natives is in the use of platitudes, profanity, and medical reports. Summer people of both sexes utilize platitudes for casual communication; male natives utilize profanity for the same purpose. Female natives utilize medical reports.

One Memorial Day, I sat on the steps of the Dublin General Store for over an hour and took notes on a number of those short, casual, greeting-type conversations. Here are three of them, verbatim (but with different names). The purpose of each one was a simple "touching" between two human beings. The techniques, however, vary along the lines I suggest—platitudes, profanity, and medical reports.

Conversation No. 1 was between two elderly male members of the summer community and was very close in form to several conversations I overheard that day between female summer persons.

Conversation No. 2 was between two elderly male natives who were both slightly deaf. They spoke loudly to each other, in almost a shout at times, with no more than a foot or so between their faces.

Conversation No. 3 was between two middle-aged female natives.

Conversation No. 1:
"Well, George—so nice to see you again."
"Nice to see you, John." (They shake hands.)
"Isn't this just a marvelous day?"

"Gorgeous. Couldn't be nicer if we'd planned it. You here for a while now?"

"Yes. We're here for the summer."

"Lucky you. You know how to live, John. We can't get up until the Fourth."

"Well, we love it. Of course, there's never time to do everything we want to."

"How well I know. The best-laid plans . . . (Laughter.) How's the family?"

"First-rate, George. Mary?"

"Just fine. I'll tell her to call Jean real soon. We must get together."

"Yes, we'd love that. It's been too long. How time does fly by. . . ."

"You can say that again. Well, nice to see you, John. And do give my best to Jean."

"Will do. Wonderful to see you, George. My best to Mary."

"Yes. Good. . . . See you real soon." (They move away from each other with, as I recall, one or possibly two additional "nice to see you"s utilized to comfortably cover the disengagement.)

Conversation No. 2:

"What are ya doin'!"

"Nothin'."

"Why not?"

"Too lazy."

"Well, ya goddam sonofabitch, ya always were!"

"Whazzat?"

"I said, you always were!"

"Well, I ain't dead yet."

"No, by Jesus, you ain't. Guess we can still show a few of 'em one or two things, can't we, Ed?"

"You're goddam right we can. I guess we can remember one or two things, too!"

"I guess, by Christ!" (Loud laughter from both men. Without further conversation, they turned to go, still smiling. I noted that one of them uttered long, quiet, private Eeeeayuhs to himself as he walked away.)

Conversation No. 3:

"How are you, Beth?"

"All right *now*, I guess, Helen."

"Haven't seen you around."

"Well, I was laid up for over a week last winter with the flu, you know."

"I heard you were. I've *still* got it, by gorry! Thought I'd cough myself to death this morning."

"Of course, you knew Harry went in the hospital last week?"

"Harry sick?"

"Well, they took a cyst out of his leg the size of a brick."

"No!"

"Guess he lost a lot of blood, but they say he'll be all right." (The next few minutes were spent on specific anatomical details of the operation.)

"Well, guess I gotta go buy something for dinner today. Ed always wants a big meal on Memorial Day. I don't care much for big meals myself, but . . ."

"The doctor says I'm not supposed to eat a lot all at once." (There followed a discussion involving personal gastronomical information. Then . . .)

"Well, I'm late. 'Bye, Helen."

"Bye-bye." (The women parted, but I noticed they were conversing again a few minutes later in the store parking lot.)

As in conversation No. 2, above, profanity is often used as a substitute for descriptive elaboration and/or an expression of emotional feelings. A Stoddard, New Hampshire, man who loves to hunt raccoons with his hound dogs described the sound of the hounds' baying to me once by saying, "If that ain't the god-damnedest sound I ever heard." He meant that the sound was pure poetry to him. But it wouldn't do to say it that way!

The Lord's name, in its various forms, flows easily and comfortably among many (but certainly not all) natives, even— as on a number of occasions I can recall—in addressing several hundred people at town meeting.

"By the Jesus Christ, I'm not going to have some goddam college-educated fella tell me what kind of truck we need for this town." That's a direct quote from a Dublin town meeting somewhere in the late 1960s.

The four-letter variety of profanity, however, is never used in public and is hardly ever used in mixed company. And profanity substitutes have been the preference of many New Englanders for centuries. For instance, there was a time in some areas when even the vaguest reference to the devil or hell was considered inappropriate speech, so the word "Tophet" came to the rescue. *Hotter than Tophet* is still a handy expression. One can also *run like Tophet.*

Expressions like "gosh all hemlock," "by thunderation," "land-o-goshen," "by Godfrey" (after Godfrey De Bouillon, the great crusader), and "by George" (after the king, of course), and countless others all provide the verbal emphasis and emotional outlet often required in communicating—without taking the Lord's name in vain.

Still and all, although many New Englanders disapprove of so doing (a single "hell" or "damn" in an issue of *Yankee* invariably results in several subscription cancellations), there are those occasions when taking the Lord's name in vain seems to be the ultimate method of accurately communicating one's true feelings. The best example of that in my own life occurred years ago when my mother decided to produce a Christmas Nativity play for the residents of Vanceboro, Maine. It was to be staged on Christmas Eve in the small red schoolhouse located in a pine grove about half a mile from our farm. Everyone in town was invited.

One of the angels in the play was a little eight-year-old lad by the name of Primo. My mother made a special point of casting Primo in an angel's role because she felt it might give him some idea of the respect due the Lord's name. Up to that point, Primo had none of that sort of respect. On arriving at our school each morning, I remember he seemed unable to give even a simple greeting to our teacher without it containing some sort of blasphemy delivered in that hoarse, penetrating little voice of his.

Throughout the two weeks of rehearsals, during which time Primo and the other angels painstakingly built their wings with wire, wood, and papier-mâché, Primo seemed to respond beautifully to his angel role, and his swearing became noticeably less frequent. Finally, for the three days before the performance, Primo's language was befitting an angel. He wasn't heard to swear at all.

Then the performance. There were more than a hundred people in attendance, waiting in a reverent silence for the curtain to rise. A light snow was falling among the pines outside the schoolhouse. My family and friends were in elaborate costumes, complete with wire halos, behind the curtain, quietly taking their places and soothing the restless farm animals that were a part of the Nativity setting. A moment of hushed expectancy.

It was a moment suddenly shattered by the instantly recognizable voice of Primo.

"Some sonofabitch," he bellowed, "stole my goddam wings!"

The immediate reaction throughout the building was a shocked intake of breath in unison. Then came the explosion of laughter. It lasted, as I recall, at least five minutes, during which time my mother found Primo's wings in a closet behind the stage, strapped them on him, and raised the curtain—and we were into the performance, which I'll bet everyone present remembers to this day as well as I do.

Profanity is, of course, a universal phenomenon. But like certain words and expressions, it can be utilized in subtly varying circumstances and with varying accents to help produce a regional language. To be sure, New England's language is still English (with some French, Portuguese, and other languages thrown in for good measure), and for the most part, it can be understood by an occupant of any other region. But its flavor is just different enough to be recognized as being distinctive. So it is with the language of any true "region" in our country. I believe that as long as a region's occupants remain proud of their region—and pride is a prime ingredient of regionalism—our various regional languages will just naturally endure. Radio, television, the Web, and a transient population notwithstanding. After all, a leanter is a leanter is a leanter. And if you do not agree, then would you please pronounce for me the word "spoon"?

8

LOVE, SEX AND SUCH

A Bull in the Presence of Ladies is a "Gentleman Cow"

The ideal wife ֍ the ideal husband ֍ sex without enjoyment—i.e. the Puritan view and teachings ֍ why New Englanders still feel "chosen"—and used to deliberately build their furniture to be uncomfortable ֍ how to keep warm in church ֍ the Puritan work ethic ֍ the New England Conscience and why no lady with it would remove her clothes for artistic purposes ֍ remembering the "Old Howard" ֍ selling votes in rural Maine ֍ the sexual image we must endure ֍ the image of the New England male ֍ banned in Boston, or no kissing, cussing, or cuddling ֍ Frank Merriwell and, at last, the real definition of "clean living" ֍ a possible substitute for saying "I love you" ֍ the quarrelsome wife ֍ when and when not to "fall senseless to the floor" ֍ the strong he-man woman ֍ women named Submit, Desire, Silence, and Freelove ֍ the art of bundling ֍ shift marriages ֍ and a couple of changes in the sexual scene —i.e., holding hands vs. fornicating

ASKED SEVERAL YEARS AGO BY A *Boston Globe* reporter for his description of the "ideal wife," Captain Eliot Winslow, a well-known tourist-boat operator out of Boothbay Harbor, Maine, replied, "She ought to be able to dig clams. She ought to be able to split wood. And she ought to be able to row my dory standin' up."

As to the "ideal husband," an elderly lady in Saco, Maine, supplied that definition in a letter to *Yankee* that we once published. "The ideal husband," she wrote, "is a man who is careful of his clothes; don't drink no spirits; can read the Old Testament without spelling out the words; and can eat a cold dinner on wash day to save the women folks from cooking."

While we New Englanders may smile at these two definitions of the man-woman relationship, we also feel comfortable with them. We're comfortable with the emphasis on practicalities and we're comfortable with the omission of sentiment or (perish the thought!) romance.

When it comes to love, sex, and romance, our New England image, reflecting from this region out to the country as a whole, is that we're prudish, unemotional, not at all romantic—maybe even cold.

> There was a young lady of Boston,
> Whose manner had such a deep frost on,
> That she invariably froze
> Every one of her beaus
> With her high plane of thought they got lost on.

It's not at all surprising that this image persists to this day. If our present mode of living does little to support it, our past is *more* than adequate to do so into the foreseeable future.

What Caused It All

As we all know, the blame or credit for our New England image must be ultimately laid at the feet of our English Puritan forefathers—particularly those who established the Massachusetts Bay Colony some ten years after the Plymouth Rock landing in 1620. The late Perry Miller, one of this country's foremost scholars in the field of American intellectual history, wrote in his foreword to *The American Puritans* that "because their societies were tightly organized and, above all, because they were a highly articulate people, the New Englanders established Puritanism—for better or worse—as one of the continuous factors in American life and thought."

And the Puritans *were*, of course, puritanical. That does not mean that sex was not a part of individual Puritans' private lives and thoughts. They did not advocate celibacy. As Samuel Eliot Morison wrote, "Puritanism taught that . . . a farmer or merchant who conducted his business according to Christian ethics was more agreeable in the sight of God than one who withdrew from the world and escaped his responsibilities by a celibate or monastic life." Puritans did believe, however, that there was a certain commonly held perception of what was *right*. It was expressed through their laws, through the writings of John Winthrop, Cotton Mather, William Stoughton, and the other leaders, and through parents' advice to their children. A fundamental cornerstone of this perception of right was that it was neither necessary nor desirable to seek *pure pleasure* in this world. In other words, pleasure for pleasure's sake was a definite no-no. In fact, pleasure would, they feared, actually replace God as humankind's highest priority. As Puritan minister Thomas Hooker (1586-1647) harangued his attentive congregation over and over again, sin tended to "jostle the Almighty out of His glorious sovereignty and indeed be above Him."

On the deck of the *Arbella* in the middle of the Atlantic Ocean, John Winthrop delivered a lay sermon that stated: "if we . . . prosecute our carnal intentions . . . the Lord will surely break out in wrath against us." "Carnal intentions" and "sin" were, and always have been, somewhat synonymous with the pursuit of worldly pleasures.

In this same occasionally dreary sermon, Winthrop made it plain that the Puritans, and the generations of New Englanders who would follow them, were "God's chosen people," destined to perpetuate and implement Puritan beliefs. New England was often likened to the promised land of Israel in the Old Testament. "The Lord make it like that of New England," said Winthrop, "for we must consider that we shall be as a city upon a hill, the eyes of all people upon us."

William Stoughton, founder of Dorchester, Massachusetts, and judge at the Salem witch trials (a role he later repented of), said "the Lord's promises and expectations of great things have singled out New England . . . above any nation or people in the world." We New Englanders still have a little of that feeling today, no matter where in the world we may live. However, in the interest of friendly relations with non–New Englanders, we have made every effort to suppress it. Better to simply admit, as we do, to the identical sentiment Americans have always had about their country as a whole. (Thanks in large part to the early teachings of our New England Puritans.)

Puritan logic outlawed bull baiting and bear baiting not because these activities represented excessive cruelty to animals but because they provided excessive *pleasure* to the spectators. Long after the creed of puritanism had passed into history, chairs were still deliberately designed to be uncomfortable. Stoves were omitted in many nineteenth-century New England churches— not to save wood or so that parishioners would be less likely to fall asleep, but rather because stoves would make going to church a more pleasurable experience. (About the only way to keep one's feet warm in church during those winter Sundays was to bring a dog into the pew and tuck one's feet under him as he lay sleeping during the long service. However, so many people caught on to that little trick that eventually some Sunday worship services were reduced to a series of horrendous dogfights. A rule was then enacted in several towns that anyone bringing a dog to church would be fined six pence. If the fine wasn't paid, the dog was taken away from its owner permanently. Sentiment had no place in a puritanical culture.)

Despite the large number of begats in the Old Testament, all begetting, even married begetting, was fundamentally sinful in certain seventeenth-century Connecticut colonies. A Connecticut "blue law" of that period (Connecticut was known as the "Blue Law State") protected ministers from contaminating themselves by performing marriage ceremonies, or in other words, by becoming involved with the sin inherent in the potential pleasure of the conjugal bed. "No gospel minister shall join people in marriage," it directed. "The Magistrate shall join only in marriage as they may do it with less scandal to Christ Church."

As to some forms of nonprocreative sexual activity, well, here's how a Connecticut law of 1642 reads: "If any man or woman shall lie with any beast or brute creature by carnal copulation, they shall surely be put to death. The beast shall be slain and buried." Connecticut was tough—even on beasts.

Logic wasn't—and isn't—always necessary in matters of sin. If a child was born healthy in body and mind, he was enjoying a "Divine mercy." If he had physical mental disabilities, he was only being justly punished for the sin of having been born.

"In Adam's fall, we sinned all," says the old New England primers from which early colonists' children learned their ABCs. (New England humorist Josh Billings suggested a more realistic rewording: "In Adam's sin, we all jined in.")

Finally, while the Puritans didn't believe that "good deeds" could cancel out human sins, good deeds were essential to "the Glory of his Creator" and the common well-being of mankind. Puritan John Cotton (1584-1652) wrote that "if thou has no calling tending to public good, thou art an unclean beast." Owning property, however, or trading codfish for rum, or throwing the Indians off one's land, or, generally, acquiring great wealth in any number of ways, were *not* sinful activities as long as one's "heart is not set upon these things." Wealth was simply an outward sign of inner grace. In other words, be successful in a worldly way, but don't be successful for the purpose of enjoying it. In New England, I've heard the phrase to describe this attitude as "loving the world with weaned affections."

It's also called the Puritan or Protestant "work ethic," an attitude stamped deep in the New England character even unto this day, which with the great migration westward became a major factor in shaping the American spirit.

⊗

During the nineteenth century, New Englanders like John Brown, Horace Mann, Margaret Fuller, and even the Brook Farm dreamers carried on the Puritan zeal for "doing good." However, these idealists, particularly the abolitionists, drove many people to utter distraction with their "moral superiority" and maddening disdain for practicalities. Perhaps if they hadn't been "right," as everyone eventually recognized, the American Puritan beat would have faded into oblivion. But they *were* right, and the Puritan instinct continued into the twentieth century, where it ran head-on into the literary revolt that was part of the Roaring Twenties, when most of the country, including many New Englanders, flamboyantly and exuberantly indulged in throwing off the so-called yoke of New England, a burden consisting of such Puritan ingredients as emotional control, "pure" thoughts, the necessity of working hard and performing good deeds, strict sexual morality, and so on. Boston's predilection for book-banning during those years was clearly a latter-day "Puritan stand" against the growing tolerance of everything, including "sin."

The fact that the basic Puritan instinct survived all that—and many scholars identify today's religious conservatism with it—is astonishing when one considers the difficulties true puritanism always presented an individual. To eliminate personal enjoyment as a top priority in the quest for fame and fortune has never been easy! Maybe the impossibility of it ensures that anyone with that old Puritan instinct is never really free of guilt! To be guiltless, one must delicately walk a fine line between impractical, visionary idealism ("do-gooders," as they say) on one side and outright hypocrisy on the other. Not even the original Puritans were all successful at that. However, they did establish a tool to help them walk that fine line and decide what was morally right in all matters. The tool has been passed down from one generation of New Englanders to the next, constitutes one of New England's major and most famous exports, and is still, depending on circumstances, either most efficient or extremely irritating. It is probably in the latter case that its uncanny power is best demonstrated.

The name we've given this tool is the New England Conscience.

The Results of It All

Other regions of the country and the world have very conscientious men and women, but, as Perry Miller pointed out in a 1958 essay in *The American Scholar*, "only in New England is there a Conscience so standardized that it must be capitalized." John Quincy Adams called New England the "Colony of Conscience."

The New England Conscience manifests itself in varying and often confusing forms. During my childhood in Vanceboro, Maine, a certain lady with a foreign accent (probably from France: anything "Frenchie" was likely to be immoral) who posed for a local artist in the nude—that is, "stark naked"—was criticized far more severely than were any of the countless young women in town who found themselves with a "come-by-chance" child. "Chance-found" babies seemed to be an accepted fact of our rural life. But no lady in good Conscience would take off her clothes for artistic purposes.

I should have remembered that when, in July 1960, *Yankee* published a reminiscence of Boston's Howard Athenaeum on Scollay Square, affectionately known as the "Old Howard" or, to old-time Bostonians, the "Dear Old Place." Once a legitimate theater featuring such luminaries as Jenny Lind, Edwin Booth, and John L. Sullivan, it became a bump-and-grind emporium (a very tame one by today's standards) frequented by red-blooded college boys "on the town," before it was torn down in the early 1960s to help make way for Boston's Government Center. In my enthusiasm to convey the history and atmosphere of the place, I included several old-time photographs, yellowed with age, of Old Howard headliners such as "Charmaine, taking all sorts of daring liberties" and "Collette, performing her world-famous feather dance." Both women were far from "stark naked," but we received several dozen subscription cancellations. I was astonished, although I shouldn't have been. The logic in many of the cancellation letters somehow reminded me once again of Vanceboro and the lady with the French accent. Here's a typical one that I've saved. It was from

Rhode Island:

> I always thought I could safely leave the *Yankee* around my house
> but this morning I discovered my grandson looking at the disgusting
> filth that people paid money to see in that place you called "dear" in
> your July issue. You should know that morality is supposed to begin at
> home. When it's time for my grandson to learn about the female body,
> he won't learn it from some dirty magazine like *Yankee*. He'll learn it
> from his own family. Please cancel my subscription.

Back in Vanceboro, I recall politicians from Augusta coming
through town and buying votes openly and blatantly. I think the
going price was a dollar per vote or even less. This common practice
in rural Maine during those days had no connection with morality
and thus in no way involved the New England Conscience. That is,
not until after the vote had been sold. At that point, no person of
Conscience would think of selling his vote *again*, to the opposition
candidate coming into town a few days later. *That* wouldn't be right.

I heard a Boston government official, convicted a few years ago
on bribery and extortion charges, explain in a television interview
after the trial that, sure, he had in effect stolen some money from
people, but, he said, "I didn't get any enjoyment out of what I
stole." His particular Conscience seemed a somewhat distorted,
distant echo of those men of long ago who had names like Mather,
Sewall, Hooker, and Cotton. As my uncle Robb Sagendorph told
me, "The New England Conscience doesn't keep us from doing
anything. It just keeps us from enjoying it."

But of course it's more than that. The New England Conscience
is a key element of that difficult combination of reforming spirit
and business acumen derived ultimately, as Perry Miller once put
it, "from the tremendous earnestness of the Puritan heritage."

Thus it is that our New England attitude toward matters of
love, sex, and romance remains a bit stodgy, like our image. As the
late actor John Houseman once famously told viewers of a series
of television commercials about the profitability of an investment
firm, "We've *earned* it!" (To be pronounced without an *r*.)

"Descendants of the Puritans," wrote Perry Miller, "have carried traits of the Puritan mind into a variety of pursuits and all the way across the continent. Many of these qualities persist."

It is ironical that the English share with us the same stodgy sexual image, inasmuch as the original Puritans were reacting against, as Miller says, "the foul heritage of medieval corruption," which included the debauchery of Elizabethan England. For years, the Puritans and their descendants refused to even celebrate Christmas here in New England because Christmas observances of any kind smacked of the wild and woolly, merry, merry Christmases of Olde Englande.

Some years after the Plymouth and Massachusetts Bay colonies were founded, however, the rigid austerity of Puritanism was established for a time in England too, and so the English and New England stereotypes began to develop in tandem. Today, the Boston Brahmin or New England aristocrat seems to have much in common with the stuffy Britisher, particularly in matters of sex and romance. To eliminate this or any other stereotype in our minds would be to eliminate an essential ingredient of humor throughout the world!

Here is an example, once told to me at the Peterborough, New Hampshire, diner:

It seems that a certain young man was walking along an almost deserted beach one summer day when he came across a beautiful, bikini-clad young lady lying in the sun. The young man attempted to strike up a conversation with her, but she refused to respond in any way. Finally, in exasperation, he knelt down beside her and planted upon her pretty mouth a rather long, amorous kiss. Still no response. At that point, several men were seen running along the beach toward them, carrying a stretcher.

"What do you think you're doing kissing that woman, you oaf," one of the men yelled as they approached. "She's dead, you know. Drowned just a while ago!"

"Dead?" the young man replied. "My heavens! I thought she was English."

The story would still work if "English" were replaced by "a New Englander." Such is the image to be endured.

A Vermonter returned home after calling upon a young lady for the first time and was asked how he liked her.

"Oh, I liked her first-rate," he said. "She swept the floor all around me and never asked me to move."

A Dartmouth classmate of mine, Jere Daniell, former chairman of the history department up there, told me this one:

FEMALE VOICE: "Edward, you know we used to sit a lot closer together back when we was courtin'."

MALE VOICE: "I ain't moved."

We just don't much want to talk about things in the area of sex and romance, particularly in mixed company and even when the mixed company is one's own spouse. New Englanders may be noted for calling a spade a spade, but all of us country people over forty remember that we never, for instance, referred to a bull as a bull when ladies were around. And I'm told that ladies never referred to a bull directly even in all-female company. I recall the two farmhands we had on our Vanceboro farm hand-milking our sixty or seventy Guernsey and Holstein cows and chatting away, in very explicit fashion, about farm sexual matters and even sex in general—until my mother or my sister happened into the barn. Then the bull would become a "gentleman cow" or "he one" or just plain "him." I think "the old gentleman" was occasionally used too.

But we can also be very direct. In Wilmington, Vermont, where Brigham Young was born, there stands a plain marble slab on the site of his birthplace. The legend on the tablet reads: "Brigham Young, born on this spot in 1802, a man of much courage and splendid equipment."

Perhaps that's an exception. Same as a little advertisement I have stashed away in my files, taken from a nineteenth-century newspaper on Nantucket Island. Before reading it, one should know that many women on Nantucket were alone in those days because their husbands were off whaling for months and even years. The ad reads: "Wanted: A job! I will sleep in the homes of timid women for 15¢ a night, or two nights for a quarter."

The general atmosphere in New England, however, has been one of verbal restraint in words of "carnal overtones." Bulls, chicken breasts (to say nothing of chicken thighs and legs), as well as countless other subjects (women never "sweated"—they "glowed" or sometimes "glistened"), were downright uncomfortable to express in New England—and elsewhere too. It is no wonder, therefore, that Boston banned so many books during the first half of the twentieth century. Aside from the official power struggle to maintain Puritan standards in the face of what some considered national licentiousness, many ordinary people just hadn't become adjusted to that sort of language right out there in bold print. Not everyone has adjusted yet! A simple "hell" or "damn" in any new issue of *Yankee* will invariably result in cancellations and scolding letters.

Actually, the first book officially banned in Boston was *The Woman Who Did*, banned in 1894. It was written by an English author, Grant Allen, who stated that his aim in writing the book was to "stamp out prostitution forever." The Boston city fathers, who banned books on the recommendation of Boston Public Library officials until, eventually, an official censor was appointed, definitely favored banning prostitution, too. But they could not see their way clear to approving anyone's *writing* about or even *speaking* on the subject. (Incidentally, an original copy of *The Woman Who Did* is extremely valuable today.)

Books were banned for far milder reasons. For instance, censors were able to point out exactly seventy-four scenes in Theodore Dreiser's classic *The Genius* containing either (1) kissing, (2) cussing, or (3) cuddling. When John Kennedy's grandfather was mayor of Boston and, as such, the official censor, he banned a play because a city mayor was depicted as being corrupt. Mayor Curley refused to allow the United States Marines in the film *What Price Glory* to utter the words "hell" or "damn," which for all intents and purposes rendered them speechless.

As is well known, books by Ernest Hemingway, Sinclair Lewis, Sean O'Casey, Upton Sinclair, Elliot Paul, H. G. Wells, and many, many others were banned. Not so well known, perhaps, is the fact that Boston banned a Walt Disney film. (In fact, this 1938 banning was not made public until after Disney's death in 1966.) It seems the censor objected to a certain verse Sneezy was supposed to sing in *Snow White and the Seven Dwarfs*, and after a hushed-up wrangle, the film was allowed to play with the objectionable verse omitted. (This is the verse: "The minute after I was born / I didn't have a nightie. / So I tied my whiskers 'round my legs / And used 'em for a di-ah-dee.")

Many of us still feel that a clean-living, clean-thinking hero has the strength of at least ten dirty "bad" guys. Even though I can intellectualize to myself that this is ridiculous, I feel it anyway. Can't help it. It's been the American way for years. Thanks, in large part, to New Englander Gilbert Patten of Corinna, Maine.

Under the alias "Burt L. Standish," Patten wrote all the Frank and Dick Merriwell "dime novels," which, along with similar books read by millions of American youths, emphasized and rewarded the "good guy" attributes—loyalty, purity, integrity, honesty, perseverance, valor, humility, stamina, and "clean living."

"Clean living" is never specifically analyzed. But since it is always *added* to the above list rather than summarizing its components, I feel the only interpretation *left* for the term "clean living" is "no sexual activity" of any kind. One would *not* find a "clean-living" young lady working in a house of ill repute, for instance, even if she were otherwise loyal, courageous, pure, honest, humble, and of integrity and incredible stamina.

"Did you love your character Merriwell?" Patten was once asked late in his life. "Well, at first he seemed more like a joke," he answered, "but then, yes . . . I loved him. And I loved him most because no boy, if he followed in Merriwell's tracks, ever did anything he need be ashamed of."

Guilt and shame are the strongest weapons of that ever-present New England Conscience.

A bull is a bull in New England nowadays—even in mixed company—but the Puritan abhorrence of excess emotion, blatant pleasure, and romantic expression is still very much a part of our regional character. Just the simple little phrase "I love you" can catch in the throat of many New England men today. I have real difficulty with it myself. One *feels* the love and prepares for an amorous, softly spoken "I love you," or perhaps even a matter-of-fact rendition, spoken more or less off-handedly. Suddenly one's throat tightens, one's soft romantic smile becomes a grimace, and a mysterious, helpless feeling of revulsion for the utterance permeates one's entire body almost to the point of nausea. To say "I love you" at that instant is not only downright impossible but also somehow a betrayal of our very New England heritage!

Back in August 1973, we published an article in *Yankee* about the dearth of sentiment, particularly in Maine men. A week or so later, I received a letter from a Midwestern lady (she will remain nameless at her request) who said she felt this attitude applied to all New England men. Her husband, she said, was originally from Massachusetts and he "nearly choked on the marriage vows being's they contained the word, love.'" Here's the ending of her letter, which I've saved to this day:

> "You look all right," is the highest compliment I ever get and once when I bawled (all right, so I was younger then) and said he never told me he loved me, he muttered darkly, "I show it in other ways," and went back to whittling on his woodcarving.
>
> There is some evidence that he may be mellowing, however. One night last winter he got out of bed to go to the bathroom and I think he must have thought I was asleep, which I almost was, being barely aware he was up, because when he came back to bed he said out loud, "I love you!" It startled me awake so's I got up and wrote down the date and time (Feb. 28,1:10 a.m.), but I'd appreciate if you'd omit to print my

name and address if you print this letter, as I'd hate for his relatives
back in Massachusetts to get the idea he's become maudlin.

I've found that the Micronesian term for "I love you," brought
back from the South Pacific to this country by all the New England
Puritan do-gooder missionaries who have been going out there
for years, is much more comfortable to say. So when it appears
apparent that something along the romantic line ought to be
expressed, I say "Yokwe yuk." (There is some evidence to indicate
the effect isn't quite the same.)

"A New England man doesn't make love," the late Burt Willard,
once a Dublin neighbor of mine, told me. "He maybe buys his wife
a new ironing board and she is enchanted by his thoughtfulness.
Because he doesn't drag her around by the hair, she is ravished by
his negative caress."

While the commonly accepted image of the New England
male is a pretty fair reflection of reality, the image of the New
England female is a series of contradictions. This is probably
because males historically have been, in their position of power,
the ones who created the images—and how can one create an
image of something one doesn't understand?

First of all, there's the quarrelsome wife. New England
literature refers to her all the time. It's the same general image
as the talkative woman. Somebody named Seth says he'd like to
divide his house with his quarrelsome wife. "I'd keep the inside for
myself and give her the outside."

Or we've all heard about a Vermont man named Payson, who
complained he'd had bad luck with his two wives. "One left me and
the other one didn't."

An elderly woman who ran the cash register at a New
Hampshire country store along Route 101 once told me, in
the course of casual chitchat, that she would advise any young
woman not to worry about being quarrelsome but rather to simply
concentrate on finding someone looking for his *second* wife. "His
first wife helps him to get his property together," she said, "and then

comes along 'number two,' who spends it like a woodchopper at the end of the season. For a smooth, easy journey, I'd advise any young woman to take her chances on being a second wife every time."

This same lady once told me that when she was a young girl, she had received a lot of marriage proposals. "But," she said, "you had to be on your toes to recognize them as such."

My favorite "quarrelsome wife" story takes the image we males enjoy perpetuating about our New England women and heaves it back into our chauvinistic faces! I heard it told some years ago in Newington, Connecticut, and was assured it was true. It seems that back around the turn of the twentieth century, a very religious, wealthy, and conscientious gentleman (the perfect Puritan!) of Newington surprised his friends and neighbors by suddenly marrying a woman reputed to be one of the most quarrelsome, talkative, troublesome females in the entire community. One of his neighbors later found him in a quiet, reflective mood while sitting on his veranda and, during the course of the conversation, ventured to ask him if there was a reason for his choice. The gentleman replied that yes, there was. He felt that he was very well off, that he had no troubles, and that because of these circumstances, he was fearful of becoming "too much attached to things of time and sense." He went on to explain that he felt experiencing some afflictions would enable him to become more "weaned from the world."

The best part of the story is that the gentleman's wife somehow found out, through the usual village grapevine, what her husband had said. She was furious. So out of revenge, she instantly, and for the rest of their lives together, became one of the most pleasant, quiet, dutiful wives one could ever imagine, saying to her friends on more than one occasion, "I'll be damned if I'll be made a packhorse to carry my husband to heaven!"

A gravestone in Sargentville, Maine, gives the quarrelsome wife image a fitting epitaph:

> Beneath these stones do lie,
> Back to back, my wife and I.

When the last trumpet the air shall fill,
If she gets up, I'll just lie still.

Then there is the image of the weak, dutiful, obedient, attractive little lady of no account whose only function in life is to learn to serve a husband and, once married, to do so. While it may be that no female human being has ever existed in such a simplified, robot-like form, the general type is very real indeed.

Cleveland Amory tells the story of a New York girl who married into a prominent Boston family and named her firstborn child after her husband. When the second child came along, she wanted to name him Alfred, after her brother. Upon hearing this disturbing news, an elderly lady of the husband's family came to visit and said, "I hear you are intending to give your son the name Alfred. You know, I've studied our family genealogy back through many generations, and I cannot find that name recorded anywhere." As Amory points out, it probably would have been useless for the young woman to protest she had a family, too. In the New England sense and in accordance with the no-account attitude concerning the female gender, she didn't.

In New England literature, this type of lady "swoons" a lot at the announcement of bad tidings, or better still, "falls senseless to the floor." I'm sure many young ladies did just that without at all losing consciousness. It was simply the approved reaction under certain circumstances and was doubtless a fine substitute for conversation.

It has never been good form for a male to faint—unless it's from loss of blood resulting from a wound. Several years ago, when the son of a close friend of mine, then living outside Concord, New Hampshire, received from his fiancée on the morning of their scheduled wedding a note saying she couldn't go through with it, he reportedly "fell senseless to the floor." If only the rejection had been his and the reaction hers. As it was, the episode made everyone distinctly uneasy.

In sharp contrast to the image of the weak, dutiful female is that of the strong, independent New England woman. There's nothing she cannot do "just as good as a man." In the long list of our New England folk heroes, it's interesting to note that the women included are of this strong, capable variety, possessing so-called masculine qualities, such as physical courage. Women like Ida Lewis of Newport, Rhode Island, who rescued more than forty people from drowning during her nineteenth-century lifetime; or nineteen-year-old Mary Patten of Boston, who, when her clipper ship captain became ill, took charge of the great ship *Neptune's Car* and sailed her around the Horn; or Revolutionary War soldier Deborah Sampson; or Indian-scalping Hannah Dustin.

Two articles that once appeared in *Yankee* that drew particularly favorable reactions concerned a seventy-five-year-old retired schoolteacher, Mary Heather, who had bought and was operating a water-powered electric generating plant in Stockbridge, Massachusetts, and a Norwichtown, Connecticut, woman (she looked like everybody's grandmother) who had built her four-room house from scratch with her own hands. "How about those foundation rocks?" we asked her. "When they're too big to handle," she replied, "I just break 'em up with my sledgehammer." Judging from their letters, our readers love that sort of thing.

In a 1976 *Yankee* magazine interview, we asked Professor T. Gerald Foyp, head of the Department of Geopolitics at Mentor College, Mentor, Maine, and the outrageous creation of writer Bill Conklin, if he thought a woman would ever become President of the United States. His answer:

"I'll tell you something. A woman has already *been* President of the United States. I can't say which one but you'd recognize the name. Please don't press me on this, for obvious reasons of confidentiality."

Not all famous New England women fit our standard stereotypes exactly—for instance, Louisa May Alcott, Lydia Pinkham, Julia Ward Howe, Harriet Beecher Stowe, Sarah Josepha Hale, Margaret Fuller, Sarah Orne Jewett, Emily Dickinson, et al. Perhaps they *would* have if they'd been forced to proceed through life with true Puritan names like Lowly, Mindwell, Obedience, Submit, Charity, Mercy, Prudence, Comfort, Delight, Thankful, Desire, and Silence. These names are all listed in genealogist Donald L. Jacobus's book *Genealogy as Pastime and Profession*. Mr. Jacobus goes on to say, "It is odd that Wait and Waitstill should be masculine [names], Hope and Hopestill usually feminine [names]; that Lovewell should be a man's name and Freelove a woman's."

What's so odd?

"If New Englanders were always so stuffy about love, sex, and romance, then how come it was commonly approved practice for young couples to go to bed together before they were married? And also to get married in the nude?" A common question. And it's true. Young New England unmarried boys and girls *would* indeed go to bed together as part of the courting routine—*but* with their clothes on. It was called bundling. When I was a teenager, I knew about people who "courted" in bed with their clothes on, but I have never met anyone who called it "bundling" or who remembers their parents or grandparents admitting to the practice. Yet bundling is written about so much in New England literature that there must be a little flame creating all that smoke!

Most accounts I've read indicate that a centerboard was lowered between the bundled couple. Or sometimes a straight stick, called a "whispering rod," was secured between the boy and the girl at both ends of the bed, to which, also, a few sleigh bells were tied.

Joe Allen of Martha's Vineyard once told me, "I've seen 'em roll the young folks up in quilts and then haul a wool sack over 'em and tie it around their necks. But somehow, by Gorry, they always cleared themselves before morning." (I so loved Joe and everything he said—but I couldn't always tell if he was putting me on. However, I have heard from other sources that wool sacks were often substituted for centerboards.)

Marrying in the nude, or "shift marriage," was not a New England invention, but until 20th century it *was* quite common in

New England, particularly Rhode Island, as well as in New York and Pennsylvania. It occurred when a man was marrying a widow, and it was only the lady who was nude, or in a shift, to symbolize that she brought nothing to the marriage but herself and was not responsible for any of her former husband's debts. Sometimes her presence at the ceremony was represented only by her arm, thrust through a "widow's hole" from behind a closed door. Unlike bundling, this awkward and probably embarrassing little custom is well documented.

For instance, there is a so-called shift-marriage entry in the old registration books at the town hall in South Kingston, Rhode Island:

> Thomas Calverwell was joyned in marriage to Abigail Calver-well his wife the 22. February, 1719-20. He took her in marriage after she had gone four times across the highway in only her shift and hairlace and no other clothing. Joyned together in marriage by me.
>
> *George Hazard*, Justice

And How It Is Today

As we all know, not very long ago it was thought that an unmarried couple living together was scandalous.

My maternal grandfather, George A. Sagendorph of Boston, used to love to tell the story about a certain Framingham, Massachusetts, older gentleman who insisted on living with a young servant girl and calling her his "wife" even though everyone knew there had never been a marriage ceremony. The community was outraged. One morning the city magistrate happened to meet them on the street and bluntly accosted them.

"John Rogers," he said, "do you persist in all your stubbornness in calling this woman, a servant so much younger than yourself, your wife?"

"Well, yes, I do," the old gentleman retorted, immediately on the defensive.

"And you, Mary"—the magistrate gruffly turned to the young girl—"do you wish such a crotchety old man such as John Rogers here to be called your husband?"

"Indeed I do," she replied a little angrily, "and I don't think there's call for you to speak of him in that manner."

"Then by the laws of God and this Commonwealth of Massachusetts," was the rather disconcerting response, "I, as a magistrate, do hereby pronounce you man and wife."

As everywhere, much has changed in New England over the years in the area of love, sex, and romance, and in the roles of women—and men. To be sure, the stuffy but wonderful old Boston Athenaeum tolerated a woman way back in 1829 when Miss Hannah Adams applied for and was granted "reading privileges." In all candor, the fact that she was related to the Athenaeum's head librarian *and* to the President of the United States didn't hurt. Today her portrait is a part of the Athenaeum's permanent collection.

However, it was only in 1972 that the historic male sanctuary at Yale celebrated in "The Whiffenpoof Song" no longer baa-ed (sorry!) women from "the tables down at Mory's, at the place where Louis dwells," on York Street in New Haven, Connecticut.

Walking across Boston's Public Garden and along Beacon Street recently after dinner with a family friend who is a retired attorney and a Yale graduate, I was musing about all this—and also about the fact that right along here the likes of Daniel Webster and Ralph Waldo Emerson once strolled, too, during summer evenings.

"You know, in the days of my youth," my friend reminisced, "if a young man and a young lady walked along here together in the evening after dinner, it was a sign they were engaged."

We continued on slowly, in a brief silence.

"Now," he began again, "in the summer along here at night, they'll be fornicating."

Another moment of steady pacing along together in the balmy evening air.

Finally, "... and I don't know if that's a sign that they're engaged or not."

We both laughed—and for some reason or another, I suddenly felt a little uncomfortable.

9

THE DARK SIDE

I Have Seen, in the Moonlight, a Latch Rise . . .

The Smuttynose murders ❧ the hidden dark side of rural life ❧ living next door to Lizzie Borden ❧ "Frozen Death" ❧ a stuffed wolf in a haunted cave ❧ ghosts I have met in the Massachusetts State House ❧ how the whole world was spooked from a men's room in New Milford, Connecticut ❧ what Dr. James Huntington swore he saw ❧ the malevolent "presence" atop Mount Washington ❧ communications from the dead ❧ the standard New England reaction to a real ghost ❧ superstitions and how we don't believe in them—much ❧ why Captain Kidd's skull ought to be sent into outer space ❧ horrible evidence of a Rhode Island vampire ❧ the afternoon I "imagined" I heard Mary Howe moan and groan from beneath the ground ❧ precautions to be taken against being buried alive ❧ why some were buried sitting in a chair or standing up ❧ preparing for forever

I T WAS THE FIRST CALM NIGHT OF THE YEAR. A quarter moon shone dimly on the sea around the Isles of Shoals off Portsmouth, New Hampshire. The only people on the island known as Smuttynose were three women—Maren Hotvet, Maren's sister, Karen, and her sister-in-law, Anethe. Their three men had set sail the previous morning for a day of commercial fishing. They planned to sell their catch in Portsmouth and return to Smuttynose the following morning.

Sometime during that calm, dark night of March 3, 1873, two of the three women on Smuttynose were hacked to pieces with an ax in one of the most brutal and notorious murders in New England history. The survivor was Maren Hotvet, found by residents of nearby Appledore Island at eight o'clock the next morning. She was wandering around "in her nightdress crying and hallooing and blood all over her clothes," but other than having almost frozen feet, she was unhurt. This is essentially what she said occurred:

Sometime after the three women had gone to sleep, Maren said, she heard her dog begin to bark somewhere inside the house. Then there was a bloodcurdling scream (is there any *other* kind?) from her sister, Karen, in an adjacent bedroom. Maren leaped from her bed and reached her bedroom door just as Karen fell through it and lay sprawled, unconscious, on the floor. She was bleeding from several blows administered with a chair by the figure of a man behind her. Maren testified at the trial that both she and her prostrate sister were hit several additional blows by this person before she somehow managed to push him back out through the bedroom door and bolt it shut against him. Meanwhile, the third woman in the house, Anethe, was awakened by all the screaming and managed to climb out a window to the outside, where she stood transfixed within full view of Maren's bedroom window. Maren, in her later testimony, said she screamed to Anethe, "Run! Run!" but Anethe seemed "frozen with terror" as the figure, who had abandoned trying to break through Maren's bolted bedroom door, went outside, grabbed an ax from the nearby woodpile, and walked over to the terrified Anethe, who merely "stretched out her hands before him." Then, "in one swift motion he raised the instrument high into the starry night and drove the steel blade into Anethe's head."

As the body of her sister-in-law "shuddered and slumped lifeless to the ground" under a rain of additional blows, Maren, watching all this from her window, said she suddenly recognized the attacker. It was one Louis Wagner, a drifter who had once been a boarder at the Smuttynose house and was now working at the fishing docks in Portsmouth. He is described in the old-time accounts of the crime, including that of author Celia Thaxter, as a "dark, muscular, 28-year-old Prussian with a thick accent." One description I've seen says he was "dark, lowering, skulking."

At this point, realizing she could no longer help either her dead sister-in-law or her unconscious sister, Maren said she clambered out her bedroom window just as Louis Wagner entered the house again, ax in hand. Once outside, she said she ran over the bloodied snow to hide along the shore of the island for the rest of the night. Karen must have regained consciousness, she speculated, and also attempted an escape out the now-open bedroom window, because Maren heard more screaming from the house, and the next day, Karen's body was found strangled and hacked beneath the window, which was split in several places from blows that obviously missed their mark.

It was a grisly, horrifying, ghastly little event that has absolutely *fascinated* us New Englanders ever since. We've published accounts of it in *Yankee* from time to time, principally because new readers are always asking us to. The last time was in the March 1980 issue. This brought me a letter from an associate professor at the University of Southern Maine, L. Morrill Burke. Professor Burke's well-documented view of the murder contradicted every other account of it that I have ever read, to say nothing of the subsequent trial. Oh, yes. Louis Wagner was arrested in Boston the evening after the murders, found guilty in what Professor Burke refers to as virtually a "public lynching," and on June 25, 1875, protesting his innocence, was hanged at the state prison in Thomaston, Maine.

Professor Burke maintained that "Louis Wagner was almost certainly innocent." More startling was his assertion that Maren "was almost surely guilty." What's more, he presented a convincing case, pointing out that the blood on Wagner's clothes, recovered by the police, could well have been fish blood, as Wagner stated it was. No tests were made. The wounds found on the two victims were erratically placed, superficial wounds obviously inflicted by a relatively weak "feminine" arm rather than by the arms of a man who could row the twelve miles to Smuttynose and back in a stolen dory, as Wagner was accused of doing that night. Maren not only survived but was unhurt.

Perhaps the most intriguing new piece of information that Professor Burke brought out in his letter was that Louis Wagner was *not* dark, lowering, and skulking. A witness to the execution, *Lewiston Journal* reporter Edward Mitchell, described him as a "rosy-faced Prussian. His face was round and good-natured, his eyes mild: no wickedness." To make him evil we New Englanders had to make him dark. That's where evil lurks. He was in fact blond!

At the time of the Smuttynose murders, people like Whittier, Longfellow, and Emerson were saying, in effect, that evil—as personified by Louis Wagner, the "dark, scowling Prussian"— always came to New England from without. But Melville and Hawthorne found the truth and it was otherwise.

The "black weeds" on a dead man's grave, as described in *The Scarlet Letter*, had "sprung up out of a buried heart, to make manifest an unspoken crime." The devil could "drop into her tender bosom a germ of evil that would be sure to blossom darkly soon, and bear black fruit betimes." Guilt, sin, evil, Hawthorne and other writers said, are mixed together somewhere deep in a darkness inside each and every one of us. Evil comes from *within*.

To be sure, New Englanders have always had a particular fascination for murders, ghosts, curses, monsters, grotesque and macabre behavior, death, and mysteries involving death. *Yankee* magazine has been full of these things from its very first issue, in 1935. My files are overflowing with letters commenting, often in astonishing detail, on the spooky, scary, and sometimes downright revolting articles we have published.

It has often occurred to me that there is something about the New England landscape that is particularly nourishing to the dark side of the New England character. A chill east wind off the ocean on a gray February day reminds me of it. So do the silent graveyards with markers going all the way back to the Salem witch trials and executions; our black mountains outlined against cold night skies; old cellar holes deep within our forests.... Perhaps the very continuity of New England, representing strength and hope on one hand, also has a way of emphasizing death. Generation after generation of New Englanders, as Hawthorne describes, are "planted and replanted in the same worn-out soil."

There are those interminably long, dark, often depressing New England winters, and then, too, the isolation, loneliness, alcoholism, poverty, and yes, the inbreeding of the northern rural countryside. One doesn't run across *that* side of New England in the travel brochures, but it's there. An 1899 article in the *Atlantic Monthly* isn't all that outdated in certain isolated areas even today. "Nearly everyone you meet is a Glenn-Glenn," it says of one remote village. "So were his parents and theirs and theirs and theirs. He is a Glenn of the nth power. Accordingly, the town abounds in 'characters.' One of our families is 'muffle-chopped.' Another whole family is deaf and dumb. The proprietor of the sawmill stands three feet two and one-half inches with his boots on. Israel Glenn is a giant, measuring seven feet in height.... Glenns should stop marrying Glenns."

Several years ago, when I was still a volunteer fireman in Dublin, a strange incident one night after a bad fire brought into sharp focus the hidden "dark" side of rural life. The chief asked me and two others to stand watch over the smoldering ruins of an old farmhouse that had burned to the ground during the evening, to make sure the fire didn't flare up again and burn the outbuildings we'd managed to save. We'd had a hectic time. About a hundred men from Dublin and neighboring towns plus plenty of equipment had been utilized and now, suddenly, the three of us were left there alone in the darkness. The smoldering wood in the cellar hole behind us occasionally shifted and spat while we stood quietly together drinking a beer. About fifty yards in front of us was the black outline of a huge old barn that had definitely seen better days. After about ten minutes of silence, all three of us distinctly heard a door creak open in that direction. There was no wind at all. Something had opened it. We stood like statues. I've never felt so spooked in all my life, and worse was yet to come!

We felt rather than saw something approaching us from the direction of that barn. At last one of us (not me!) had the presence of mind to act. He snapped on his flashlight and there, shuffling along slowly toward us, was a very old, bent-over man, his upper body deformed like that of a hunchback and his mouth seemingly frozen wide open, as if he'd been trying to scream for the last forty years. I remember he had long white hair coming out from under a wool cap, a thin, scraggly beard, and was dressed in several layers of wool pants and wool sweaters, which had so many holes and tears that all the layers were visible.

We spoke to him—I don't recall what anybody said—but he shuffled silently by us in the dark, his mouth still locked wide open, and stood at the edge of the smoldering cellar hole. All our efforts to communicate with him were futile. Because we really didn't know what else to do, we got on the radio in the fire truck and told the chief about him. About a half hour later, during which time the pitiful old creature continued to stand at the edge of the cellar hole, a man and two women who were evidently part of the family who owned the farm arrived in a pickup truck, quietly carried the old fellow from the cellar hole into the truck, called him "Pops," as I recall, and drove away. No explanations.

The rumor that drifted back to me days later was that this was the family's insane grandfather, who had been stored away in that barn for many, many years. I cannot be absolutely sure that was true, but the image of him, his mouth opened so unnaturally wide, still haunts me.

The premier murder case of New England, perhaps of the entire United States, occurred in Fall River, Massachusetts, around eleven o'clock on the sweltering-hot morning of August 4, 1892, when elderly, wealthy Andrew Borden and his second wife, Abby, were done in—by *someone*. Interestingly enough, it is somewhat similar to the Smuttynose murders of about twenty years before. In both cases, two people were hacked to death with an ax (although the Borden murder weapon was never found, officially). In both cases, an upright, churchgoing, respectable woman was very possibly the culprit. In both cases, said woman was never convicted of the crime. And both cases seemingly sparked that "dark side" imagination of us New Englanders far beyond what might be called normal, passing interest. For some, like writers Edmund Pearson and, more recently, Edward D. Radin (*Lizzie Borden, The Untold Story*), the Borden case became a fascinating obsession.

A big difference was that while Maren Hotvet wasn't suspected of any crime, Lizzie Borden was always considered as guilty as guilty can be, even though she was found innocent at her trial. Most of the books, poems, and plays about the Borden murders leave no doubt whatsoever that "Lizzie Borden took an ax, and gave her mother forty whacks. Then to show she wasn't done, she gave her father forty-one."

The interesting part of the Borden murders to me is that so many New Englanders with truly *personal* pieces of the Borden puzzle surfaced after we published a story about the murders in 1966. In New England, Lizzie Borden is as real as one's next-door neighbor—in fact, one letter was from someone who *had* lived next door to Lizzie. That was after she and her sister, Emma, moved to the house on Fall River's Second Street where Lizzie lived out her life in relative seclusion until her death in 1927. The letter-writer, a man from Swansea, Massachusetts, stated "for a fact" that Emma was "afraid Lizzie would kill her, too." He said Emma told him so. It's true that Emma stayed with Lizzie for only a short time after the murders, before moving to a secret residence somewhere in New Hampshire.

This same Swansea man heard secondhand, but "from a lady I trust," that Lizzie had once been thrown by a beautiful, spirited white horse, and in an insane rage, had returned to her house, fetched a gun, and proceeded to shoot the horse then and there.

A New Hampshire woman wrote us recalling an astonishing story told her family by a frail mentally handicapped little man who did odd jobs around their farm back in the 1920s. The little man said he once lived in Fall River and often did odd chores for the Bordens. Around noon of the murder day, when he was cleaning up behind the Borden house, Lizzie came to the back door wiping off a hatchet! She handed him the hatchet and the rag with which she'd wiped it off, and told him to put the hatchet in the barn and dispose of the rag, along with a bundle wrapped in paper, which she went back into the house to fetch. She said to throw it all in a nearby lot where fill was being dumped every day. This he did.

An hour or so later, he heard the Bordens had been murdered "with a hatchet," and so, with what may have been mentally deficient reasoning, he hid the hatchet behind the horse stalls "so no one else could use it to hurt someone." As to the rag and bundle, they were shortly buried, he related, beneath tons of fill. He never told the police any of this because he was afraid he would somehow be punished. Yet he evidently felt guilty and soon left Fall River so that he could be sure he would never run into Lizzie Borden again. My correspondent said she believed he spent the rest of his life moving from town to town, doing odd jobs on local farms. Occasionally he would tell his story, as he did with her family, and then immediately move on to another locality so that he wouldn't be "punished." An intriguing tale—but true? I personally believe the woman who wrote me, but who can say whether or not the man's story was a figment of a feeble mind. Maybe.

A Fort Lauderdale, Florida, man wrote to say he knew for a fact that Lizzie Borden was accused of shoplifting in the Tilden & Thurber Jewelry Store in Providence, Rhode Island, some years after the murders. According to his "unimpeachable source," the Tilden & Thurber people agreed not to prosecute Lizzie if she signed a confession, which she did (after all, the law had already found her innocent). It was his "understanding" that this signed confession, saying both murders were "by my hand and mine alone," remained in the Tilden & Thurber vaults until a fire destroyed the entire store, including everything in the vaults. What a collectors' item *that* little slip of paper would be today!

"I was a member of the crew of carpenters who remodeled the Borden home in Fall River back in 1949," a Springfield, Massachusetts, man wrote me, "and we came upon a rusty old hatchet concealed behind a partition there." He was referring to the second Borden home, but still . . .

Someone telephoned my uncle Robb Sagendorph after our 1966 article came out, to say she had personally known the maid in the Borden house, Bridget Sullivan, whom a number of people, including writer Edward D. Radin, always considered to be the guilty party rather than Lizzie. She said Bridget told her in confidence (but not at the trial, "out of fear of reprisal"), that she discovered Lizzie stuffing a brand-new dress into a roaring fire in the kitchen stove that hot day of the murders. She said Lizzie told her the fire was "to heat her iron" and that she was destroying her dress because she'd ironed a hole in it too large to fix. (Bridget Sullivan, incidentally, died in Montana in 1948 at age eighty-two.)

There were other letters and other personal anecdotes too. And where the truth lies in all this is anyone's guess—and guess and guess and guess! There are two things, however, that are certain: (1) We'll *never* know exactly what happened in the Borden house on August 4, 1892. (2) We New Englanders will never, ever, tire of speculating about it.

It's not possible to freeze old people in the beginning of winter, store them outside, almost naked, and then thaw them out in time to help with the spring planting. Is it? Well, in 1939, Dr. Temple S. Fay of Philadelphia, who had done some experiments freezing human organs, gave a talk in Providence, Rhode Island, in which he related a grotesque story *he* believed to be true. He said it occurred just outside Montpelier, Vermont, about the turn of the twentieth century.

If I were asked to name the most popular story we have ever printed in *The Old Farmer's Almanac* since we purchased the publication from Little, Brown in 1939, I'd probably have to name this story of Dr. Fay's. We called it "Frozen Death," and for reaction and sustained interest, it even noses out by a whisker our "Artificial Insemination by a Bullet" article. (The latter describes how a New England soldier in the Union Army was hit in an extremely sensitive area between his legs by a Confederate bullet, which continued on its path until it came to rest in the lower abdominal region of a young Southern girl who was observing the fight from the front steps of her house. Accepting the remainder of this allegedly true story significantly extends one's believability frontier, because the young girl suddenly became pregnant while still a virgin, recovered from the wound, gave birth to a boy, and eventually married the Union soldier, who, also recovering, came to visit her after hearing what happened to the bullet that had hit him first! The story blandly goes on to say that the couple had two more children, "conceived in the more conventional manner.") Anyway . . .

"Frozen Death," or as Dr. Fay called it, "A Strange Tale," isn't quite as sensational, but its slightly higher popularity rating may be due to the appeal of its macabre, deathlike images set in the isolation of a long, dark New England winter. It makes one's spirit shiver.

Dr. Fay quoted the tale from an old diary kept by his late uncle Williams, who visited a remote community outside Montpelier one January 7 and found all the community's old people lying on the floor of a cabin, drugged into unconsciousness. The diary goes on to describe how, during that evening, the drugged people were stripped of all clothing "except a single garment," carried outside into the bitter-cold air, and placed on logs.

> . . . and the full moon, occasionally obscured by flying clouds, shone on their upturned, ghastly faces, and a horrible fascination kept me by the bodies as long as I could endure the severe cold.
>
> Soon the noses, ears, and fingers began to turn white, then the limbs and faces assumed a tallowy look. I could stand the cold no longer and

went inside, where I found the friends in cheerful conversation. In about an hour I went out and looked at the bodies. They were fast freezing.

The next day the bodies were covered with straw, placed in layers in a huge wooden enclosure to protect them from animals, and left there. The diary relates that when the writer returned to the community the following May, all the frozen old people were brought inside and placed in tubs of warm water with hemlock boughs until they revived, after which they went about their business "rather refreshed by their long sleep of four months."

I once asked an old Vermont farm couple in the Montpelier area if either one of them truly believed the "Frozen Death" story.

"Certainly do," the husband answered emphatically, without hesitation.

Then his wife added, "The only part I doubt is the thawing out."

New Englanders *want* to believe in ghosts—and we have so many of them—but we are often too practical and hardheaded to believe anything we haven't seen. There's the old story, for example, about the New Hampshire farmer who was cornered by a scholar researching New England religious history and asked if he believed in baptism by immersion in water.

"Yep," replied the farmer. "I seed it done."

There are several New England ghost stories I know to be absolutely true. I "seed" the ghosts myself!

One was a photograph I saw years ago in some Connecticut museum showing a wolf's ghost standing just inside the entrance to a rock cave in Mashamoquet State Park, Pomfret, Connecticut. That's the cave from which Israel Putnam dragged his famous wolf back in 1743. (A few years later, Old Put, as Israel came to be known, said, "Don't fire until you see the whites of their eyes" at Bunker Hill.) One day about the turn of the century, a photographer doing a story on the legendary Putnam wolf incident propped a moth-eaten stuffed wolf or coyote just inside the cave entrance and began taking photographs, when he realized he needed some additional equipment. He left the wolf there for a few hours while he went home, and it was during this period that two hikers happened by. They later swore to anyone who would listen that they had actually seen a wolf's ghost in Old Put's cave. Ever since that time, the cave has been haunted.

I have also viewed, in daylight, with my own incredulous eyes, a ghost in the Massachusetts State House Hall of Flags. It was—and is to this day—clearly discernible in one of the Italian marble columns there. A tourist attraction right up there in popularity with the flags themselves, it's been known for years as the "Bride in White." If you've had the benefit of several glasses of wine at lunch, as I had, you can also view the "Kissing Cavalier" on the outer portion of the marble stairway leading up from Doric Hall, the ghost of a chicken on the marble fireplace in the Senate Reading Room, the ghost of an English bulldog just outside the Reading Room, and perhaps most startling, the ghost of William Cullen Bryant on the lower portion of another marble column outside the Hall of Flags. The Massachusetts State House is a historic and eerie place.

In 1968, *Yankee* writer Dale Hartford talked with several of the dozen New Milford, Connecticut, men who were responsible for the world-famous "New Milford ghost" of 1930. The New Milford ghost was a series of faint, ghostlike voices emanating from the small shed behind a restaurant on the north end of Railroad Street.

"Someone please help me," the ghost moaned. "I'm a little baby buried forty feet underground. Help!" Another time the voice was that of a murdered man seeking revenge. Then there was a Native American chief who had lived in the area two hundred years earlier. And others.

At one time, more than three thousand outsiders, including members of the clergy, spiritualists, newspaper reporters from around the country and even from Europe, as well as the merely curious, were in New Milford to hear the voices. Even Gabriel Heatter, the Walter Cronkite of his day, reported on the ghost in one of his nightly radio broadcasts. After a few weeks of bedlam — and very good business for the restaurant—the police barricaded the shed, the voices stopped, and everyone went home.

It seems that when an old refrigerator in the shed was sold, the wiring that went underground to the restaurant kitchen was removed. But the old cable that encased the wires was not. By accident, two of the "ghosts" discovered they could communicate between the kitchen and the shed via this cable, which weirdly distorted their normal voices. In a clandestine night operation, they extended the cable through three adjacent stores to a hidden outlet in the men's room of Garcia's Tailor Shop. It was from there that they proceeded, for about two chaotic weeks, to spook the entire Western world!

Some New England ghosts are not so easily explained. The late Dr. James Huntington, a Boston obstetrician, who gave his beautiful eighteenth-century house, Forty Acres, in Hadley, Massachusetts, to the Porter-Phelps-Huntington Foundation, which maintains it today (open to the public during the summer), was absolutely *convinced* of the existence of a ghost in his house.

"I have seen, in the moonlight in the small hours of the night, a latch rise and the door silently open," he often told people, suggesting it was the ghost of Elizabeth Porter, returning to look for her father, who was killed in the French and Indian Wars. He said the door would open no matter how securely it had been *bolted*. Swore to it.

Over the years, we have published several articles on the so-called presence atop Mount Washington. In the weather station buildings up there, it has lifted curtains off their hooks and tossed them on the floor, pushed a man off the precipitation-measurement platform, made footsteps sound in an empty hall—all sorts of things. In January 1980, *Yankee* writer and illustrator Austin Stevens went up there to investigate, and returned convinced that almost all the people stationed on Mount Washington during the winter have, at times, experienced "a force—a curious, watchful, malevolent force."

During the earlier years of this century, New Englanders even went through what might be called a spiritualism craze; it featured such things as "psychic photographs," in which faces of dead people, usually relatives, would pop up in the negatives of otherwise ordinary family photographs. My maternal grandmother frequently attended Boston gatherings in which a medium in a trance would serve as a go-between for spirits—often Native Americans, it seemed—who would speak to and answer questions from those assembled. Following the death in 1930 of Sir Arthur Conan Doyle, the creator of Sherlock Holmes and an ardent spiritualist, a voice, supposedly Doyle's, was heard at a stance, warning his sons Denis and Adrian, racing car enthusiasts, that there was a fault in their racing car. As it turned out, a steering column *was* about to give.

Most New Englanders react to this sort of story, as well as to most of the thousands of New England ghost tales, stories of sea monsters in Lake Champlain and elsewhere, black panther sightings, or even the innumerable "buried treasure" legends, in a rather blasé manner.

"Well, now . . . maybe there's *something* to it. Ya never know." That's a typical summation by someone who has just been subjected to a "true story" filled with, for instance, an avalanche of ghostly happenings, none of which could *possibly* be explained except by saying they were all manifestations of the supernatural.

"The vase simply rose for no reason at all about two or three feet above our fireplace mantel," a young woman who lived in a Stoddard, New Hampshire, haunted house earnestly explained to my uncle and me one day, "and then it suddenly dropped to the brick hearth and broke into a thousand pieces. I saw it with my own eyes. Nothing bumped the vase or was even near it. There was no wind, no earthquake, nothing! Now, how can you explain that? It *had* to be our ghost!"

Robb's reaction was as sympathetic as he could make it. "Well, now . . . maybe there's *something* to it. Ya never know." The young woman, I noticed, rolled her eyes upward and sighed deeply.

Most of the fishermen in the picturesque village of Port Clyde, Maine (the late Andrew Wyeth's home town), are descendants of the English, Finnish, and Swedish stonecutters who came to Maine to quarry paving blocks for the streets of New York and Philadelphia. They became fishermen when cobblestone streets went the way of the horse and most of the quarries went out of business.

"These Port Clyde fishermen are a wonderfully lovable, superstitious, and rowdy bunch," a retired businessman friend of mine wrote me after moving permanently from New York to the town of Saint George, of which Port Clyde is a part. So a few months later, *Yankee* writer and photographer Larry Willard and I moseyed down the Maine coast to fill out a story we were planning to do on New England superstitions.

"We're not any of those things," a fisherman we found on the town docks told us when I read him that portion of my friend's letter. "People may think we're rowdy because we go up to Rockland and have a few drinks on Saturday night. Or maybe once in a while during the week, if the weather report is bad and we know we won't have to get up at three in the morning the next day and go out on the trawler.

"And what do you mean by 'superstitious'? In what way are we supposed to be superstitious?"

There was nothing for Larry and me to do but tell him a few of the many, many things that we'd heard most New England fishermen believe to denote some sort of ill fortune—such as painting a boat blue, mentioning the word "pig," having an umbrella on board ship, or leaving a hatch cover turned upside down.

For several minutes during and after our brief explanation, the fisherman worked silently on the net he was repairing and puffed on the cigarette that remained dangling from his mouth.

Finally, I prodded him with: "For instance, it doesn't look to me as though there is a blue fishing boat in this whole harbor."

"Well," he said thoughtfully, "I wouldn't paint a boat blue

myself. I don't like the color. But I don't call it a superstition. Maybe it once was a superstition, but the younger fellows don't follow the old ways. I think there is one blue boat in the harbor —and she's still afloat."

Then I told him I'd always been led to believe that most fishermen simply do not allow the word "pig" to be used around or on their boats and that some fishermen won't even eat pork.

He seemed a little uneasy as I went on to say that I'd heard a young boy in Port Clyde had made an "oink" sound near a fishing boat the previous summer and had been punished when the boat returned from its next trip because its nets had been ruined in some sort of mishap at sea.

"I don't eat pork myself," he responded after a pause, "but it ain't that I'm superstitious about it. I just don't like pork."

"What about your friends?" I asked.

"I'll admit a few of my friends won't use the word 'pig,' " he said, "but it don't bother *me* none . . . so long as I'm clear of the boat."

"What about having an umbrella aboard ship or leaving a hatch cover bottom side up?" Larry asked, entering the conversation for the first time.

Visibly relieved and feeling on solid ground once again, the fisherman turned to Larry and fairly shouted, "Why in the world would anyone *want* to bring an umbrella on board a ship? And as to leaving a hatch cover bottom side up—that's no superstition. Only a goddamn fool would leave a hatch cover bottom side up!"

With that, he left the nets and walked away, obviously somewhat disgusted with the ignorance of writers and editors.

Individual superstitions vary from area to area within our region, but I believe that particular fisherman's *attitude* about them is typical of New Englanders everywhere. Superstitions are so deeply ingrained in the New England character that we seldom recognize them—or admit to them. Myself included.

For instance, it's not that it's necessarily "bad luck" to return for something you forgot after beginning a trip. It's just that the delay will be worse than going without the forgotten item. Even if it's your suitcase. They say it's bad luck when the first person a man speaks with after beginning a trip happens to be a woman. I don't believe silly superstitions like that, although sometimes that combination *is* trouble! I think it's stupid to avoid moving into a new house on a Saturday—but why take the chance? I don't know whether swallowing the bubbles in a cup of coffee or tea *really* brings money, but I've always made sure I do. Simply for the pure fun of it. And every time I've made a wish on a passing load of hay, my wish has come true. Coincidence, no doubt.

There's no real point in *challenging* superstition. A case in point is my friend the late Edward Rowe Snow, author of more than seventy-five books on New England lore, legends, and mysteries, who somehow acquired the skull of Captain Kidd. Got it in Red Rank, New Jersey, of all places, via some obscure shenanigans which, he told me, "I'll reveal when everyone involved, excluding me, is dead." I'm still waiting.

Ed was very cocky about the well-known "curse" on the skull, which allegedly brings misfortune after misfortune on anyone owning it. He said the curse was a "pirate's curse," and because he believed Captain Kidd to be privateer, not a pirate, it did not apply. Kidd was, of course, hanged twice (the rope broke on the first attempt—a fine example of *good* luck) for piracy at Execution Dock in London, England, the morning of May 23, 1701. Ed maintained that evidence proving Kidd's innocence was suppressed for political reasons. Still, I would have felt uneasy with that grisly-looking thing, minus the jawbone, hanging around my house. "Nonsense!" Ed said. "How can there be a pirate's curse on the skull of someone who wasn't a pirate?" and he proceeded to write a short article for *Yankee*, which he entitled "I'm Not Afraid of Captain Kidd!"

After that, I didn't hear from Ed for over a year. Then he wrote me, saying that during the previous twelve months all his valuable gold and silver coins had been stolen while he was giving a talk at the Statler Hilton in Boston; his car had been stolen while he was escorting a group of tourists out to Peddocks Island in Boston Harbor; twenty-seven of his original book manuscripts had been swiped; a treasure chest and valuable dagger were gone . . . Well, the list of misfortunes went on and on. The only *good* thing that happened to Ed during the year, it seemed to me, was that somebody saw Kidd's skull on the front seat of his car one day and took *off* with it. But Ed didn't view the matter in that light, and a few days later, he managed to ransom it for $145.

Just before Ed's death in 1982, I spoke with his wife on the telephone. At the time, Ed lay seriously ill in a respirator. I asked about Kidd's skull and she said her husband still owned it. I told her I realized that, of course, owning an old piece of bone couldn't possibly have anything to do with Ed's present health crisis or with anything else. But, I said, "Why not just get rid of it anyway?"

"That's a good idea," she replied.

New Englanders have always seemed a little preoccupied with death. Elaborate paintings of tombs, complete with flowers and weeping willow trees made with the real hair of a recently departed family member, were popular until the beginning of the twentieth century and are today, I'm told, coming back as antiques. Same with hair wreaths, framed photographs of dead babies, and mourning rings with hair in them.

Tourists still visit the graves of Mrs. Mary E. Brown and her two daughters, Mary and Mercy, in the Chestnut Hill Cemetery in Exeter, Rhode Island. After all three had died, so many of the Brown family became weak and ill that they decided maybe a vampire was at work. So in 1892 they dug up all three women. Two were skeletons. Mercy's body (which had been dead a much shorter time) was whole, and filled with blood. "Obviously" a vampire was making her body its permanent home. So they burned the corpse and fed some of the resulting ashes, mixed with medicines, to ailing members of the Brown family. Then they all died too. Lovely little story.

I'll admit I have myself looked around the Glidden Cemetery in Newcastle, Maine, for the gravestone of Mary Howe. Mary was a medium who, as such, often put herself into trances. In the summer of 1882 she went "into" one of these and remained that way for a number of weeks. Finally, several doctors examined her, found no pulse, and said she was dead. Yet she remained warm (possibly because of the warm rocks her family placed around her), her limbs were flexible, and it is said there wasn't the slightest odor from the body. Over the protests of her family, the town authorities ordered her buried anyway. And she was. But for years afterward, people in that area of Maine insisted they sometimes heard low moans and groans coming from the ground around her gravestone in the Glidden Cemetery. I couldn't locate the stone when I wandered around there one cold, foggy November day several years ago. I truly thought I heard a moan, though. One soft, short little moan.

There have been stories of people *actually* returning from the dead. An old-time New England favorite concerns the funeral of a strong-willed Vermont woman during which the carriage bearing her body hit a wooden post as it was leaving the house for the cemetery. The force of the collision was so great that she was thrown from the carriage onto the ground. The shock of that brought her back to life and she went on to live another five vociferous years before she died once again. This time, as the carriage carrying the body was preparing to leave for the cemetery, the woman's meek and soft-spoken husband approached the driver and said solemnly, "Be careful now that you don't hit that post again."

Some people have taken precautions against being buried alive. Ulysses Smith of Middlebury, Vermont, left instructions in his will that his coffin be equipped with a glass window that would be plainly visible through a glass-covered shaft extending to the surface of the ground. Further, he stipulated that a string should extend from inside the coffin up through the shaft, connected to a small bell attached to his tombstone. He felt secure in the knowledge that if he was mistakenly buried alive, he would be able to ring the bell and signal for help. After his death all this was done, exactly per his instructions. Rumor has it that one day a slightly inebriated passerby thought he heard the bell tinkling, staggered over to the tombstone, looked down through the glass at the body far below, and yelled several times, "What do you want?"

For reasons rather more obscure, John Smith of Amesbury, Massachusetts, who died in 1899, requested that he be buried sitting up in a chair—and that's no doubt the position his skeleton is in today inside a sealed marble tomb in the Mount Prospect cemetery in Amesbury. It is said that his will offered all his money to any woman who would agree in *her* will to join him in the same position in the same vault after her death. There were no takers. (He probably didn't have much money.)

A lady by the name of Peggy Dow is buried "standing up" beneath a small tombstone in the Burrows Hill Burying Ground in Hebron, Connecticut, but her reasoning is clear. She was married to nineteenth-century evangelist Lorenzo Dow, and they both figured she would be in a better position to "rise in the morning of the resurrection" if she was already standing when the trumpet sounded.

Perhaps, as in the case of Peggy Dow, our somewhat excessive interest in death is more a matter of simple practicality than any manifestation of the "dark side" of our natures. One day during my growing-up years in Vanceboro, Maine, my father was passing the time of day at the railroad station with the rather impoverished elderly man who operated the roundhouse (that's where steam engines were turned around to face in the opposite direction). He happened to tell my father that he had recently purchased a $500 tombstone for himself and his wife. My father asked why he felt he could afford $500, an enormous sum in those days, for something neither he nor his wife were even using.

The man answered, "Well, we calculate to use it quite a spell once we get started."

As it happened, both he and his wife were buried beneath it within three months, and there's no question they'll be there for "quite a spell."

As will we all.

10

THE SIX STATES

Yankee Come Home

The real origin and correct definition of the word "Yankee" ᐪᐩ why each New England state feels superior to the other five ᐪᐩ Maine of the soul, of sheet-metal roofs, of the wilderness, and of potatoes ᐪᐩ communicating in Maine ᐪᐩ the differences between New Hampshire and Vermont ᐪᐩ New Hampshire's split personality, frugality, and uncertain place in history ᐪᐩ the six responsibilities of being a Vermonter ᐪᐩ why Massachusetts stories are not funny and why Joshua Slocum was no sailor ᐪᐩ how the North Shore views the South Shore ᐪᐩ western Massachusetts, Ralph Nader country ᐪᐩ why everything began in Rhode Island ᐪᐩ what happens if you make a mistake in Rhode Island ᐪᐩ Connecticut Yankees ᐪᐩ Yankee Ingenuity ᐪᐩ the hydraulic cigarette lighter ᐪᐩ the origin of "Swamp Yankees" ᐪᐩ changing the words of "Yankee Doodle" ᐪᐩ the Gold Coast ᐪᐩ Sunday dinner with Katharine Hepburn ᐪᐩ the image of New England ᐪᐩ and coming home

A YANKEE HAS BEEN VARIOUSLY DEFINED as an American, a northern American, a New Englander, an old native of Vermont, Maine, or Cape Cod, and an old Vermont native who eats apple pie for breakfast—with a knife.

[239]

There is no real consensus on the word. Some define it by geography; others maintain it is more a state of mind.

Dr. Cornelius Weygandt, professor of English at the University of Pennsylvania in the 1930s and author of many New England books, said, "There are Yankees in all but local color and dialect everywhere in the world. Yankeeness, blessedly, is an essential human quality."

Dr. Weygandt probably agreed with an 1870 definition written by the editor of a magazine called *Assembly*, published in Peabody, Massachusetts: "A Yankee is self-denying, self-relying, and into everything prying. He is a lover of piety, propriety, notoriety, and the Temperance Society. He is a bragging, dragging, striving, thriving, swapping, jostling, wrestling, musical, quizzical, astronomical, philosophical, poetical, and criminal sort of character whose manifest destiny is to spread civilization to the remotest corners of creation."

In the 21st century it's probably a rather small minority of Yankees who are lovers of the Temperance Society. Anyway, I belong to the geography school. To me, a Yankee is someone either native to New England or whose ancestors were. That encompasses a large portion of Americans alive today—and surely the others just naturally accumulate Yankee "traits" by osmosis!

As to the origin of the actual word, opinion seems to be about equally divided between the Dutch and the Native Americans. Advocates of the Dutch theory say the early English settlers sold cheese to the Dutch settlers, so the latter began calling the English "John Cheese" which is "Jan Kaas" in Dutch. The word "Yankee" just naturally evolved. (Perhaps we can all be grateful they didn't sell pumpernickel!)

Those who favor a Native American origin cannot decide on which Native Americans.

"Yankee comes from the Cherokee word *eankke*, meaning slave or coward," Tom Aytos, a New England scholar from Reading, Massachusetts, told me in 1975. "It was applied to the inhabitants of New England by the residents of Virginia when the New

Englanders would not assist them in a war with the Cherokees."

James Fenimore Cooper, in a footnote in *The Deerslayer* (1841), said, "All the old writers who speak of the Indians say the Indians pronounce 'English' as 'Yengeese.' "

Then there's Professor Edward Taube of Racine, Wisconsin, a scholar of the early Algonquin Indian languages, whose work suggested Yankee evolved from the Algonquin word *awaunaguss*, which means "this stranger." As in "Awaunaguss go home!"

Professor Taube wrote: "Awaunaguss, awenoch, wanuy, menoh, Yanokie, Yankee, etc., are all distinct and independent descendants of the same Algonquin ancestor, each one mutilated a little but differently during its individual transfer from the Algonquinian *spoken* word to the English *written* record."

The late Joe Allen once explained to me very seriously that "Yankee" evolved from tugs of war in colonial Maine in which there was an "anchor," pronounced "yanker," and a "yankee," who often suddenly and shrewdly yanked the rope out of his opponent's grasp a split second before the contest was to begin. (Joe also maintained that the outstanding accomplishment of New Englanders down through history was the perfection of the art of whittling.)

A few years ago on I-95 going into Boston, I passed an interstate trailer truck with huge lettering on the tailgate: "Serving New England, New Jersey, New York, and Maine." *Yankee* magazine subscribers from upper New York state will occasionally write to ask whether or not their area is "more New England" than, say, southern Connecticut. My answer is "yes" in terms of the state-of-mind theory many people have about New England and Yankees in general. However, in actual fact, New England consists of everything within the geographical boundaries of Maine, New Hampshire, Vermont, Massachusetts, Rhode Island, and Connecticut. No more, no less. Six very proud, very independent, and very different entities, which together represent a formidable political, economic, and spiritual force in America. The American character, as it's generally perceived, derived historically from the people who inhabited and migrated west from these six states.

"To endure, a people must treasure the image of itself," writer Lew Dietz wrote to me once, and I think America indeed treasures the image of New England as, in large measure, the image of itself. Nonetheless, while each individual New England state truly possesses all the many and varied characteristics inherent in our region's "image," each also has a personality unto itself.

Furthermore, each feels superior to the other five.

In 1967, there began a running debate among *Yankee* subscribers throughout the United States that was to last almost two years. The subject of the debate was *why* each New England state feels superior today, and what precipitated it all was a letter we published from New Hampshire that claimed the Granite State felt superior because "the first military action of the Revolutionary War" occurred at Fort William and Mary, New Castle, New Hampshire, in December of 1774 (see Chapter 5). Then the flood of letters began. We published arguments and rebuttals almost every month. Here are some highlights:

Vermont: "The Fort William and Mary episode was simply a mob action prior to the Revolution. The New Hampshirites were not led by a commissioned officer in the American army, the British did not surrender, there were no casualties on either side even though a few guns were fired, and nothing is recorded about it in American or British archives.

"The first offensive action of the American Revolution was taken by Vermonters. Oh, sure, the Minutemen of Concord and Lexington fought back along the stone walls and from behind trees, and their *defensive* action is considered to be the beginning of the Revolution. But the first *offensive* military action of the war, in which captives, cannon, ammunition, and rum were captured, was when Ethan Allen and his Green Mountain boys rowed across Lake Champlain on May 10, 1775, and captured Fort Ticonderoga."

Connecticut: "If Ethan Allen, his brother Ira, and Remember Baker led the Green Mountain boys on the first bona fide military action of the Revolution, then Connecticut deserves the credit. All three hailed from Litchfield, Connecticut!"

Massachusetts: "The first armed resistance to the British occurred before Lexington and Concord and before New Hampshire's Fort William and Mary episode. It was August 16, 1774, when 500 armed men stopped the king's judges from holding court in Great Barrington, Massachusetts. In fact the local DAR chapter there is called the 'First- Resistance Chapter.'"

Rhode Island: "Rhode Islanders feel superior in the certain knowledge that the first military action of the American Revolution was the burning and sinking of *HMS Gaspee*, a British man-of-war, on June 9, 1772. A bunch of Rhode Islanders, whooping it up at Sabin's Saloon, heard the *Gaspee* was aground waiting for a high tide, so they piled into eight longboats, rowed out there, boarded her, shot the captain, overpowered the crew, and sank the ship by setting her on fire. In fact, she's still out there on the bottom off Pawtuxet today. King George called it an act of 'war against the king,' and I don't think you need a better authority than that!"

Connecticut: "What we're *really* proud of here in Connecticut was that we had our own 'Declaration of Independence' on June 18, 1776—some twenty days before our first national Independence Day on July 4, 1776."

Rhode Island: "Connecticut may be interested to know that Rhode Island adopted a declaration of independence a month and a half before Connecticut did. Rhode Island, not Connecticut, was therefore the first sovereign state in the new world."

Vermont: "The first declaration of independence in America was written on October 10, 1774—long before either Rhode Island or Connecticut did any such thing. On that date, the citizens of Chester, Vermont, stated 'that all the acts of British Parliament tending to take away rights of freedom ought not to be obeyed.'"

Massachusetts: "They may have talked and shouted a lot in other states, but Massachusetts was the first to shed *blood* for the cause of liberty. And this occurred at North Bridge in Salem, Massachusetts, one month and 21 days before the fight at Concord's North Bridge. In a confrontation between a British regiment in search of colonial arms and a group of citizens bent on blocking their passage across Salem's North Bridge, 'a scuffle ensued between the soldiers and those in the gondolas,' according to the 1878 *Standard History of Essex County*, 'and Joseph Whicher, a foreman in a local distillery, received a wound from a British bayonette, drawing blood, and of which he was afterwards exceedingly proud.'"

Maine: "Maine was settled sixteen years before anybody but the Indians stepped on Plymouth Rock."

The writer James Russell Lowell described the Yankee as "a strange hybrid of contradictions" and certainly Maine, considered with Vermont to be the most "Yankee" of the New England states, conforms to that definition, with, in Lowell's words, its "niggard-geniality, calculating fanaticism, cast-iron enthusiasm, unwilling humor, and close-fisted generosity." *Yankee's* late poetry editor, Jean Burden, always said that of the many complaint letters she regularly received about our "high falutin', modern, no-rhyming, senseless poetry that's only fit for some egghead publication," the majority came from Maine. Yet writer and lecturer John Cole once told me that an art show, put on by himself and others in Brunswick to raise money to restore the town common, sold hundreds of fine paintings in a matter of a few days.

Maine is beautiful and Maine is ugly. I remember driving from Sedgwick to Brooksville several summers ago and stopping at the top of Caterpillar Hill. There before me was Maine the beautiful —Walker Pond in the foreground, the ocean beyond dotted with dark, pine-covered islands of all shapes and sizes, the bridge crossing Eggemoggin Reach, so familiar to yachtsmen, Deere Isle with its thin road winding down toward Stonington, and in the far distance, the Camden hills. This is the Maine that lives in the hearts of all New Englanders as well as visitors—the Maine of artists, of poets, of the soul.

Then there is backcountry Maine, "the Maine that artists do not paint, writers do not usually describe, and visitors do not talk about," wrote Charles E. Clark in *Maine, A History*. It is "the Maine where scrubby woodlands alternate with bleak, unshaded villages marked by an old general store and a Baptist Church, but also by a laundromat, a couple of gas stations, and a Dairy Joy, and where the houses may have sheet metal roofs." People in backcountry Maine say a house is a house, but a house with a shed is a village. This is the Maine that shows up near the bottom of annual United States per capita income listings.

A third Maine is the forested wilderness, the Maine of white water canoeing, hunting, fishing, mosquitoes big enough to carry you away, old Maine guides, lumbering, and tall tales. In one of my favorite Maine books, *The Jonesport Raffle*, author John Gould recalls a fishing story contest in Montana that a Maine backwoodsman decided to enter by mail. "The prize was to be a new fly rod, but he [the Mainer] said he never used a rod—he hid on the bank of the stream and clubbed the trout with a baseball bat when they came up to pick blueberries."

The Maine man won the contest, but the Associated Press was careful to assure readers that it was a typical Maine woodsman's "tall story" and not to be believed literally. Gould, however, doesn't give an inch. "Truthfully," he writes, "it is nothing to see men with ball bats lined up along a brook in Maine—not for taking trout, but for self defense. The vicious, man-eating trout of Franklin County have been known to drive a man up a tree, and then jump at his feet."

Still another Maine is potato Maine, hugging the New Brunswick border for over a hundred miles, an open, rolling area that everyone in the United States has heard about but fewer than several outsiders have ever been to. School starts in Aroostook County in mid-August, and that's bad news for kids. On the other hand, all the schools then close for three whole weeks in September to enable children to spend (legally) dawn-to-dusk days harvesting potatoes. Up there, that's known as a bad news-bad news story.

I once asked a little New Hampshire first grader touring the *Yankee* offices if she'd like to pick potatoes in Maine in September instead of going to school. She said, "Sure—it wouldn't last long anyway. No one lives in Maine all year round. Maine's closed in the winter."

Although traditionally Down Easters are noted for their plain and direct manner of communicating, I think Mainers are actually the most *indirect* of all New Englanders. To obtain a straight answer to a straight question in Maine is often next to impossible.

For example:

VISITOR: "Can you tell me where the hotel is in this town?"
MAINER: "What hotel?" (Mainers like to answer a question *with* a question.)
VISITOR: "Oh, is there more than one hotel here?"
MAINER: "Didn't know there was any."

Or (and this is verbatim from the transcript of a Bangor assault and battery court case of some years ago):

COUNSEL: "Did you see the defendant throw the stone?"
WITNESS (*a Bangor native*): Well, I saw that he did have a stone— and I suppose he might have thrown it."
COUNSEL: "How large a stone was it?"
WITNESS: "Why, I should call it a largish stone."
COUNSEL: "Would you please say how big it was?"
WITNESS: "It appeared to me to be a stone of some bigness."
COUNSEL: "Yes, but please describe the bigness."
WITNESS: "As near as I can recollect, it was a considerable of a stone."
COUNSEL (*becoming agitated*): "Well, Guard sakes, man, can't you compare it to something—like, say it was as big as this thing or that thing that all of us in this court would understand?"
WITNESS: "Well, if I should say now, I should say it was as big . . . well, as big as a piece of chalk."

Somewhere deep within the Maine psyche is a strong instinct to avoid being pinned down. There are definite pitfalls, Mainers feel, in being too direct too soon in any conversation. Here's a story I heard when I was growing up in Vanceboro, which explains what can happen when that instinct is ignored:

It happened at Eastport, the easternmost United States town (Quoddy Head at nearby Lubec is the easternmost mainland point, Eastport being on Moose Island) and concerns a large hound dog belonging to an Eastport lawyer. One day this particular dog grabbed a sizable chunk of meat—well, it was a considerable of a chunk—from the back shed of the local butcher shop and ran off with it. The butcher spotted him in the act, recognized the dog, but couldn't catch up with him. So the next morning the butcher confronted the lawyer in his office and said, "If—and I mean just supposin'—a dog should steal a piece of meat from a butcher shop and the butcher was sure of the dog's owner—and, well, if that happened would the butcher have the legal right to collect the value of the meat from that owner?"

"Why, yes," said the lawyer, "if that butcher were to go to the owner of the dog and explain what happened, I think the owner would have a legal and moral obligation to pay the butcher for the value of the lost meat."

"All right," said the butcher, misplaying his trump card, "you owe me fifteen dollars. It happened—it was *your* dog that took my *meat* yesterday afternoon."

"Well," said the lawyer, a fifth-generation Mainer himself, "my legal advice to you is worth twenty dollars. You owe me five dollars."

In light of Mainers' inclination for indirect approaches, I've often pondered the meaning of their state motto, which is simply *Dirigo* or "I Direct." "Put the emphasis on the 'I'" someone told me, and that does clarify it some. I still can't figure out how they came to make the chickadee the state bird, though.

New Hampshire and Vermont are often lumped together in outsiders' view, but residents of both states are aware how remarkably different each is from the other. New Hampshire is mentally oriented to small businesses and manufacturing. On the other hand, there's probably no other state in the Union as rural in complexion as Vermont. Traditionally, New Hampshire has been politically conservative, though that has changed some. In recent years, Vermont has enacted some of the most liberal legislation in the nation. I'm always conscious of the immediate difference one "feels" when crossing the Connecticut River from Vermont to New Hampshire or vice versa. Much of Vermont is open farmland. New Hampshire is almost completely forested. So many of Vermont's villages appear almost unreal—as if they had been created by Grandma Moses. New Hampshire's villages seem totally unconscious of whether or not they are picturesque. (Thus, many are not.)

In a cultural sense, the two states lean away from each other too—Vermont, in spite of itself, toward New York and New Yorkers; New Hampshire toward Massachusetts and southern New England. As to shape, New Hampshire has always described Vermont as an "upside-down New Hampshire." Vermont sees it the other way around.

During the years between 1915 and 1934, the two states wrangled over which of them owned the Connecticut River. The final settlement said the river was New Hampshire property all the way across it to the low-water mark on the Vermont side. New Hampshirites considered this a great victory until they realized it meant New Hampshire would be responsible for the upkeep and construction of all the bridges. Score one for Vermont. Incidentally, New Hampshire used to imply that it was only the Vermont side of the Connecticut River that was polluted. Vermont said it was the New Hampshire side. Fortunately, the river is now clean on *both* sides.

Like Maine, New Hampshire has more than one personality. There's the prosperous, booming if somewhat faceless southern half of the state, which has all but become a suburb of Boston. Then there's the northern half. Up there are towns like Pittsburg, the largest town east of the Mississippi River, with a thirty-mile main street that rambles through a wilderness of lakes, mountains, and evergreen forests, inhabited by moose, bear, deer, loons, a few humans, and snowmobiles. Movie theaters, department stores, and hospitals are as far as twenty miles away. Many jobs are farther.

Northern New Hampshirites would like more economic opportunities, particularly for their young people, but they're a proud, independent lot who also cherish their isolation.

"Pittsburg is getting crowded," a native told writer Gail Kelley when she was up there on a *Yankee* assignment many winters ago. "In the last few years, I have begun to sense that things are getting away from us." So they went ahead and abolished a meddling planning board and zoning laws enacted just the year before.

"When people ask us how we like living up here in the northern New Hampshire woods," a Colebrook man told me recently, "it's like asking someone who has eaten porridge every single day of his entire life, 'How's the porridge?' "

Though frugality and shrewdness in business dealings are traits characteristic of New Englanders as a whole, I think New Hampshirites are the most frugal of all. Possibly it has something to do with the overall conservative and business orientation of the state.

A typical New Hampshire story, for instance, concerns two Berlin (remember—pronounced *Berlin*) men discussing the hard financial times. One asks the other how in the world he has managed to feed his large family on such a low income.

"I'll tell you," is the reply. "I find out what they don't like and then I give 'em plenty of it."

A neighbor of mine who deals in antiques points out how this frugality coupled with a general regional stubbornness can make negotiating with a New Hampshirite a pretty difficult process. Several years ago, he spotted a nice chest of drawers standing in a woodshed of an old farmhouse in Gilsum. He stopped and asked the owner if he'd care to sell it for, say, seventy-five dollars. The man, an elderly, slow-moving gent who'd obviously enjoyed better days, said no, he guessed not. The next time my friend drove by, about a month later, the chest of drawers was still there, and he offered the old fellow a hundred and twenty-five dollars, which is about what he felt its value was. Still no. Almost a year later, he stopped again and, in a display of his own stubbornness, tried out a figure higher than he figured the chest was worth. "Well, what do you say?" he asked. "Shall I take it away for two hundred dollars cash?" The old man reflected for several minutes and then said slowly, "I guess she can set there for a spell longer. She ain't eatin' nothin'."

She was also increasing in value faster than most anything he could put money into.

Several years ago, *Yankee* writer Ned Comstock wrote me a letter, which I published, that described a New Hampshire church supper he'd attended. After enjoying one dish of fresh-baked, feather-light biscuits loaded with fresh strawberries, dripping with juice, and smothered in whipped cream, he'd noticed a sign next to the woman guarding the cash box.

"Strawberry Shortcake," it read. "First Plate: Fifty Cents. All You Want: One Dollar."

As Ned prepared to pay his bill, the lady asked him if he wanted more strawberry shortcake before he left. Ned said no, he'd enjoyed his piece very much but was full.

"That will be one dollar," the lady said firmly.

Conceivably because it has gotten the better of so many people so many times and for so long, New Hampshire has had to endure more criticism than any other New England state. "The God who made New Hampshire," wrote Ralph Waldo Emerson, "taunted the lofty mountains with little men." Neal Peirce, in writing his book about "people, politics, and power" in the six New England states, couldn't find much of anything worthwhile in all New Hampshire except *Yankee* magazine publisher Rob Trowbridge, then a state senator, the Sandwich Mountain Range, and Newfound Lake, on which Peirce owns property.

He says he "read and reread the state's history" in search of anything distinctive and found little or nothing. No great leaders, no important tradition in literature, nothing significant in the arts or public policy, no sense of historic mission. Nothing. Even Daniel Webster, he pointed out, moved permanently to Massachusetts. And Franklin Pierce, the state's only United States president, suffered from two specific problems: "an over-fondness for alcohol and a violent allergy to it."

> She had one President (Pronounce him Purse,
> And make the most of it for better or worse).
> —*Robert Frost, "New Hampshire"*

I do recall that when President Pierce's former home in Concord was in danger of demolition, New Hampshire saved it in a rather characteristic manner. Sufficient funds were raised by selling over $75,000 worth of bourbon in $15 commemorative bottles.

Incidentally, Neal Peirce *and* Emerson are wrong about the lack of historic figures associated with the Granite State. Where, we New Hampshirites might well ask them, but Gilmanton Iron Works do they think Grace Metalious came from?

Being a Vermonter carries with it some heavy responsibilities. To be precise, six of them.

1. First of all, a Vermonter must possess a great deal of common sense. Although a number of adults living in Vermont today never finished high school, ignorance is not a lack of education but rather a lack of common sense.

"That Hardwick road sign back there is pointing off in the wrong direction, isn't it?"

"Sure it is, but anyone with a little common sense knows how to get to Hardwick."

Ask a man if he'll split a pepperidge (black gum) log; if he shakes his head, he's smart enough for most any job. A pepperidge log cannot be split.

In his book *Vermont, A Bicentennial History,* Charles T. Morrissey, the former editor of *Vermont Life* magazine, quotes from a survey taken of Nevada, Utah, and Vermont judges to "ascertain philosophical outlook, legal competency, and social background." In the questionnaire, "common sense" was one of seven choices concerning factors influencing judicial decisions. The results showed 37.7 percent of the Nevada judges marked "common sense," 47.3 percent of the Utah judges, and 72.2 percent of the Vermont judges.

2. A Vermonter is expected to display a certain amount of dry humor. Senator George Aiken fulfilled this Vermont duty throughout his political career—as did Cal Coolidge—and the country appreciated the effort. It's somehow comforting to Americans when a Vermonter acts like "a Vermonter." We all smiled and felt good inside when Aiken advised President Lyndon Johnson to declare the Vietnam War won and pull out the troops. It would not have been as amusing or even as wise if someone from another state had said it.

3. A Vermonter must have integrity. Its state government does. Neal Peirce ranked it as one of only five states in America—and the only state in New England—that is free of political corruption. (The others: Minnesota, Wisconsin, Oregon, and Hawaii.) The old story is that there are so few nickels in Vermont that every politician knows where each one is located, making it impossible for anyone to steal one.

It's often been said that James Curley of Boston "could no more have been governor of Vermont than Joe E. Brown could have been the Shah of Iran." And though Vermont voted for Warren Harding for president in 1920, Harding would have had about as much success as a Vermont politician as, in the words of writer Leonard Morrison, "a peanut shucker at a corn husk." George Aiken drove fellow senators and would-be senators to distraction with his meticulous campaign expense accounting. While they were spending thousands of dollars in categories such as "entertainment" and "travel," Aiken reported the sum of $17.09 in total expenses for his 1968 campaign. He also apologized for spending a dollar more than in 1962 because of the increased cost of postage stamps. "I had to thank people who circulated papers for me even if I didn't ask them to," he explained.

The closest thing to official "manipulating" of finances I've ever heard about in Vermont—and the story is actually more an example of honesty—occurred at a small country church then located outside Rutland. Because the congregation had dwindled down to almost nothing, the members decided to disband. The question of the disposal of funds in the church treasury came up during the final meeting, when the treasurer reported a sum of eighty dollars on hand. One of the members suggested that forty dollars of this be given to Zeke Tuttle, a church member who was ill with tuberculosis at the time.

Several months later, a member who had not attended the final meeting ran into the church treasurer in town and asked him whatever became of the money in the treasury of the now disbanded church.

"At our last meeting, we voted to give forty dollars of the eighty we had to Zeke Tuttle because he was sick," the treasurer replied.

"What about the rest?"

"Well," said the treasurer without a hint of hesitation, "I wasn't feeling any too good myself, so I kept the rest."

4. Vermonters, unlike Mainers, are expected to speak in a simple, direct, no-nonsense manner. Possibly it's all part of the Vermont version of honesty and integrity. The late Allen R. Foley, a Dartmouth College history professor for many years and a state senator from Norwich, Vermont, used to tell the story of the wealthy, well-meaning lady in Cavendish who decided to invite a certain old Vermont handyman to her family Christmas dinner. The handyman lived alone in a shack near the town dump, and during the winter, always wore several layers of underwear, pants, and shirts, which he never removed until spring. When she asked him to come, he said he'd like to think it over and get back to her in a few days. The following week she happened to run into him again, outside the post office, and he gave his reply:

"I want you to know how much I appreciate your kind invitation, ma'am," he said, "but I've got to thinking it over and, well, you see,

I'd have to take off all my clothes and then take some sort of bath somewhere and then I'd have to find something else to wear and, well, you know, I guess I've about decided it just ain't worth it."

Many, many Vermont stories, like those collected in Keith Jennison's book, "*Yup . . . Nope*" *and Other Vermont Dialogues*, feature this sort of direct approach in conversation:

QUESTION: "What do you suppose they'll do when old man Appleby dies?"
ANSWER: "Bury him."
QUESTION: "Think it's ever going to stop snowing?"
ANSWER: "Always has."
QUESTION: "Can you tell me when the next train leaves for Boston?"
ANSWER: "It left more'n ten years ago."

There must be a thousand more of these.

5. A Vermonter has the responsibility to be a free and independent thinker. Independence and freedom are honored throughout New England, but in Vermont they are virtually a religion. An Ethan Allen statement along that line is a popular quote: "I am as determined to preserve the independence of Vermont as Congress is that of the Union, and rather than fail I will retire with my hardy Green Mountain boys into the caverns of the mountains and make war on all mankind."

Years ago, when I started writing the first edition of this book, my friend Vrest Orton dashed off a letter to me to make *sure* I understood the background of Vermont's present-day feeling of independence.

"You must remember," he wrote, "that Vermont was *never* a colony of Great Britain nor was it a state until 1777 when we declared it to be an independent, sovereign Republic or Commonwealth. Then, when we entered the Federal Union (a colossal mistake) in 1791, we became the 14th state. And during those fourteen years prior to 1791, we were threatened by the British, the greedy New Yorkers, the New Hampshirites who lost us, and even Massachusetts who forgot to keep us. And all five of the other New

England states had a period of aristocratic oligarchy. We didn't. All Vermonters were middle-class, hard-working, and young! No other state was like that.

"We were and are stubborn about our convictions and remained so while the other states lost their convictions early and had nothing to be stubborn about!"

Cal Coolidge said, "If ever the spirit of liberty should vanish from the rest of the Union ... it all could be restored by the generous store held by the people of the brave little state of Vermont." Trivia enthusiasts would know that Cal Coolidge was not Vermont's only United States president. Chester Allen Arthur, though a New York resident when he succeeded Garfield, was born in North Fairfield, Vermont.

6. Finally, some Vermonters are expected to be willing to put in a hard day's work for a meager day's pay. Throughout the state, but particularly in the three northern counties known as the Northeast Kingdom, there is poverty.

Charles Morrissey described it with brutal clarity:

"Do the touring shutterbugs who snap pictures of scenic Vermont vistas ever wonder who lives in all the trailers and all the shacky houses they don't record on film? Do they notice the sad and ugly towns they drive through to get to the pristine villages which outsiders have restored?"

"Woodchuck" is a derisive term used for Vermont's poor by newcomers or those with some affluence. "Everything about a woodchuck is poor," said Morrissey. "His housing, his health, his nutrition, his schooling, his children and their schooling, the condition of his pickup truck, and his behavior on Saturday nights after a ferocious round of drinking. He views the world with a sullen stare; behind his back the comfortable make jokes about him—like the one that claims his idea of a banquet is boiled woodchuck and a six-pack of beer."

Yes, being a Vermonter carries with it some heavy responsibilities. The role requires common sense, a dry sense of humor, impeccable honesty, a direct manner of speaking, a healthy obsession with freedom, and for those who are poor, a lot of hidden suffering. Most Vermonters, I think, feel it's a duty and a privilege to play that role—at least, all but the last part of it, and that, as they say, "just goes with the territory." So much so that perhaps there is very little role-playing required during their lifelong performances.

Most residents of the Green Mountain State would agree that Vermont is "an experience" as well as a geographic area of New England, but to outsiders, who own most of the state anyway, Vermont is a place you feel homesick for even before you've left it.

Massachusetts is called the Hub of the Universe. That's not a name given in jest. As a Massachusetts native, I can say that pride in the Bay State has always bordered on or spilled over into what outsiders might consider to be arrogance. The Massachusetts image exported to the outside seems to consist of Harvard, Boston Brahmins, the Puritans, the Kennedys and their accent, liberalism, do-gooders, Concord/Lexington, and a sort of "we know best" attitude toward the rest of America. Not included in the exported image are the high taxes and cost of living, the interminable political corruption, racial antagonism, and the fact that besides lawyers the Massachusetts legislature has been at times dominated by funeral directors.

The notion that a region's humor often is based on regional personality traits, much exaggerated, is borne out by Massachusetts. Its high self-esteem shines forth in all the old favorites, such as:

Two Massachusetts (or Boston) women went to San Francisco and ran into a particularly hot spell there. As they were stewing on Treasure Island, one said to the other, "My dear, I never expected to be so hot in San Francisco." To which her companion replied, "But, my dear, you must remember that we're three thousand miles from the ocean."

Or—and there are many variations to this one—

A visitor sought to speak with A. Lawrence Lowell, then

president of Harvard, who had been called to Washington by President William Howard Taft for a White House conference on education. The visitor was informed by the secretary in Lowell's outer office: "The president is in Washington seeing Mr. Taft." Tell that story to many Massachusetts residents, most Bostonians, or *any* Harvard graduate, and they won't understand why it's funny.

Massachusetts is still fueled by the Puritan ethic, probably more so than any other New England state. When Mary Peabody, mother of Governor Endicott Peabody and wife of Malcolm Peabody, Episcopal bishop of central New York, went to St. Augustine, Florida, at age seventy-two to join in a civil rights demonstration and ended up in jail, she was considered by many people across America as simply a meddling, do-gooding old coot looking for headlines. New Englanders knew better. While not everyone agreed with her actions, she was recognized as being sincere. The tradition she was exemplifying runs strong and deep in Massachusetts.

"Do your duty, do your part in life—that's what being a New Englander means to me," she later told my Dublin neighbor, author Richard Meryman, when he talked with her in her Cambridge home fourteen years later. "Doing your duty, caring for things that are good and true, being a terrible prig, I suppose."

The fuel shortage had begun at the time of Meryman's *Yankee* interview. "I don't allow myself a fire if I don't have anybody here," said this frail, then-eighty-six-year-old widow lady, as she sat covered by a shawl, the thermostat set at sixty, in her ancestral home surrounded by memorabilia of her distinguished, wealthy, and influential ancestors.

"In my mother-in-law's Bible, after she died, I found a little note she had written to herself. It said, 'Remember to be cheerful.' I think that's very important, not to complain, to say you're lonely all the time. All I say is, I'm cold all the time. . . . I'm very frugal. Also, the thing to do is to save energy. So I put on layers like the Chinese. My layers of clothes."

After reading this, I felt like calling John Winthrop, Cotton

Mather, or any of the old-time Massachusetts Puritans (perhaps via my grandmother's medium) and asking them to let poor old Mary Peabody off the hook. Tell her she can have a fire now. She can say she's lonely. Let her alone! But of course that wouldn't help. *She* would tell *them* how it ought to be. The Puritan tradition doesn't depend upon "permission" from anybody, past or present. For Mary Peabody, the only voice of authority was that which was deep within her—the voice of her New England Conscience.

To be fair, I must add that the Puritan instinct for "doing good deeds" is viewed as just plain "meddling" by many people all over the world. Certainly Massachusetts, the cradle of do-gooders, isn't immune to the same confusion. When the great evangelist Dwight L. Moody returned to his native Northfield, Massachusetts, after years of journeying around the country and the world preaching against ignorance and vice, he decided to devote some time to improving his own hometown. The story goes that one morning he met a local farmer, whom he'd known from boyhood, and immediately began suggesting ways in which he might make his farm more productive.

The farmer, who suffered from a rather severe stutter, finally interrupted him by saying, "D-D-Dwight, y-y-you have been all over the w-w-w-world and people think you're a g-great m-m-m-man, but there's one thing you c-c-can't do, D-D-Dwight."

"Oh," said Moody pleasantly, "I guess there are many things I can't do, but what special thing are you thinking of?"

"You c-c-c-can't m-m-mind your own business, D-D-Dwight."

Perhaps it is pride that insulates Bay Staters from being overly impressed with "reputations." Movie stars and other celebrities attract less public attention in the state of Massachusetts than anywhere else in the country—unless, perhaps, they're from Massachusetts. One day I noticed then California Governor Pat Brown being videotaped, hatless, strolling down Boston's Commonwealth Avenue while speaking with an interviewer walking beside him. I don't think anybody else noticed—at least, I didn't see anyone stop to look.

Back in 1895, a Fairhaven, Massachusetts, man by the name of Joshua Slocum sailed all the way around the world alone in a small sailboat called the *Spray*. It took him three years. In 1961, I met a very elderly lady from Fairhaven who had actually been at sea with Joshua Slocum. Her name was Alice Charry and when she was a young girl, Slocum had taken her for a couple of sails. One time they set out for Newport out of Fairhaven and ended up in Marion, forty-two miles east of Newport. Another time, she said, Slocum couldn't seem to find the island of Cuttyhunk, just fourteen miles off Fairhaven.

So in spite of Slocum's reputation and worldwide honors as the first man to sail around the world alone, Miss Charry was convinced he was "no sailor."

I remember a local newspaperman, who was interviewing her that day also, pointing out to her that Slocum was a dreamer and probably didn't really care whether he ended up at Newport or Marion or whether or not he found Cuttyhunk Island.

"He was more a writer and a philosopher," he earnestly pointed out to Miss Charry. "More of a seagoing Henry David Thoreau."

"Well, I don't know about *that*," replied Miss Charry emphatically. "All I know is that I don't understand all this fuss about his being a *sailor*."

Although there are various regions within Massachusetts, I don't consider the state as a whole to be a region (at least, not as defined in Chapter 3). Perhaps it's too diverse. I notice that Bay Staters visiting elsewhere will announce themselves as being from New England rather than from Massachusetts. But Cape Codders, who consider themselves in a world apart, will say they're from Cape Cod. Off Cape islanders—such as those living on Martha's Vineyard and Nantucket—never leave, so they aren't faced with the problem.

The late writer Jerome Beatty, who moved to Cape Cod a number of years ago, wrote about life there with the sensitive perspective of the sympathetic but ultimately dispassionate observer. He pointed out that nowadays one ought to be rather wary of Cape Cod "local color," and told me about an incident involving a Newton, Massachusetts, doctor who summers near him in Waquoit. Daily, the doctor's wife sent him to one of those Cape Cod roadside stands that advertise "native produce."

"It was so quaint it hurt—even to the honor system where you make your own change," recalled Beatty, who frequented the place himself. One day the doctor couldn't find the particular vegetable he wanted, so he made his way to the farmhouse, where he found the colorful old Cape Codder—opening a crate of California tomatoes and putting them into quaint little Cape Cod bags for display at his roadside stand.

The other Massachusetts "regions" are named for their geographical relationship to Boston. There's one to the north, another to the south, and still another to the west of Boston. And each, like a miniature version of the six New England states, feels superior to the others. North Shore resident Joseph E. Garland, in his book *Boston's North Shore: Being an Account of Life Among the Noteworthy, Fashionable, Wealthy, Eccentric & Ordinary 1823-1890*, describes the South Shore as simply "a sandy prelude to the Cape." He goes on to say: "its few small harbors, though filled with pleasure boats, are half emptied by every tide. Miles of flats, marsh, and bog provide a haven for waterfowl and avaricious insects. It is simply incomprehensible to the North Shore summerer how his counterpart below Boston can with evident satisfaction spend the season sweltering and smacking 'skeeters while *he*, enlightened soul, enjoys the 10 or 15 degree discount in Fahrenheit with which geography and climate have rewarded his good sense."

West of the general Boston area is, naturally and logically, western Massachusetts. Because of its political isolation, growing educational institutions, and curious mixture of old-time natives and idealistic but maturing dreamers left over from the hippie generation, Ralph Nader once referred to western Massachusetts as "the most interesting part of the United States." In what's known as the Pioneer Valley, bankers are likely to grow organic vegetables, communes are running hard-nosed businesses for profit, and as a food cooperative worker was heard to remark, "It's hard to find a good Swiss cheese that's politically acceptable."

In a *Yankee* article, writer Tim Clark referred to Berkshire County from June through September as "a comic-opera kingdom, inhabited by wealthy city folks pretending to be farmers, Hollywood stars pretending to be actors, natives pretending to be picturesque, and the Boston Symphony Orchestra masquerading as the Berkshire Festival at Tanglewood." It was his cultural dig at the last that infuriated everybody.

"I'm so sick and tired of outside media always thinking anything cultural in this area has to come from Boston," an art museum director in Amherst wrote me after reading Clark's description, "and that once the summer people go home in the fall there's a cultural wasteland here until the following spring. That is simply not true, as anyone who lives here and attends the art shows, concerts, and excellent theater year-round knows full well."

Sure. Anything you say, sir.

Boston (and environs) *is*, of course, the cultural center not only of Massachusetts but of all New England. Down deep, we all know it. The real trouble is—Boston knows it too.

The State of Rhode Island and the Providence Plantations is the official name. Other names for it have been "The Plantation of the Otherwise-Minded" and "Rogues Island." At one time the greatest slave-trading colony in America, Rhode Island was the first civilized community anywhere that allowed freedom of religion. Of its Roger Williams psyche emphasizing freedom of conscience and action, Massachusetts Puritan Cotton Mather said, "If a man has lost his religion, he might find it at this general muster of opinionists."

Little Rhody or the Ocean State is still a "general muster of opinionists," and as such, has just naturally developed a reputation for tolerance. It calmly abides various elements such as the Mafia in its little midst; Brown is the only city university in New England without the "town and gown" problems one encounters in, say, Cambridge or New Haven; it has the highest proportion of Roman Catholics of any state in the Union; and when he was mayor of Providence, Buddy Cianci, "the working man's mayor," was often seen riding horseback down wealthy Blackstone Boulevard in Providence with his spurs pointing forward so they wouldn't hurt the horse.

Of course, it's small. Only forty-seven and a half miles long and, at most, forty miles wide. Yet it has more people than Vermont. If you live in the Rhode Island countryside you can, as they say, be in the city in seven minutes. And like a person of small stature, Rhode Island absolutely refuses to be overlooked or ignored in any situation. Once a Rhode Islander gets started on the subject of Rhode Island, he or she can almost, but not quite, become downright belligerent.

"Do you realize Rhode Island was the *first* colony to disregard the British stamp act?" a museum curator suddenly sprung on me as we were sifting through some photographs of nineteenth-century Cranston (pronounced "Creeanston").

"We were also the *first* to officially renounce allegiance to Great Britain," the little bombardment continued, "among the *first* to adopt the Articles of Confederation, and *first* to fire a cannon at any British naval vessel."

"Really?" I responded, attempting to lift the appearance of my own interest to his earnest level. "Oh, sure," he continued, "and the *first* Baptist church is in Providence, the *first* Jewish synagogue in America is in Newport, the country's *first* cotton mill, started by Samuel Slater, was begun in Pawtucket in 1790, the *first* lighthouse on the American coast was built at Beaver-tail back in 1749, the *first* spinning jenny in the United States was—" I interrupted here with a hearty "By Gorry!" and then, "That's something! Do you have any literature about all this I could borrow and take back with me to the *Yankee* office?" Did he! But at least we were eventually able to return to selecting the old photographs.

Concern for accuracy—particularly historical accuracy—is

a trait shared by all New Englanders, but it seems most highly developed in Rhode Islanders. Their noted tolerance in other matters evidently does not extend to errors. Whenever we publish something containing even the most minor mistake, we hear first and most often from Rhode Islanders.

"Your December cover painting by Maxwell Mays, showing the church choir in a 'New England Christmas Service,' is nice but inaccurate. The American flag just visible on the left of the clergyman as he faces the congregation in the painting, is in the wrong position. According to Public Law 829, 77th Congress, Chapter 806, second session HJRES. 359, it should be on the right." This from Wakefield, Rhode Island.

Some years ago we mentioned in some article that the distance from Rhode Island to New York was many miles, we heard not a word from our subscribers in New York, the second-largest state in number of *Yankee* subscriptions. From Rhode Island we received an avalanche of mail, each letter and postcard pointing out to us that the two states actually border one another—out in Long Island Sound. Many gave us a seagull analogy. "A seagull, should he choose to, might sit in the water at a certain point in Long Island Sound and have his tail in New York, his beak in Rhode Island, and his left wing in Connecticut."

In southern Massachusetts just south of Worcester is a lake we once called in *Yankee* Lake Chargoggagoggmanchauggauggagoggchaubunagungamaugg. A few days after the issue was sent out, we heard from several Rhode Islanders who told us we had misspelled it. It should have been Lake Chargoggaggoggmanchaugagoggchaubunagungamaug. We noted and corrected the error in our next issue.

In the interest of further accuracy, I would add a linguistic observation or two for those wishing to assimilate quickly into the community that is Rhode Island. First of all, never refer to Rhode Island Reds as communists. Rhode Islanders don't think that's funny anymore, if they *ever* did. Even more important, the state should be pronounced "Ruh Dilan." If that seems stupid, then call it ustupit"—pronounced *stoo-pit*. Of course, the Rhode Island language is a whole other story in itself.

Historically, Connecticut is the most "Yankee" of all the New England states. If you are of the school that believes the Dutch were responsible for the word "Yankee" (i.e., the "John Cheese" theory), then it is logical to believe it was the Dutch in New York who began applying the term to their English neighbors in Connecticut. "Connecticut" and "Yankee" are two words that are very comfortable when combined, and so they were long before Mark Twain wrote *A Connecticut Yankee in King Arthur's Court*.

Connecticut Yankees were principally responsible for establishing the smart, shrewd, clever, and, well, slippery reputation of Yankees everywhere. Early Connecticut peddlers, with their leaky calf weaners, wooden nutmegs, defective clocks, and cigars that would not draw, traveled from town to town around New England and eventually the entire country—always moving fast enough to be out of town before anyone realized they'd been had. It was often said, "You might as well try to hold a greased eel as a live Connecticut Yankee."

Now, when two Connecticut Yankees bargained together, that was the stuff of stories—hundreds of them. This one's typical:

While plowing one spring, a Connecticut farmer's horse suddenly expired and fell lifeless in the field. The farmer left it lying there, still hitched to the plow, and walked several miles to the house of his neighbor, who, it so happened, had tricked the farmer's wife into buying what turned out to be a fake nutmeg the year before. He found his neighbor whittling something out on his back doorstep. "Ben," he said after suitable exchanges on the weather, "I feel like swapping something today. You know that black-and-white horse of mine?"

"Yes," replied his neighbor as he continued to whittle. "I know him well."

"Well, then you know he's younger than your big bay but he

may not be as big and strong. How would you like to swap your bay horse for him?"

"Even?"

"Yes. Even."

"You've got a deal," said his neighbor, and they solemnly shook on it, whereupon the farmer, typically honest about his double dealings and with a pleased smile on his face, said, "Well, Ben, your brand-new horse is dead. He's lying out in my field. Keeled over while I was plowing with him this morning."

"All right, fine," replied his neighbor. "My big bay horse died night before last, and his skin is hanging out in the back shed."

But there was a more positive side to the Connecticut Yankee. In time his ingenious approaches, clever ideas, original thinking, and skillful craftsmanship evolved into a virtue proudly claimed by *all* New Englanders today. In fact, it's claimed by all Americans. Usually preceded by the words "good" and "old," it's now known as Yankee Ingenuity, and it's credited with, among other things, winning World War II.

Connecticut has a valid point in claiming Yankee Ingenuity as its own. Since the United States Patent Office opened in 1790, Connecticut has often averaged more patents each year per thousand of population than any other state in the Union or any other country in the world! Nutmeggers have invented everything from the submarine, anesthesia, radar speed detectors, sky hooks, the grinder for the cotton gin, pistols with revolving cylinders, lattice-truss covered bridges, and the lollipop. And it was a Connecticut inventor, one Samuel Morey, who *steamed* down the Connecticut River in 1787, fourteen years before "Tricky Bob" Fulton did *his* steamboat thing.

My own favorite Connecticut invention is the "hydraulic cigarette lighter" that I saw demonstrated in a Wallingford knick-knack shop many years ago. Its "advantage" was that it used plain water rather than lighter fluid. The water was poured into a funnel, from which it flowed through a hose to a showerhead, which sprinkled it onto a sponge located on a small wooden platform.

As the sponge became heavy with water, it lowered the platform to raise the gate of a mouse's cage. The mouse, seeing a piece of cheese, jumped out and landed on a paddle that extended from one end of a lever. When the paddle dropped with the mouse's weight, a pin on the opposite end pricked a balloon, allowing a weight to fall, which in turn provided the power to revolve an emery wheel to which a match was held. Connecticut Yankee Ingenuity!

I believe Connecticut can also be credited for "Swamp Yankees," although the term has always been a derogatory one anywhere in New England when applied by outsiders. Like "hillbilly," the term is acceptable only when utilized in good humor "amongst the family." Back during the summer of 1776, a few people in Thompson, Connecticut, spent a night down in a local swamp to avoid the oncoming British. The next day, the citizens who had remained in the village and fought off the British soldiers gave their bedraggled, wet, mosquito-bitten neighbors a very hard time as they emerged from the swamp, and the term "Swamp Yankee" was born.

("Blue-Bellied Yankees," however, cannot be attributed to Connecticut alone. During the Civil War, many Union soldiers, particularly those from Maine, were issued long underwear colored by a runny dark-blue dye that made their tummies turn blue.)

In 1978, the Connecticut legislature went so far as to adopt the song "Yankee Doodle" as its very own official State of Connecticut song. Even had the gall to change the words. The Connecticut version has Yankee Doodle going "to town" instead of the original "to London" and had him "with the folks be handy" instead of "with the girls be handy." I'm not sure what being handy with "the folks" entails, but perhaps it has something to do with Connecticut Yankee ingenuity.

Like New Hampshire, Connecticut has a split personality. There's Fairfield County, with its "Gold Coast" New York bedroom towns of New Canaan, Darien, Westport, Stamford, Greenwich, et al. And then there's the rest of Connecticut. From time to time, a movement begins to lop off Connecticut's Fairfield County from New England and either give it to New York or make it a state on its own. That will never happen, of course. One doesn't disown one's own brother simply because he has become, over the course of many years, rich, white, Protestant, successful, country-clubby, and in love with New York City and the train ride to and from.

At a 1982 legislative hearing on transportation and tax issues, the contrast in interests between the Fairfield County representatives and those representing the rest of the state was notable. From Fairfield came talk of pollution, noise, accident rates, and the amenities of life. Speakers from Hartford and other upstate areas stressed the need for revenue and jobs.

At one point in the debate, according to a report in *The New York Times*, State Representative John A. Miscikoski, a Democrat from Torrington, good-naturedly, but with a measure of bite, jabbed the Fairfield contingent by asking, "All I'm hearing from are people with names like Roberts and Harris—doesn't anyone down there have a name like Miscikoski?"

The coast of Connecticut is divided too. From New Haven on down to the New York line is general industrial ugliness occasionally relieved by fancy yacht sanctuaries. Yet many harbors from New Haven east have lobster boats and a "Down East" look. The towns in the general area around the mouths of the Connecticut and Thames rivers—Groton, Stonington, Old Saybrook, Old Lyme, Essex—are among the most picturesque and well-to-do in all New England. They're also *very* protective of their privacy. In Garson Kanin's *Tracy and Hepburn*, the late Spencer Tracy told a story about a Sunday dinner with Katharine Hepburn, a Connecticut native, and her family at their beach house in Old Saybrook. They were all debating the basic "rights of the common man" when the actress's father, in the middle of an impassioned speech on the subject, spotted a lone stranger walking along the beach in front of the house. In an instant, the whole family was out on the porch, yelling, "Hey—this is private property! Get off the beach immediately!" When the intruder had been properly routed, Dr. Hepburn and family returned to the table and, a bit short of breath, took up the defense of the common man once again.

To the west, especially in the Litchfield hills and lower Connecticut valley, stretches of the state's pristine natural beauty remain unspoiled by the rapid overall growth that so many say is now polluting Connecticut's historic regional character. I must disagree with that oft-repeated lament, but not just because much of Connecticut is still pretty. Odell Shepard refers to the "pollution of the spirit" in his book *Connecticut Past and Present*, saying, "Connecticut streams have been winding down to the sea by the same worn paths since before the Pyramids were imagined. You can bring from a thousand new and different sources the water that flows through one of these ancient channels, you can even pollute it with all defilement, but it will nevertheless pour over and around and among the boulders of its bed with the same everlasting curves and lazy meanders, as though it were carved in bronze."

The very nature of the Connecticut Yankee is that of a survivor. So if the future can be called an everlasting extension of the past, Connecticut will always be Connecticut—Fairfield County and all, insurance companies and all, changes and all—forever and ever.

What other state in the Union can *ever* truthfully say that one of its existing daily newspapers reported the story of the Boston Tea Party as straight news? The *Hartford Courant* did, and, in 1796, counted among its real estate advertisers a Virginian named George Washington.

Each New England state shares the characteristics of the other five to some degree. Mix Maine's tall stories and runaround manner of answering questions with New Hampshire's frugality and Vermont's common sense, integrity, and laconic, wise humor. Then add the Puritan ethic of Massachusetts with a generous dash of Rhode Island tolerance, pride, and concern for historical details. Top all that with a dose of Connecticut's shrewdness and Yankee Ingenuity, and behold, New England! For authentic additional flavoring, garnish with the ethnic influences of the

French, Portuguese, Irish, Italians, Poles, and Armenians, and for good measure, throw in some fickle weather, five thousand or more legends, a ghost or two, exactly nine ayuhs, and a good old-fashioned Rhode Island clambake.

And yet New England means something slightly different to each New Englander.

At a church supper in Springfield, Massachusetts, following a talk about New England I gave to a historical society there, we all started discussing what New England meant to us.

"New England is where neighbors help neighbors mend each other's fences, and New England is where they say what they *mean*."

"New England is where it all began and where a feeling of continuity is still strong."

Several people chose to describe it in physical or visual terms.

"New England is the little village in the Christmas cards—and what many outsiders are surprised about is that the little village really exists!"

"New England is coming into Northeast Harbor under sail after a beautiful day in Frenchman Bay—and picking up the buoy the first time around!"

"New England is eating homemade coffee ice cream and sitting on the cannon in front of the Old Sloop Church in Rockport, Massachusetts, watching some fife and drum corps march by in the Fourth of July parade."

A visitor from Cleveland, Ohio, at the table said, "New England—it all seems so *substantial*. "

Finally, a distinguished-looking elderly gentleman at the head of the table said quietly, "To me, New England is coming home." We all nodded in agreement, but none of us wished to risk diminishing the statement by attempting further explanation.

However, I think we could all *feel* his meaning. "Coming home" constitutes, perhaps, an image that doesn't necessarily have anything to do with maple-shaded village greens, lobsters, Beacon Hill, Vermont's orange hills in autumn, or anything else commonly associated with our region. "Coming home" is a personal, very private image of New England.

At a certain time when I'm as old as or older than the Springfield gentleman, I know where I'll be, wherever I am. It will be very early on a calm, warm late-June morning on New Hampshire's Lake Winnipesaukee. I'll walk down to the water's edge below my camp on Sleepers Island, rest on the bench I built there years before, and sip from a mug of hot coffee. The sun will glisten through the tall pine trees behind me. From the distance, I'll hear the faint sound of an outboard motor, but the huge lake before me, lying there in its myriad of undulating reflections, will be otherwise free of human activity. Then, far down near The Witches and Forty Islands, I'll see a dark, faintly ominous-looking band of ruffled water creeping slowly toward me along the entire breadth of the lake from Meredith Bay to Moultonborough Neck. There'll be long-ago voices and laughter like distant music. A solitary leaf on the poplar tree leaning over the shore near me will flap lazily as if in preparation for the daily summertime wind—inevitably on its way as always. While I wait for it calmly in the temporary magical stillness of early morning, just as I have done a thousand times before, I'll look across the water to the hills that rise over the faraway shores and then on and on beyond for miles and miles of misty blue mountains to the north.

BIBLIOGRAPHY

Amory, Cleveland. *The Proper Bostonians*. New York: E. P. Dutton, 1947.

Baltzell, E. Digby. *The Protestant Establishment*. New York: Random House, 1964.

—. *Puritan Boston and Quaker Philadelphia*. New York: Free Press, 1979.

Borland, Hal. *A Place to Begin*. Photographs by B. A. King. San Francisco: Sierra Club Books, 1976.

Hal Borland's Twelve Moons of the Year, ed. Barbara Dodge Borland. New York: Alfred A. Knopf, 1979.

Bridgman, Howard Allen. *New England in the Life of the World*. Boston: Pilgrim Press, 1920.

Chamberlain, Samuel, and Stewart Beach. *Lexington and Concord*. New York: Hastings House, 1970.

Cole, Arthur H. *The Charming Idioms of New England*, Freeport, Maine: Bond Wheelwright, 1960.

The Connecticut Almanac, ed. Robert O'Brien. West Hartford, Conn.: Imprint, and Green Spring, Inc., 1981.

Daniels, Jonathan. *A Southerner Discovers New England*. New York: Macmillan, 1940.

Emerson, Ralph Waldo. *The Complete Poetical Works of Ralph Waldo Emerson*. Boston: Houghton, Mifflin, 1867.

Foley, Allen R. *The Old-Timer Talks Back*. Brattleboro, Vt.: The Stephen Greene Press, 1975.

Gould, John. *The Jonesport Raffle*. Boston: Little, Brown, 1969.

Hawthorne, Nathaniel. *The Complete Novels and Selected Tales*, ed. Norman Holmes Pearson. New York: Random House, 1937.

The Scarlet Letter and Other Tales of the Puritans, ed. Harry Levin. Boston: Houghton Mifflin, 1961.

Herman Melville, ed. R. W. B. Lewis. New York: Dell, 1962.

Holbrook, Stewart H. *The Yankee Exodus*. New York: Macmillan, 1950.

Jacobus, Donald Lines. *Genealogy as Pastime and Profession*. Baltimore: Genealogical Publishing Company, 1968.

Jennison, Keith. *"Yup . . . Nope" and Other Vermont Dialogues*. Photographs by Neil Rappaport. Taftsville, Vt.: The Countryman Press, 1976.

Johnson, Malcolm L. *Yesterday's Connecticut*. Miami, Fla.: E. A. Seemann Publishing, 1976.

Jones, Evan. *American Food—The Gastronomic Story*. New York: Random House, 1981.

Leavitt, Richard F. *Yesterday's New Hampshire*. Miami, Fla.: E. A. Seemann Publishing, 1974.

Lee, Albert. *Weather Wisdom*. Garden City, N.Y.: Doubleday, 1976.

Longfellow, Henry Wadsworth. *The Complete Poetical Works of Henry Wadsworth Longfellow*. Boston: Houghton, Mifflin, 1893.

Ludlum, David. *The Country Journal New England Weather Book*. Boston: Houghton Mifflin, 1976.

Maine, "A Guide Down East," ed. Dorris A. Isaacson. Rockland, Maine: Courier-Gazette, Inc., 1970.

Mayflower Families Through Five Generations, ed. Robert M. Sherman. Plymouth, Mass.: General Society of Mayflower Descendants, 1978.

McGovern, James R. *Yankee Family*. New Orleans: Polyanthos, 1975.

Miller, Perry. *The American Puritans*. Garden City, N.Y.: Doubleday, 1956.

The Responsibility of Mind in a Civilization of Machines, ed. John Crowell and Stanford J. Searl, Jr. Amherst, Mass.: University of Massachusetts Press, 1979.

Mitchell, Edwin Valentine. *It's an Old New England Custom*. New York: Vanguard Press, 1946.

Morrissey, Charles T. *Vermont*. New York: W. W. Norton, and the American Association for State and Local History, 1981.

The Old Farmer's Almanac. 1976 through 1982 editions. Dublin, N.H.: Yankee Publishing Incorporated.

Orton, Vrest. *The Voice of the Green Mountains*. Rutland, Vt.: Academy Books, 1979.

"Over to Home and From Away." Ed. by Jim Brunelle. Portland, Maine: Guy Gannett Publishing, 1980.

Patenaude, Michael. "We Americans Don't Speak the Same Language After All." 1981 *The Old Farmer s Almanac*. Dublin, N.H.: Yankee Publishing Incorporated, 1981.

Rhode Island Yearbook. Providence, R.I.: The Rhode Island Yearbook Foundation, Inc., 1969.

Rice, Benjamin. *Book of Country Essays*. Dublin, N.H.: Yankee Publishing Incorporated, 1974.

Shepard, Odell, *Connecticut Past and Present*. New York: Alfred A. Knopf, 1939.

Skotheim, Robert Allen. *American Intellectual Histories and Historians*. Princeton, N.J.: Princeton University Press, 1966.

Stevens, William O. *Old Nantucket—The Faraway Island*. New York: Dodd, Mead, 1936.

A Subtreasury of American Humor, ed. E. B. White and Katharine S. White. New York: Coward-McCann, 1941.

A Treasury of New England Folklore, ed. B. A. Botkin. New York: Bonanza Books, 1965.

Tree, Christina. *How New England Happened*. Boston: Little, Brown, 1976.

Wenkam, Robert. *New England*. Chicago, New York, San Francisco: Rand McNally, 1974.

Wilson, Harold Fisher. *The Hill Country of Northern New England*. New York: Columbia University Press, 1936.

Yankee magazine, September 1935-April 1982. Dublin, N.H.: Yankee Publishing Incorporated.